Archives
and the Digital Library

Archives and the Digital Library has been co-published simultaneously as *Journal of Archival Organization*, Volume 4, Numbers 1/2 2006.

Monographic Separates from the *Journal of Archival Organization*™

For additional information on these and other Haworth Press titles, including descriptions, tables of contents, reviews, and prices, use the QuickSearch catalog at http://www.HaworthPress.com.

Archives and the Digital Library, edited by William E. Landis and Robin L. Chandler (Vol. 4, No. 1/2, 2006). *An examination of various innovative perspectives and the latest technological advances for archives and archivists in the digital library.*

Encoding Across Frontiers: Proceedings of the European Conference on Encoded Archival Description and Content (EAD and EAC), Paris, France, 7-8 October 2004, edited by Bill Stockting and Fabienne Queyroux (Vol. 3, No. 2/3, 2005). *A collection of the finest presentations from the European Conference on Encoded Archival Description and Context (EAD and EAC) held in Paris, France in October 2004.*

Archives
and the Digital Library

William E. Landis
Robin L. Chandler
Editors

Archives and the Digital Library has been co-published simultaneously as *Journal of Archival Organization*, Volume 4, Numbers 1/2 2006.

Routledge
Taylor & Francis Group
LONDON AND NEW YORK

First Published by

The Haworth Information Press®, 10 Alice Street, Binghamton, NY 13904-1580 USA

Transferred to Digital Printing 2009 by Routledge
270 Madison Ave, New York NY 10016
2 Park Square, Milton Park, Abingdon, Oxon, OX14 4RN

The Haworth Information Press® is an imprint of The Haworth Press, Inc., 10 Alice Street, Binghamton, NY 13904-1580 USA.

Archives and the Digital Library has been co-published simultaneously as *Journal of Archival Organization*, Volume 4, Numbers 1/2 2006.

© 2006 by The Haworth Press, Inc. All rights reserved. No part of this work may be reproduced or utilized in any form or by any means, electronic or mechanical, including photocopying, microfilm and recording, or by any information storage and retrieval system, without permission in writing from the publisher.

The development, preparation, and publication of this work has been undertaken with great care. However, the publisher, employees, editors, and agents of The Haworth Press and all imprints of The Haworth Press, Inc., including The Haworth Medical Press® and Pharmaceutical Products Press®, are not responsible for any errors contained herein or for consequences that may ensue from use of materials or information contained in this work. With regard to case studies, identities and circumstances of individuals discussed herein have been changed to protect confidentiality. Any resemblance to actual persons, living or dead, is entirely coincidental.

The Haworth Press is committed to the dissemination of ideas and information according to the highest standards of intellectual freedom and the free exchange of ideas. Statements made and opinions expressed in this publication do not necessarily reflect the views of the Publisher, Directors, management, or staff of The Haworth Press, Inc., or an endorsement by them.

Library of Congress Cataloging-in-Publication Data

Archives and the digital library/William E. Landis, Robin L. Chandler, editors.
     p. cm.
     "Co-published simultaneously as Journal of archival organization, Volume 4, numbers 1/2."
     Includes bibliographical references and index.
     ISBN 13: 978-0-7890-3437-3 (alk. paper)
     ISBN 10: 0-7890-3437-9 (alk. paper)
     ISBN 13: 978-0-7890-3438-0 (alk. paper)
     ISBN 10: 0-7890-3438-7 (alk. paper)
     1. Archives–United States 2. Digital libraries–United States. 3. Archives–California. 4. Digital libraries–California I. Landis, William E. II. Chandler, Robin L. III. Journal of archival organization.
CD3021.A83 2006
027.073–dc22
                                                         2006029961

The HAWORTH PRESS *Inc.*

Abstracting, Indexing & Outward Linking

PRINT *and* ELECTRONIC BOOKS & JOURNALS

Journal of Archival Organization

This section provides you with a list of major indexing & abstracting services and other tools for bibliographic access. That is to say, each service began covering this periodical during the the year noted in the right column. Most Websites which are listed below have indicated that they will either post, disseminate, compile, archive, cite or alert their own Website users with research-based content from this work. (This list is as current as the copyright date of this publication.)

Abstracting, Website/Indexing Coverage . . . . Year When Coverage Began

- *Academic Search Premier (EBSCO)*
  <http://www.epnet.com/academic/acsearchprem.asp> **2006**

- *(CAB ABSTRACTS, CABI) <http://www.cabi.org>* **2006**

- *Cabell's Directory of Publishing Opportunities in Educational Technology & Library Science <http://www.cabells.com>* **2006**

- *EBSCOhost Electronic Journals Service (EJS)*
  <http://ejournals.ebsco.com> **2002**

- *Education Research Product Family (EBSCO)* **2006**

- *Elsevier Eflow-D <http://www.elsevier.com>* **2006**

- *Elsevier Scopus <http://www.info.scopus.com>* **2005**

- *FRANCIS INIST <http://www.inist.fr>* **2005**

- *Google <http://www.google.com>* **2004**

- *Google Scholar <http://scholar.google.com>* **2004**

- *Haworth Document Delivery Center*
  <http://www.HaworthPress.com/journals/dds.asp> **2002**

- *(IBR) International Bibliography of Book Reviews on the Humanities and Social Sciences (Thomson)*
  <http://www.saur.de> **2006**

- *(IBZ) International Bibliography of Periodical Literature on the Humanities and Social Sciences (Thomson)*
  <http://www.saur.de> **2002**

(continued)

(continued)

Bibliographic Access

- **_Magazines for Libraries (KATZ)_**

- **_Ulrich's Periodicals Directory: International Periodicals Information Since 1932 <http://www.Bowkerlink.com>_**

Special Bibliographic Notes related to special journal issues (separates) and indexing/abstracting:

- indexing/abstracting services in this list will also cover material in any "separate" that is co-published simultaneously with Haworth's special thematic journal issue or DocuSerial. Indexing/abstracting usually covers material at the article/chapter level.
- monographic co-editions are intended for either non-subscribers or libraries which intend to purchase a second copy for their circulating collections.
- monographic co-editions are reported to all jobbers/wholesalers/approval plans. The source journal is listed as the "series" to assist the prevention of duplicate purchasing in the same manner utilized for books-in-series.
- to facilitate user/access services all indexing/abstracting services are encouraged to utilize the co-indexing entry note indicated at the bottom of the first page of each article/chapter/contribution.
- this is intended to assist a library user of any reference tool (whether print, electronic, online, or CD-ROM) to locate the monographic version if the library has purchased this version but not a subscription to the source journal.
- individual articles/chapters in any Haworth publication are also available through the Haworth Document Delivery Service (HDDS).

As part of Haworth's continuing committment to better serve our library patrons, we are proud to be working with the following electronic services:

AGGREGATOR SERVICES

EBSCOhost

Ingenta

J-Gate

Minerva

OCLC FirstSearch

Oxmill

SwetsWise

FirstSearch

Oxmill Publishing

SwetsWise

LINK RESOLVER SERVICES

1Cate (Openly Informatics)

CrossRef

Gold Rush (Coalliance)

LinkOut (PubMed)

LINKplus (Atypon)

LinkSolver (Ovid)

LinkSource with A-to-Z (EBSCO)

Resource Linker (Ulrich)

SerialsSolutions (ProQuest)

SFX (Ex Libris)

Sirsi Resolver (SirsiDynix)

Tour (TDnet)

Vlink (Extensity, *formerly Geac*)

WebBridge (Innovative Interfaces)

LinkOut.

SerialsSolutions

((extensity))

WebBridge

Archives
and the Digital Library

Archives and the Digital Library has been co-published simultaneously as *Journal of Archival Organization*, Volume 4, Numbers 1/2 2006.

Archives
and the Digital Library

CONTENTS

ABOUT THE EDITORS

William E. Landis is Head of Arrangement and Description and Metadata Coordinator in Manuscripts and Archives, Sterling Memorial Library at Yale University. He previously served as Metadata Coordinator in the Data Acquisitions unit of the California Digital Library focusing on prototyping metadata harvesting tools and leveraging metadata enhancement strategies in support of new CDL access systems. His other professional positions have included Manuscripts Librarian in Special Collections and Archives at the University of California, Irvine; and Production Coordinator for JSTOR. Mr. Landis received his MILS from the University of Michigan. He contributes to metadata standards efforts for the Digital Library Federation, and teaches a data content standards workshop for the Society of American Archivists.

Robin L. Chandler serves as Director, Data Acquisitions, for the California Digital Library. Her responsibilities currently include managing the online Archive of California and supervising a variety of mass digitization projects underway at the University of California. Her previous professional positions include Head of Archives and Special Collections and Director of the Tobacco Control Archives at the University of California, San Francisco; and Laboratory Archivist and Public Services Librarian at the Stanford Linear Accelerator Center. Ms. Chandler received her MA in History from San Francisco State University, and her MLIS from the University of California, Berkeley. She has been an active member of the Society of American Archivists, and is a past president of the Society of California Archivists.

INTRODUCTION

Archives and Archivists:
Key Collaborators in the Digital Library

BACKGROUND

What is a digital library anymore, anyway? Carl Lagoze and his co-authors posed this question in the November 2005 issue of *D-Lib Magazine*,[1] exploring some answers and open issues from their perspective as researchers in a computer science department. Archivists, too, bring a unique perspective to and have a significant stake in our collectively evolving notion of the digital library. Contributions by archivists to digital library developments range across a wide variety of areas, including: digital collections, whether materials are reformatted to digital or born in digital formats; technical infrastructures that support the capture, management, and preservation of, and access to digital information resource objects; tools for both end users and workers in the world of digital information resources; and innovative services that help us and end users leverage the promise of information technologies as they apply to our work.

An important current and future challenge for the archival profession is to articulate what is unique and valuable to others working on digital library efforts about our approach to the appraisal, accessioning, and management of information resources. What do the complicated mix of

[Haworth co-indexing entry note]: "Archives and Archivists: Key Collaborators in the Digital Library." Co-published simultaneously in *Journal of Archival Organization* (The Haworth Information Press, an imprint of The Haworth Press, Inc.) Vol. 4, No. 1/2, 2006, pp. 1-9; and: *Archives and the Digital Library* (ed: William E. Landis, and Robin L. Chandler) The Haworth Information Press, an imprint of The Haworth Press, Inc., 2006, pp. 1-9. Single or multiple copies of this article are available for a fee from The Haworth Document Delivery Service [1-800-HAWORTH, 9:00 a.m. - 5:00 p.m. (EST). E-mail address: docdelivery@ haworthpress.com].

Available online at http://jao.haworthpress.com
© 2006 by The Haworth Press, Inc. All rights reserved.
doi:10.1300/J201v04n01_01

theoretical background and practical training that constitutes a professional archivist add up to, and how can our strategies and expertise be leveraged in an increasingly digital world? At the same time, how do we prevent our unique approaches to information management from blinding us to the opportunities for collaboration and cross-fertilization with other professional communities coalescing around the digital library? We need to continue as a profession to value and maintain the access paradigms we've developed over time where they remain valuable and useful to specific end users. Nonetheless, while doing so, we need collectively to better understand users and usability issues relating to digital content, regardless of how it became digital, and to collaborate with allied digital library professionals in integrating archival content with other information resources in ways that make it easy for Web-based users to find it. Settling on the right balance, which will be different depending on the institutions in which we work, promises to engage archivists for many decades to come. The one-size-fits-all, manna-from-heaven solution will undoubtedly elude us indefinitely.

"Archives in the Digital Library," brings together a variety of perspectives on archives and archivists in the digital library. In no way comprehensive of all of the issues and perspectives that are possible under the broad rubric of this volume's theme, it nonetheless is intended to function as a snapshot in time, situating archival repositories, professional archivists, and archival perspectives and issues in the current digital library landscape. The articles, collectively, are reflective both of contributions made by archivists and archival repositories to digital library initiatives, and of current digital library issues that should be of broad interest to archivists.

The first group of articles, under the heading "Developing Non-Licensed Content," reports on several innovative explorations into programs for coordinating and facilitating inclusion of unique, non-licensed content in digital library collections. The focus of these articles is on digitally reformatted surrogates of non-digital items from archival collections, primarily textual and graphic materials. Collectively they probe roles that archivists can play in broadening the scope of digitization efforts by contributing to developments in policies, procedures, and tools that facilitate this kind of digital-content creation.

The previously cited Lagoze et al. article is representative of much of the conversation in the literature on digital library efforts thus far. It focuses on technical issues and solutions, and is driven by a "proof of concept" research approach. In another vein, the years 2005-2006 have given us mass digitization efforts on a scale that would have been almost impossible to imagine just a few short years ago: witness efforts like Google Books and the Open Content Alliance.[2] But the focus of these early mass digitization efforts is on published resources, the largely duplicative, relatively mass-produced materials that inhabit the shelves of research and other libraries around the world, which is understandable given the conversion economies for which the mass digitization effort is striving. These and other current developments in the digital library world, while extremely important, sometimes do little to engage archivists, responsible as they are for unique content in information resources not generally created and distributed through traditional publishing routes.

Despite the current focus on artifacts of the publishing process, archival collections represent a window into unique content that, once digitized, promises to truly blow open the new knowledge-creation potential inherent in a mass digitization approach to reformatting non-digital information resources. This first group of articles in "Archives in the Digital Library," we hope, suggests that archivists are poised to be champions for inclusion of unique content in a stepped up mass-digitization effort. The collections for which we are currently responsible represent a real gold mine for efforts to surface information in non-digital holdings for discovery and understanding via tools and techniques for mining digital content, many of which are either currently available or under experimental development.[3] The challenge for archivists is to be willing and flexible partners in arriving at solutions to some of the challenges for mass digitization that the content in archival collections presents.[4] It would be to the detriment of all if we allow our traditions of uniqueness and specialty to be a conversation stopper within the broader digital library world. Our past access paradigms and descriptive traditions present hurdles that, while not insurmountable, will likely require creative and collaborative strategies for integration with digital library content.

In the first group of articles, Adrian L. Turner reviews a model for digital library outreach to smaller institutions in order to reformat valuable and unique information resources and make them available to digital library users. Dayna Holz explores the potential for collaboration between a special collection, a digital library, and a university press to produce an interwoven resource that integrates primary sources and secondary scholarly commentary in unique ways. Genie Guerard and Robin L. Chandler supply a case study of the convergence of digitization tools, best practices, curatorial expertise, and end-user input to make previously difficult to access content available for broad public use as a virtual collection within the digital library.

The second group of articles, "Usability Issues and Options for the End User," raises important issues for archivists to consider, especially as we move increasingly towards integrating access to electronic records and other born-digital archival materials with our traditional collections. We face challenges in maintaining our important in-person reading rooms and services, while not allowing the assumptions and tools wrapped up in our past understandings of access to constrain how we can serve new populations of users of our digital content. The digital library world is far ahead of us in taking advantage of end-user assessment techniques to help design and implement access mechanisms for digital content, and this group of articles reports on work in a broad variety of contexts to listen to end users and design access tools and services that meet their needs. One thing is crystal clear from usability work in general: end users want single-point, integrated access, or something as close to that as possible.

In the second group of articles, Rosalie Lack summarizes user assessment techniques and articulates the top-ten themes that have emerged from four years of evaluation and assessment activities on a variety of archival and bibliographic resource portals at the California Digital Library. Merrilee Proffitt documents a life-cycle approach to user-centered design, presenting the development of RedLightGreen, a tool designed for an undergraduate audience, as a case study in applying qualitative and quantitative data gathering to interface and service design. Maureen A. Burns explores a range of issues relating to access and service mechanisms for digital image collections, especially focusing on the assessment of tools designed to integrate finding and using licensed, non-licensed, and personal collections for teaching and research by visual arts faculty and graduate students.

The final group of articles in this collection, "Technology, Preservation, and Management Issues," brings together wide-ranging explorations of issues that weave inextricably with those in the first two sections. In fact, several of these articles could as easily have been placed in one of the earlier groupings. They explore issues that may not resonate immediately with many archivists who have little familiarity with current work in digital library settings, but nonetheless are of critical importance to archivists, especially because they represent areas where our profession is likely to need to integrate our expertise, needs, and concerns with the broader information management community.

In the final group of articles, Rebecca Guenther and Leslie Myrick explore description, preservation, and access issues for one specific class of born-digital resources that will likely be a significant portion of many archival collections in the future: archived Web sites. They provide instructive, concrete examples of the application of current digital library standards like the Metadata Encoding and Transmission Standard (METS) structural schema and the PREservation Metadata Implementation Strategies (PREMIS) preservation data model to Web archiving files. Jerome McDonough and Mona Jimenez present a cogent, highly readable overview of important technical and metadata-related issues regarding video capture that should inform any archival collection aspiring–alone or in a collaborative setting–to deal with digital reformatting of legacy videotaped materials. Ronald Jantz and Michael Giarlo explore the issues and implications of establishing "trusted digital repositories" to serve as the infrastructure for long-term preservation of and access to digital content. They frame their exploration with a case study of planning and implementing a digital repository at the Rutgers University Libraries. Joanne Kaczmarek ponders the need for clearer role definition and articulation in both academic and state government repositories, necessitated by the fuzzier boundaries that surface as greater proportions of collections and resources are being accumulated, managed, and accessed digitally. She frames these thoughts in the overarching context of a continuing foundational requirement to support end users' information needs, regardless of the formats in which the resources they require are available. And in the final article, Bradley D. Westbrook, Lee Mandell, Kelcy Shepherd, Brian Stevens, and Jason Varghese provide an overview of the eagerly anticipated Archivists' Toolkit, scheduled to be beta tested in the course of 2006. They review the functional requirements–based on an analysis of collection management processes in archives and special collections units–that underpinned the development of this software application, and detail possible alternatives for insuring long-term support for sustaining and expanding the application.

Taken together, these eleven articles serve as a clear and understandable overview of a wide variety of standards, technologies, and open issues that face the digital library world writ large, and archivists engaged therein, in 2006. As mentioned earlier, this special collection is meant to record a specific point in time, when many archival repositories have approached digital activities primarily under the rubric of project-based, largely grant-funded reformatting activities.

As important as the wealth of information that *is* here, is what *is not* included in this special volume. This is primarily a result of space limitations and failure to identify willing volunteers with enough time on their hands to tackle committing an exploration of these issues to paper. But more importantly, it is a reflection of the increasing complexity and interconnectedness of archival practice in an increasingly digital information world. In closing this introduction, we want to review a few of the issues and concerns that are not explicitly included here, but that nonetheless spark our interest. We do this to highlight the ongoing need for a sustained stream of contributions from archivists to the literature not only of this profession, but also to that of the broader world of research and practice relating to digital content repositories, whatever label they masquerade under.

- Considerations of approaches to Web "archiving" that fit into the more holistic, provenance- and appraisal-based methodologies through which archivists identify information of enduring value that should be maintained in the context of other materials that can't be captured by Web archiving. It would be especially useful to apply current work at the state and national government level to the records of individuals, communities, and small organizations.[5]
- Case studies of successful strategies in smaller archival repositories for appraising, capturing, describing, and preserving born-digital materials, and integrating them into access systems for non-digital materials.
- Explorations of the potential for using the Open Archives Initiative Protocol for Metadata Harvesting (OAI-PMH) for surfacing metadata about archival materials so that anyone who wants to can harvest it, enhance it, aggregate it with other interesting materials, and develop specialized access mechanisms to it for targeted groups of end users.[6]
- Summaries of ongoing work on metadata normalization and enhancement tools, some of which may form the basis for future extremely useful tools for automated extraction of metadata from and categorization of text-heavy electronic records and born-digital materials.[7] It is clear that the tools archivists need will not be available to us until we engage in their planning and development.
- Assessments of end user understandings of and responses to archival materials accessed through one-stop-shopping interfaces like those spawned following the success of Google.
- Considerations of the relevance of more tailored, targeted access portals for materials, designed with and for specific audiences, and

meant to enhance the experience of those audiences in their use and understanding of cultural heritage materials.

• Experiments with archival authority systems and their applicability for identification of born-digital content of enduring value, and for enhancing name-based access to archival materials held across institutions.

One could springboard from the title of the previously cited Lagoze et al. article and wonder whether a digital library is really a library anymore in any meaningful sense of the word. Does the notion of "library" succeed or fail in matching end users' expectations for increasingly open and comprehensive access to relevant digital information resources from a single entry point on their home computer's Web browser? Are libraries and librarians as constrained by their legacy as archivists sometimes are by their own? This collection of articles strives to explore two broad notions:

1. That archivists and the content they have been and will continue to be responsible for identifying, preserving, and serving up to end users are as important now as ever.
2. That collaborative efforts with allied information professionals in endeavors and developments that generally fall under the rubric of digital libraries promise solutions for many of our professional challenges.

We do ourselves a collective disservice when we aren't proactively front and center in critical digital information resource issues to which we can make important contributions.

William E. Landis
Robin L. Chandler

AUTHOR NOTE

William E. Landis, MILS, currently serves as Metadata Coordinator at the California Digital Library (CDL), University of California Office of the President, 415 20th Street, 4th Floor, Oakland, CA 94612 (E-mail: bill.landis@ucop.edu).

Robin L. Chandler, MA, MLIS, currently serves as Director of Built Content at the California Digital Library (CDL), University of California Office of the President, 415 20th Street, 4th Floor, Oakland, CA 94612 (E-mail: robin.chandler@ucop.edu).

NOTES

1. Carl Lagoze, Dean B. Krafft, Sandy Payette, and Susan Jesuroga, "What is a Digital Library Anymore, Anyway?: Beyond Search and Access in the NSDL," *D-Lib Magazine* 11, no. 11 (November 2005). Available online at: http://www.dlib.org/dlib/november05/lagoze/11lagoze.html. Accessed 2006-06-27.

2. For more information on the Open Content Alliance see http://www.opencontentalliance.org/, and for Google Books see http://books.google.com/. URLs accessed 2006-06-27.

3. For a few examples of these types of tools, see David J. Newman and Sharon Block, "Probabilistic Topic Decomposition of an Eighteenth-century American Newspaper," *JASIST* 57, no. 6, 753-767, and the interesting data mining work of the Stanford University InfoLab, http://www-db.stanford.edu/, especially their searchable database of publications at http://dbpubs.stanford.edu:8090/aux/index-en.html. URLs accessed 2006-06-27.

4. Issues like dealing with varying sizes and formats of materials within archival collections; representing arrangement relationships in ways that don't impede end users, but preserve important contextual information; generating searchable text from handwritten documents; developing economically viable strategies for representing archival materials and mining archival descriptive tools effectively for appropriate metadata are all challenges for which archivists need to be part of the solution.

5. For information about theme-based Web capture projects currently underway in conjunction with the Library of Congress, see http://www.loc.gov/webcapture/projects.html. Two projects funded by the National Digital Information Infrastructure and Preservation Program (NDIIPP) at the Library of Congress that are exploring Web archiving technologies and strategies for government materials are the Web at Risk project (http://web2.unt.edu/webatrisk/index.php) and the ECHO DEPository Project (http://www.ndiipp.uiuc.edu/). Internationally, seminal Web archiving projects are underway in a variety of places, including Australia (http://pandora.nla.gov.au/). URLs accessed 2006-06-27.

6. For more information about OAI-PMH, see http://www.openarchives.org/. Chris Prom, Assistant University Archivist at the University of Illinois at Urbana-Champaign, did very interesting research in 2003 on using OAI for EAD-encoded finding aids. A Microsoft PowerPoint presentation, "Do Real Archivists Use OAI?," and accompanying remarks on this research are available at http://web.library.uiuc.edu/AHX/workpap/MARAC03.ppt and http://web.library.uiuc.edu/AHX/workpap/MARAC03.pdf. See also Christopher J. Prom, "Reengineering Archival Access through OAI Protocols," *Library Hi Tech* 21:2 (2003), 199-209. See also Christopher J. Prom, "Does EAD Play Well with Other Metadata Standards? Searching and Retrieving EAD Using the OAI Protocols," *Journal of Archival Organization* 1, no. 1 (2005) 51-72. Ongoing work within the OAI metadata harvesting community since Prom's research in 2002-2003 suggests that another look at OAI for use in disseminating information about archival materials might be valuable; see especially the *OAI Best Practices* developed by the Digital Library Federation (DLF) and National Science Digital Library (NSDL) OAI and Shareable Metadata Best Practices Working Group (http://oai-best.comm.nsdl.org/cgi-bin/wiki.pl?MetadataContent) and the *Summary of OAI Metadata Best Practices* developed by the DLF. (http://www.diglib.org/architectures/oai/imls2004/training/MetadataFinal.pdf). URLs accessed 2006-06-27.

7. There is a whole host of interesting research in the computer science world, with which the editors of this special volume are only passingly acquainted, but for an example of this, see the Web site for the previously cited Stanford University InfoLab at http://www-db.stanford.edu/. For a discussion of a more practical attempt to explore the utility of some of these strategies to surface consistent topics from heterogeneous aggregations of metadata records, see the CDL's May 2005 *Metadata Enhancement Feasibility Study: Final Report*, available at http://www.cdlib.org/inside/projects/amwest/ cdl_clusteringOAI_final.pdf. This is just one example of the space that is rapidly opening up for archival experimentation with and assessment of these types of automated or semiautomated metadata extraction and remediation tools.

DEVELOPING NON-LICENSED CONTENT

Committing to Memory:
A Project to Publish
and Preserve California
Local History Digital Resources

Adrian L. Turner

SUMMARY. This article highlights the LSTA-grant funded California Local History Digital Resources Project (LHDRP) as a case study of a collaborative statewide program involving three primary groups: cultural heritage institutions, grant funding agencies, and digital library service providers. It explores how the infrastructure of the California

Adrian L. Turner, MA, MLIS, is Data Consultant and LHDRP Project Manager, California Digital Library (CDL), University of California Office of the President, 415 20th Street, 4th Floor, Oakland, CA 94612 (E-mail: adrian.turner@ucop.edu).

The author would like to acknowledge the assistance of Ira Bray, Robin Chandler, Bill Landis, and Bradley Westbrook in reviewing and providing comments on early drafts of this article. The introductory section of this article includes a restatement of text from the initial LSTA grant proposal for the LHDRP, developed by Robin Chandler.

[Haworth co-indexing entry note]: "Committing to Memory: A Project to Publish and Preserve California Local History Digital Resources." Turner, Adrian L. Co-published simultaneously in *Journal of Archival Organization* (The Haworth Information Press, an imprint of The Haworth Press, Inc.) Vol. 4, No.1/2, 2006, pp. 11-27; and: *Archives and the Digital Library* (ed: William E. Landis, and Robin L. Chandler) The Haworth Information Press, an imprint of The Haworth Press, Inc., 2006, pp. 11-27. Single or multiple copies of this article are available for a fee from The Haworth Document Delivery Service [1-800-HAWORTH, 9:00 a.m. - 5:00 p.m. (EST). E-mail address: docdelivery@haworthpress.com].

Available online at http://jao.haworthpress.com
© 2006 by The Haworth Press, Inc. All rights reserved.
doi:10.1300/J201v04n01_02

Digital Library (CDL) is utilized to preserve and promote public access to digitized local history collections, and discusses challenges and technical solutions to integrating heterogeneous resources into METS-based repositories. Project building blocks are also discussed, including digital object encoding and transmission tools, scanning services, metadata and imaging standards, and training programs. doi:10.1300/J201v04n01_02
[Article copies available for a fee from The Haworth Document Delivery Service: 1-800-HAWORTH. E-mail address: <docdelivery@haworthpress.com> Website: <http://www.HaworthPress.com> © 2006 by The Haworth Press, Inc. All rights reserved.]

KEYWORDS. California Local History Digital Resources Project, digitization projects, digital preservation, digital objects, METS, Metadata and Encoding Transmission Standard, metadata standards, imaging standards, scanning, CONTENTdm, Institute of Museum and Library Services, IMLS, Library Services and Technology Act, LSTA, California State Library, California Digital Library, Online Archive of California

INTRODUCTION

Multiple institutions throughout California–public and academic libraries, archives, historical societies, and museums–are enabled to digitize collections and disseminate them via the Internet through the support of the US Institute of Museum and Library Services (IMLS) under the provisions of the Library Services and Technology Act (LSTA), administered in California by the State Librarian.[1] The process of creating these materials requires a significant amount of effort. It is possible that the amount of resources allocated by institutions towards creating digital facsimiles, including metadata creation, scanning, storage, and ongoing maintenance of the digital assets, exceeds investments in maintaining the physical collections from which those facsimiles are derived. Because LSTA-funded digitization projects are supported substantially with public funding, it is important to ensure that these digital resources are made available in perpetuity to the public, and not just to the local communities served by institutions.

This article focuses on the California Local History Digital Resources Project (LHDRP), a multiyear (2000-present), LSTA grant-funded project that seeks to explore a model for aggregating, preserving, and providing persistent public access to local history digital collections throughout the state, leveraging the infrastructure of the California Digital Library

(CDL).[2] The LHDRP is a collaborative endeavor involving supporting agencies that provide a long-term framework for the program: public and academic cultural heritage institutions serve as digital content producers and primary reference points for the users of that content; the California State Library (CSL) guides the objectives of the program as part of the statewide plan for LSTA funds; and digital library service providers extend content creation tools, training opportunities, image scanning assistance, and resources that can be utilized by cultural heritage institutions to preserve and broaden access to their collections. In particular, the work of the CDL as a digital library service provider within the context of the LHDRP framework is highlighted.

FOUNDATIONS AND CONTEXT FOR COLLABORATION: A PROJECT SCAN

Background and Goals

The CSL Library Development Services Bureau and CDL conceived the LHDRP between 2000 and 2001, during an LSTA grant-funded planning year.[3] Under the coordination of Robin Chandler, serving as Manager of the Online Archive of California (OAC), the CDL proposed two chief objectives for a multiyear project, which was designated the LSTA Sustainability Project in its pilot phase and later renamed the LHDRP. The first objective sought to leverage CDL's infrastructure to conglomerate and extend permanent public access to local history digital object collections created by cultural heritage institutions in California.[4] The principal audiences for the LHDRP collections would be the local communities directly served by the participating institutions and specific user groups targeted by CDL Web sites: teachers for grades 3-12, University of California (UC) faculty and students, and historical researchers in general. The second objective sought to facilitate the creation of a preservation repository for the long-term retention and management of those digital assets. Ira Bray, Technology Consultant at the CSL, invited institutions to participate in the project through applications for LSTA grants.

Since the late 1990s, the CSL has been promoting the digitization of local history collections and has provided support for projects with the OAC through LSTA funds. The CSL's vision for a regional digitization program complemented the CDL's objectives for the LHDRP: the CDL was particularly interested in testing its capacity to provide scaleable, affordable, sharable collections, tools, and utilities that could be adopted and customized locally by the CDL's primary clientele, the UC campus libraries, in addition to non-UC cultural heritage institutions.

From technical, administrative, and geographical standpoints, the CDL was uniquely situated to participate in the LHDRP as a trusted digital library service provider. Established in 1997 by UC President Richard Atkinson as the eleventh "co-library" of the ten-campus UC system, the CDL was engineered to build the University's digital library, assist campus libraries by promoting a common infrastructure for sharing holdings more effectively, and provide leadership in applying technology to the creation of online collections and services. The CDL's OAC resource in particular was a logical mechanism for providing centralized access to distributed historical collections throughout the state.[5] Initially established as a catalog of Encoded Archival Description (EAD)[6] finding aids, the OAC had started to redefine its infrastructure by 1998 to deliver digital objects independent of the finding aids with which they were associated.[7] Moreover, the CDL had started to design the UC Libraries Digital Preservation Repository, a preservation system that could be extended to and replicated by CDL partners.[8] Using the repository for the LHDRP could ultimately be cost-effective: while most cultural heritage institutions share common interests in preserving collections, it is impractical, if not impossible, for all institutions to independently implement similar preservation technologies.

There were clear rationales for the multiyear project objectives. First, the digitized content was created through considerable investments of public funds. The LHDRP sought to answer a critical question posed by Paul Conway: "organizations are rearranging budgets, raising money, and anticipating income streams to make digital projects happen. Can any institution–library, archives, historical society, or museum–afford to squander this investment?"[9] Traditionally, the results of digital projects have been published online by institutions via distributed, locally hosted, and highly tailored portals. In some cases, the results have gained additional exposure through metadata-only consortial or national union catalogs, but generally have not been gathered in any coordinated fashion. Preservation efforts, beyond reprocessing and rehousing of the analog materials used to derive the digital objects, have largely been limited to storing the CDs or DVDs containing the master files. Some institutions have stored the digital objects on locally maintained hard drives with varying degrees of data backup and recovery provisions. Given the wide ranges in the capacity of institutions to devote sufficient resources in post-grant years to maintaining their digital assets, it is probable that a significant number of these Web sites are either outdated or no longer accessible. It is also conceivable that the physical media used to store the master digital files have deteriorated.

Second, the content chosen for digitization represents the result of careful selection processes carried out by each institution based on a number of considerations, with the ultimate goal of documenting a view of California's rich cultural and social history through unique, local lenses. They are digital products worth creating, providing access to, and preserving as part of California's cultural memory record, or what Conway has described as "digital products worth maintaining over time."[10]

There were no equivalent statewide programs upon which the LHDRP could be modeled, given the CDL's technical infrastructure and the particular goals of the project. The Collaborative Digitization Program (CDP), for example, provided a different framework for consolidating dispersed online collections, whereby institutions contribute digital object metadata to a centralized "referatory" maintained by the CDP. The metadata for these digital objects contains external links to the associated files, which are stored on distributed Web servers hosted by contributors.[11] While this offers contributors a high degree of local control over their content, including the ability to rapidly update objects and customize presentations for their patrons, it relies for persistence on local Web server policies and backup protocols. By consolidating both digital object metadata and associated content files in a centralized repository, the LHDRP model took a different approach to ensure the long-term viability of the collections.

Current Profile of Participating Institutions and Workflows

Following the 2001 planning year, seventeen institutions were identified by the CSL to participate in the project. As of 2005, and now in its sixth year, the LHDRP represents over forty additional institutions.[12] Approximately 18,000 digital objects have been made accessible to the public, and are being persistently managed in the UC Libraries Digital Preservation Repository. An example of some of the rich collections featured include the Society of California Pioneers' "Lawrence & Houseworth Photography Albums," comprising stereographic views of Northern California from the 1860s; Pomona Public Library's "Frasher Foto Postcard Collection," consisting of commercial black and white photographs created from 1855 through 1955 and documenting city life and scenic views throughout California; and photographs from the Silicon Valley History Online consortium of seven institutions, reflecting the rise of agriculture and technology in California's Santa Clara region.[13]

To date, the objects represent facsimiles of analog items; no born-digital items have been submitted to the CDL.[14] The vast majority of items scanned have primarily been single-sided graphic materials, the bulk of which are photographic prints and negatives. Other graphic materials scanned include printed maps, postcards, artwork, and ephemera. In a few cases, manuscript letters and maps, typescripts, and portions of multipage scrapbooks have also been digitized.

Since its inception, the project workflow has been streamlined iteratively through feedback received by the CSL and CDL, which is solicited from participating institutions using a survey administered at the end of each project year. The following generalized description of tasks conducted through the grant year reflects the current model workflow.

The LHDRP calendar follows the twelve-month State of California fiscal year, extending from July through the following June. Each year kicks off with a meeting to orient project managers from participating institutions to the project. The meeting also offers a forum for cross-institutional information sharing and networking. Following the kickoff meeting, the project managers and their teams attend a series of digitization workshops administered by two training vendors commissioned by the CDL for the project. One vendor is Infopeople, an LSTA grant-funded training organization for California libraries. The second vendor is OCLC's Western Service Center.[15] Over the next several months, the institutions focus on refining their selections of 200 objects, factoring in copyright assessments and other rights considerations.[16] Also during this time, each institution may begin recording metadata, using worksheets or directly cataloging into CONTENTdm, a shared digital asset creation tool hosted by OCLC and licensed by the CSL for the project year.[17] Project managers and CDL staff conduct joint technical assessments of sample metadata records to verify conformance with project specifications.

Scanning commences once selections have been completed. Califa, a non-profit, membership-based service bureau supported by LSTA grant funding, plays a vital role in mediating digital imaging services for the institutions.[18] From the winter through the spring quarters of the grant year, project managers ship their collections to a scanning vendor via Califa, and then receive and check for quality the vendor's deliverables. The deliverable comprises three separate image files for every object scanned: an archival TIFF master image file, a derivative JPEG access image, and a GIF thumbnail image. CD-ROMs with the image files are returned to the institutions for local retention; a duplicate DVD copy is sent to the CDL. The project managers then load the derivative image files into CONTENTdm, thereby completing their metadata records.

Towards the end of each grant year, the participating institutions export digital object metadata from CONTENTdm (with links to the derivative image files on the CONTENTdm server). To provide more context for the individual digital objects, the institutions also supply a text file with a description of the source collections used to derive the digital objects. CDL staff load the metadata and derivative image files from the submission package–with the master/archival image files received on DVD–into the CDL's access-based repository for publication via the OAC. CDL staff then stage the content for transfer into the UC Libraries Digital Preservation Repository. This includes generating technical metadata necessary for the orderly management of digital objects in the repository, using the JSTOR/Harvard Online Validation Environment (JHOVE) software.[19] Last, the data in the collection-level descriptive record worksheet is encoded by the CDL into an EAD finding aid, through a semiautomated process using CDL's EAD Web Templates. The templates are Web forms with EAD-mapped fields. Encoders simply input basic collection-level data into the form, and generate an EAD finding aid with the push of a button.[20]

A CDL project team coordinates LHDRP activities, consulting with project institutions through online discussions, e-mail, and phone.[21] The team also maintains a Web site, which serves as a forum for posting project-related documentation, and an online handbook.[22] The latter, the *LHDRP Handbook*, provides detailed information about project tasks, timelines, and instructions for creating digital assets according to specifications set forth by the CSL and CDL.

BUILDING BLOCKS FOR INTEROPERABILITY AND SUSTAINABILITY

Digital Object Creation Tools, Standards, and Guidelines

The promotion of digital object metadata and imaging standards has been a fundamental component of the LHDRP. The CSL has been proactive in promulgating standards for LSTA grant-funded digitization projects since the late 1990s.[23] With the CDL's involvement in the LHDRP, the digital object specifications needed to reflect an expanded set of descriptive and rights administrative metadata requirements needed by the CDL for the orderly management of objects in its repositories, and to power search and browse functions in its public interfaces. The specifications also needed to reflect the use of the Metadata and Encoding and Transmission Standard (METS) as a mechanism for packaging digital object metadata and associated content files.[24] The *CDL Guidelines for Digital Objects, Version 2.0* (CDL GDO) now serves as the prime blueprint for LHDRP digital objects.[25]

Since 2002, the CDL has proactively adopted the METS standard as a vehicle for ingesting and managing digital objects in its repositories of non-licensed content. This presented a particular hurdle for the CDL and participating institutions at the beginning of the project, given the dearth of METS-producing tools at the time. To overcome this challenge to data integration, two solutions have since been developed and tested by the CDL over the course of the LHDRP, involving data transformations and the compiling of descriptive, structural, and copyright metadata exports from digital asset creation tools into the METS format.[26]

The first data transformation model was formulated by CDL technical staff through an environmental scan of digital object creation processes used by participating institutions. The bulk of the institutions utilized MAchine-Readable Cataloging (MARC)-based systems, customized databases, and commercial digital asset management products to maintain their metadata and associated image files. Since there was no common record format for representing descriptive metadata in particular, the CDL proposed two primary, common standard target formats that could potentially be generated by the different systems and could also be handled by CDL systems: MARC-based encoding, comprising the MARC 21 format and its XML-based equivalents, MARCXML and Metadata Object Description Schema (MODS); and Dublin Core-based encoding, using the Resource Description Framework (RDF) in either an XML format, or an HTML format.[27] The CDL then conferred with each institution to create export routines for their digital asset creation tools to produce one of those target record formats. Given a final export from the institutions, CDL technical staff would run additional transformations on the metadata (including converting MARC 21 records to MODS) and compile the metadata and associated image files submitted on CDs or DVDs into METS.

It became increasingly clear that this model was neither extensible, nor efficient. The metadata records still contained a high degree of heterogeneous encoding practices, even when converted into common formats, that made automated ingest routines difficult. Processing still involved a significant amount of "one-off" customized work. Project institutions indicated through the yearly project assessment that they would welcome use of a centralized cataloging utility or data normalization process.

In an effort to streamline data processing, a second data transformation model was developed by the CSL and CDL in 2004 and implemented in 2005. A solution was identified in CONTENTdm, a product that had previously been utilized by some LHDRP participants. CONTENTdm affords a number of benefits. First, the tool can be configured to standardize data entry and produce predictable exports: it generates a Dublin Core RDF/XML export, a common standard supported by CDL systems. Moreover, the tool manages some degree of structural metadata for complex digital objects, a unique feature not commonly found in similar products, particularly MARC-based systems. Next, distributed institutions can catalog into a centrally administered CONTENTdm server using locally installed "Acquisition Stations." CONTENTdm is also backed by OCLC, which maintains an extensive user support and training apparatus. Last, it was possible to automate a transformation of the Dublin Core RDF/XML export into METS. In consultation with the CDL, DiMeMa, Inc., creators of CONTENTdm, implemented in Version 4.0 of the product a more robust Dublin Core RDF/XML export that exposes additional administrative and structural metadata. Structural metadata comprises a fundamental part of any given METS object: using an eXtensible Stylesheet Language Transformation (XSLT) stylesheet currently being refined by the CDL, institutions will be able to transform CONTENTdm exports "on the fly" into METS.[28]

An OCLC-hosted instance of the CONTENTdm server is currently being licensed by the CSL on a grant-year basis. CONTENTdm Acquisition Stations are installed on workstations at each institution. The Acquisition Stations are configured to promote cataloging that adheres to the CDL's specifications for digital object metadata: the data entry fields are mapped to Dublin Core RDF/XML elements that comply with the CDL GDO. The Acquisition Stations' data entry fields have also been configured by the CDL to capture "descriptive" copyright information that is vital for establishing the copyright status of a given work. This information includes details such as creator death dates (which may help establish when a given work falls into public domain), copyright holder name (when known), whether a work is published or unpublished, copyright statement (if present), and place or country of creation.[29]

Training and Educational Programs

In many cases, the project managers at the participating institutions are "lone arrangers," responsible for a dizzying array of project tasks. Concepts and practices pertaining to copyright assessment, scanning, and metadata creation are often unfamiliar to project managers at the outset. One of the guiding principles of the LHDRP is to empower institutions to build digital library collections in post-grant years. A key project building block is a suite of training workshops offered at the beginning of each grant year. Working with Infopeople and OCLC Western Service Center, the CSL and CDL developed a series of courses focusing on basic management of digitization projects; advantages and disadvantages of in-house scanning in comparison to outsourcing the work; and the creation of interoperable and standardized metadata. In 2005, two new courses were offered: a workshop exploring copyright and other rights-related issues that need to be considered when selecting materials for scanning; and a hands-on CONTENTdm workshop. A workshop concentrating on collection description practices is being planned for 2006. The majority of courses have been offered as full-day, in-person sessions. In a few cases, the courses have been offered as online tutorials.

Digital Imaging and Outsourcing

Beginning in 2004, Califa was selected by the CSL to broker digital imaging services for the project institutions in the interest of streamlining a major component of digitization projects that required significant expertise, staffing, time, and hardware and software resources.[30] In previous LHDRP years, each project institution was responsible for digitizing their physical collections, using either local in-house scanning methods or vendors. Some institutions, those with established in-house scanning capability, had greater success than others in successfully completing scanning tasks by the end of the grant year. In the summer of 2005, Califa issued a request for proposal from scanning vendors.[31] Wisconsin-based Northern Micrographics, Inc. was awarded the contract and is currently providing conversion services for the project.[32]

Califa project staff work with participating institutions through a series of outsourcing tasks. Project managers first prepare their materials for scanning. This includes completing worksheets to convey scanning instructions to the vendor, and packing materials appropriately to ship to the scanning vendor. Batch installments of fifty objects are then shipped from the institutions to the vendor over a period of five months, using a shipping service contracted through Califa. Last, Califa project staff and project managers jointly perform quality control reviews of the vendor's deliverables.

The *CDL Guidelines for Digital Images, Version 2.0* (CDL GDI) serves as a baseline scanning specification for the project.[33] Substantially informed by the U.S. National Archives and Records Administration's (NARA) *Technical Guidelines for Digitizing Archival Materials for Electronic Access: Creation of Production Master Files–Raster Images*, the CDL GDI establishes minimum requirements for all new digital image files prepared by institutions for submission to the CDL.[34]

LOOKING AHEAD: ONGOING CONSIDERATIONS

As the LHDRP moves forward into its next grant year, it continues to focus on its core objectives. It also continues to synthesize lessons learned from previous years and recommendations from the digital library community and other collaborative regional programs.[35] New developments are already underway. The CDL is currently reassessing how to deliver publicly accessible digital content via its gateways, and has embarked on designing a new Web site, to be named Calisphere. Calisphere will be tailored specifically to the California teaching community and will showcase collections previously accessible through the OAC only.[36] The CDL is also investigating two new goals: assessing pre-2001 LSTA grant-funded digital collections for retrospective capture and ingest, and exploring mechanisms for the automated enrichment and normalization of metadata–such as dates, subject terms, and form/genre headings–in those collections. Through the CDL's ongoing experimentation with using the Open Archives Initiative Protocol for Metadata Harvesting (OAI-PMH) for exposing content in its repositories to other data service providers, the LHDRP digital object metadata can potentially be shared with other regional and national consortia.[37]

Many components of the LHDRP collaborative framework represent technical solutions to challenges in aggregating and preserving digital content, and each solution brings new challenges. METS is both a technical bar and a bridge to collaboration. Many institutions still cannot generate METS-based digital objects for export, much less absorb METS digital objects into local systems to present using their own tailored websites. Yet METS was designed to facilitate data interchange and interoperability.

The feasibility of licensing a METS-creation tool such as CONTENTdm on a continued grant-year basis needs to be evaluated. A key challenge to the success of the LHDRP will lie in CDL's ability to foster the creation of affordable, easy-to-implement utilities that will output native METS digital objects. Open-source tools such as XSLT stylesheets that can transform non-native METS objects into METS are an existing solution.[38] Outsourcing of METS encoding to vendors may offer another solution. In the early stages of the project, there were no widely available tools for creating METS. But new open-source applications are now on the horizon, including the Andrew W. Mellon Foundation-funded Archivists' Toolkit and the IMLS-funded Museums and Online Archives Collaboration (MOAC) Community Toolbox.[39] DiMeMa's proactive role in updating CONTENTdm to produce a "METS-able" export is also a promising development for the digital library community, and other vendors will hopefully follow DiMeMa's lead.

Balancing the needs of consortia gateways with the needs of an individual institution for customizing presentations of content for particular communities is a general challenge faced by consortial projects. This includes balancing requirements for specific metadata elements required for CDL's gateways, such as normalized dates and Library of Congress Subject Headings (LCSH), with institutions' local cataloging practices. The CDL's exploration of methods for automatically normalizing and generating metadata may offer a future solution, but for the present time the CDL's gateways fundamentally rely on the source metadata provided by contributors. A related hurdle is the CDL's ability to provide low-barrier mechanisms that allow participating institutions to customize views of their METS objects in CDL's repositories for presentation on their local websites. The CDL's Interface Customization Tools (ICT) offer one solution that can be implemented by institutions with XSLT expertise.[40] Using HTTP protocols, institutions can query the CDL's repositories and receive the raw XML for their METS objects. The raw XML can then be converted into HTML and formatted for presentation on local Web sites, using XSLT stylesheets.

The LHDRP has thus far focused on preserving reformatted analog digital objects. Capturing born-digital materials of interest in a local history context that are being generated by individuals and organizations is another challenge. In particular, digital photographs created and collected by community members or institutional staff, blogs focused on localized issues, oral history electronic text transcripts, and digital audio/video files are examples of currently common forms of material that could be targeted in subsequent years.

In future project years, the CDL will also need to identify more sustainable methods for capturing descriptions of the institutions' collections in a standardized encoding format. Many of the institutions, particularly the public libraries and museums, do not implement EAD or arrange and describe their local history collections based on archival principles. To address the need for collection-level descriptions of these local history resources in the CDL environment, project staff at CDL developed worksheets for institutions to use to provide contextual information about their collections. Looking ahead, institutions could directly use the CDL's EAD Web Templates to generate these collection-level descriptions. Looking further ahead, the CDL may begin to investigate implementation of non-EAD schemes for representing collection descriptions. The Dublin Core Collection Description scheme offers one possibility. The scheme offers a flexible means for describing with Dublin Core elements collections that are not necessarily controlled using archival principles.[41]

The long-term viability of the LHDRP, including the benefits versus costs of participating for all participants, is an important question that is difficult to answer. But the question must be considered as the CSL and CDL continue to conduct formal assessments of the project. By the same token, taking collaborative actions now to guarantee persistent public access to statewide local history digital resources in the future will minimize chances that substantial public funds are wasted. The visible outcomes from the project are a major achievement: over 18,000 local history materials with associated collection guides, hitherto largely inaccessible to the public via a centralized gateway, are now available online and will be persistently managed for the long-term. Additionally, the less visible results of the process–a mature and collaborative framework for cultural heritage institutions, grant funding agencies, and digital library service providers–is an equally significant outcome, as it represents a powerful model for building and sustaining local history digital resources across the state.

NOTES

1. Additional information about the IMLS is available at http://www.imls.gov/. Accessed 2006-01-04.

2. The LHDRP project Web site is available online at http://www.cdlib.org/inside/projects/oac/lsta/. For more information about the CDL, see http://www.cdlib.org/. URLs accessed 2006-01-04.

3. For more information about the CSL's LSTA grant program, see http://www.library.ca.gov/html/grants.cfm. Accessed 2006-01-04.

4. The term "digital object" as used in this article specifically refers to an entity in which one or more electronic content files (e.g., image, audio/video, encoded text) and their corresponding metadata are united, physically and/or logically, through the use of

a digital wrapper, such as a Metadata and Encoding Transmission Standard (METS) file. For more information, see the *CDL Glossary* at http://www.cdlib.org/inside/diglib/glossary/. Accessed 2006-01-04.

5. For a discussion of the foundations and scope of the OAC resource, see Robin L. Chandler, "Building Digital Collections at the OAC: Current Strategies with a View to Future Uses," *Journal of Archival Organization* 1, no.1 (2001): 93-103. Additional information about the OAC is available online at http://www.oac.cdlib.org. Accessed 2006-01-04.

6. Information about EAD is available online at http://www.loc.gov/ead/. Accessed 2006-01-05.

7. This was fully realized in 2002 with the redesign of the OAC Web site and underlying technical architecture (OAC Version 2.0); see Robin L. Chandler and Genie Guerard in this volume, XXX-XXX. For a reference model for the OAC Version 2.0 redesign and a conceptualization of themed digital object collections, see William E. Landis, "Nuts and Bolts: Implementing Descriptive Standards to Enable Virtual Collections," *Journal of Archival Organization* 1, no. 1 (2001): 81-92; and Bradley D. Westbrook, "Prospecting Virtual Collections," *Journal of Archival Organization* 1, no. 1 (2001): 73-80.

8. For more information about the UC Libraries Digital Preservation Program, see http://www.cdlib.org/inside/projects/preservation/. Accessed 2006-01-04.

9. Paul Conway, "Overview: Rationale for Digitization and Preservation," in *Handbook for Digitization Projects: a Management Tool for Preservation and Access*, ed. Maxine K. Sitts (Andover: NEDCC, 2000): 16.

10. Conway, "Overview," 18-19.

11. The Collaborative Digitization Program (CDP), formerly known as the Colorado Digitization Project, is a longstanding consortium representing ten western states. For an exposition of the CDP framework, see Brenda Bailey-Hainer and Richard Urban, "The Colorado Digitization Program: a Collaboration Success Story," *Library Hi Tech*, 22:3 (2004): 254-262; Nancy Allen "Collaboration Through the Colorado Digitization Project," *First Monday*, 5 (June 2000), available online at http:www.firstmonday.dk/issues/issue5_6/allen/; and Liz Bishoff, "Interoperability and Standards in a Museum-Library Collaborative: the Colorado Digitization Project," *First Monday* 5 (June 2000), available online at http://www.firstmonday.dk/issues/issue5_6/bishoff. URLs accessed 2006-01-04.

12. The following institutions have participated in the LHDRP: Albany Public Library; Anaheim Public Library; Berkeley Public Library; California State University Sacramento, Special Collections & University Archives; California State University, Stanislaus, Library; Chula Vista Public Library; Coalinga Huron Library; Covina Public Library; DeAnza College, California History Center; Fresno County Library; Glendale Public Library; History San Jose Research Library; Humboldt State University; Intel Museum; Kern County Library; Kings County Library; Madera County Library; Marin County Free Library; Mariposa County Library; Mill Valley Public Library; Mission Viejo City Library; Oakland Public Library; Orange Public Library; Oxnard Public Library; Palos Verdes Library District; Pomona Public Library; Porterville Public Library; Redwood City Public Library; Richmond Public Library; San Bernardino Public Library; San Bruno Public Library; San Diego Historical Society; San Francisco Performing Arts Library & Museum; San Jose Public Library; San Jose State University, Special Collections Department; San Mateo Public Library; Santa Ana Public Library; Santa Clara City Library; Santa Clara University, University Archives; Society of California

Pioneers; Southern California Library for Social Studies & Research; Sutter County Library; Tulare County Library; Tulare Public Library; and Yuba County Library.

13. To view the collections online, see the list of institutions on the OAC Web site at http://www.oac.cdlib.org/institutions/. Accessed 2006-01-04. Silicon Valley History Online collaborators are listed under individual institution names on the OAC list of institutions: History San Jose Research Library; San Jose Public Library, California Room; Santa Clara City Library; San Jose State University Library, Special Collections and Archives; Santa Clara University, University Archives; Intel Museum; and California History Center (DeAnza College).

14. "Born digital" refers to materials originally created in electronic format, such as digital camera images. This is distinguished from "born analog" materials that were originally created in a non-digital format, and may subsequently be digitized. This definition based on the one for "born digital" in Richard Pearce-Moses, *A Glossary of Archival and Records Terminology* (Chicago: Society of American Archivists, 2005), also available online at http://www.archivists.org/glossary/. Accessed 2006-01-05.

15. For more information, see the Infopeople and OCLC Western Service Center training program Web sites at http://www.infopeople.org/ and http://www.oclc.org/western/. Past LHDRP training materials are available on the Infopeople Web site. URLs accessed 2006-01-05.

16. Beginning in 2005, the CSL established a limit of 200 individual items to be scanned per institution, in order to set a baseline target that could realistically be met by all institutions. This number fluctuated in previous grant years, ranging from several hundred to several thousands of objects, and not all institutions were able to meet their targeted goals within the grant year. The 200-item limit may increase in subsequent project years as the CSL assesses the degree to which institutions successfully meet this goal.

17. For more information about CONTENTdm, see http://www.contentdm.com/. Accessed 2006-01-05.

18. For more information about Califa, see http://www.califa.org/. Accessed 2006-01-05.

19. JHOVE is a software utility for the identification and validation of digital object content files. For more information, see http://hul.harvard.edu/jhove/. Accessed 2006-01-05.

20. EAD Web Templates are accessible online at http://www.cdlib.org/inside/projects/oac/toolkit/templates/. EAD mappings comply with RLG's and CDL's best practice guidelines for EAD Version 2002. Accessed 2006-01-05.

21. Primary LHDRP project staff includes: Ira Bray (CSL, State Data Coordinator and Technology Consultant), Robin Chandler (CDL, Director of Built Content), Paul Fogel (CDL, Programmer Analyst), Brian Tingle (CDL, Content Management Designer), Trudy Levy (Califa), and the author. Project staff from previous grant years includes Bradley Westbrook (UCSD, Metadata Librarian/CDL Consultant) and Lori Bowen Ayre (Galecia Group/CDL Consultant).

22. See http://www.cdlib.org/inside/projects/oac/lsta/. Accessed 2006-01-05.

23. See California State Library, *Metadata Standards*, ed., Liz Bishoff (Evergreen, Colorado: The Bishoff Group, 1999), available online at http://www.library.ca.gov/assets/acrobat/metadocfinalrev.pdf; and California State Library, *Scanning Standards*, ed., Liz Bishoff (Evergreen, Colorado: The Bishoff Group, 1999), available online at http://www.library.ca.gov/assets/acrobat/CSLscan.pdf. URLs accessed 2006-01-05.

24. METS is an emerging, open source, XML-based international standard for encoding metadata necessary for both the management of digital objects within a repository and exchange of such objects between repositories. METS provides a method for structurally binding related components of a digital object. Within a METS file, disparate content files (e.g., digital images, encoded texts) may be embedded or referenced from associated descriptive, technical, or administrative metadata. It is possible to flexibly transmute a METS object for a variety of different functions within a given repository, such as for ingest, presentation, rights management, and preservation; the standard is therefore adaptive to repository implementations based on the Open Archival Information System (OAIS) reference model. METS also supports the representation of object structures, from simple images, to complex multipage texts or multimedia resources. The CDL has adopted METS for its strengths as an interoperable encoding standard in these regards. For more information, see the METS Web site available online at http://www.loc.gov/standards/mets/. Accessed 2006-01-05.

25. Available online at http://www.cdlib.org/inside/diglib/guidelines/. Accessed 2006-01-05.

26. The CDP offers a different, highly streamlined approach for ingesting heterogeneous metadata into its Dublin Core-based metadata repository. As of 2004, the CDP uses the DC Builder system to translate metadata from different formats into Dublin Core. Institutions upload records in native formats to the DC Builder, but specify mappings from their native formats to the target Dublin Core scheme. The CDP model can be contrasted from the LHDRP model in that it is not METS based. See the previously cited Bailey-Hainer and Urban: 255-257.

27. For more information about MARCXML and MODS encoding, see http://www.loc. gov/standards/marcxml/ and http://www.loc.gov/standards/mods/. For information about Dublin Core encoding, see http://www.dublincore.org/resources/expressions/. URLs accessed 2006-01-05.

28. XSLT can be used to transform a given XML document in one encoding format into another XML document, through the use of stylesheets For more information, see the W3C Web site at http://www.w3.org/TR/xslt. Accessed 2006-01-05. The CONTENTdm export stylesheet will be a product of the CDL for LHDRP-specific purposes. Once developed, however, the stylesheet will be made available to the METS user community.

29. For additional context about this copyright data model, see Coyle, Karen, "Descriptive Metadata for Copyright Status," *First Monday*, 10, no. 10 (October 2005), available online at http://www.firstmonday.org/issues/issue10_10/coyle/. Accessed 2006-01-05.

30. For a discussion of rationales for outsourcing digitization, see Roy Tennant, "Outsourcing Digitization" in *Library Journal* (September 15, 1999), available online at http://www.libraryjournal.com/article/CA156509.html. Accessed 2006-01-05. See also Janet Gertz, "Vendor Relations," in *Handbook for Digitization Projects: a Management Tool for Preservation and Access* ed., Maxine K. Sitts (Andover: NEDCC, 2000): 150-163.

31. The following RFP's were consulted by Califa and served as models for the LHDRP: RLG, *RLG Model Request for Proposal for Digital Imaging Services* (Mountain View, CA.: Research Libraries Group, Inc., 1997); and Arkansas History Commission, *Request for Proposal: Scanning of Photographic Materials* (Little Rock: Arkansas History Commission, 2000), the latter available online at http://www.ark-ives.com/ photo/images/pdf/P000796.PDF. Accessed 2006-01-05.

32. Further information about this vendor is available online at http://www. normicro.com/. Accessed 2006-01-05.

33. Available online at http://www.cdlib.org/inside/diglib/guidelines/bpgimages/. Accessed 2006-01-05.

34. NARA's guidelines are available online at http://www.archives.gov/research/ arc/digitizing-archival-materials.pdf. Accessed 2006-01-05.

35. The Digital Library Federation (DLF) and Council on Library and Information Resources (CLIR) have also provided a number of compelling recommendations for building sustainable collaborative digitization programs. See CLIR, *Building and Sustaining Digital Collections*, (Washington, DC: CLIR, 2001), available online at http://www.clir.org/pubs/reports/pub100/pub100.pdf; Smith, Abby, *Strategies for Building Digitized Collections* (Washington, DC: CLIR, 2001), available online at http://www.clir.org/pubs/reports/pub101/contents.html; and Zorich, Diane, *A Survey of Digital Cultural Heritage Initiatives and Their Sustainability* (Washington, DC: CLIR, 2003), available online at http://www.clir.org/pubs/reports/pub118/contents.html. URLs accessed 2006-01-05.

36. Calisphere, scheduled for release in spring 2006, will comprise a redesign of the current CDL Web site for publicly available content at http://californiadigitallibrary.org/. Accessed 2006-01-05.

37. The CDL was awarded a three-year William and Flora Hewlett Foundation grant beginning in 2004 to assemble a virtual collection highlighting digitized primary resources documenting the American West, drawing from the resources of major research institutions. The project will explore the use of OAI-PMH as a method to aggregate digital object metadata from disparate online collections. The collection will be presented with a range of tools supporting extensive reconfiguration, integration with online learning environments, and continued growth through the addition of relevant research and teaching materials produced in the course of its use. For more information about the CDL American West Project, see http://www.cdlib.org/inside/projects/amwest/. Accessed 2006-01-05.

38. The CDP's DC Builder provides another useful model that could be further investigated for transforming heterogeneous data formats into a standard target METS format.

39. For an overview of the Archivists' Toolkit, see Westbrook et al. in this volume, 233-257. See also the Archivists' Toolkit Web site at http://archiviststoolkit.org/. For more information about the MOAC Community Toolbox, see http://www.bampfa. berkeley.edu/moac/community_toolbox.html. URLs accessed 2006-01-05.

40. For a discussion of ICT implementations, see the Chandler and Guerard in this volume, 47-69. See also the ICT Web site at http://www.cdlib.org/inside/diglib/repository/ customize/. Accessed 2006-01-05. CDL gateways such as Calisphere and the OAC are also designed to leverage ICT-based technology; the two gateways are essentially different customized views of subsets of the same collections in CDL's digital object repository.

41. For more information about the Dublin Core Collection Description schema see http://dublincore.org/groups/collections/. Accessed 2006-01-05.

doi:10.1300/J201v04n01_02

Technologically Enhanced Archival Collections: Using the Buddy System

Dayna Holz

SUMMARY. Based in the context of challenges faced by archives when managing digital projects, this article explores options of looking outside the existing expertise of archives staff to find collaborative partners. In teaming up with other departments and organizations, the potential scope of traditional archival digitization projects is expanded beyond the limits of a single institution. A case study of this principle is the collaboration between the Mark Twain Papers, the California Digital Library, and the University of California Press to develop TEI-encoded versions of elaborately annotated manuscript and published materials. Though not an example of a conventional archival digitization project, the Mark Twain Digital Project serves as a model of how to solicit and incorporate

---

Dayna Holz, MLIS, is Project Archivist, Environmental Design Archives, University of California, Berkeley, 230 Wurster Hall #1820, Berkeley, CA 94720-1820 (E-mail: dholz@berkeley.edu).

The author gratefully acknowledges the assistance of several colleagues in the research and completion of this article, namely, Anh Bui, formerly of the Mark Twain Papers, Catherine Candee, Director of Publishing and Strategic Initiatives for the UC Office of Scholarly Communication, Kirk Hastings and Felicia Poe of the California Digital Library, Andrea Laue of the Mark Twain Digital Project, and Betsy Frederick-Rothwell of the Environmental Design Archives.

[Haworth co-indexing entry note]: "Technologically Enhanced Archival Collections: Using the Buddy System." Holz, Dayna. Co-published simultaneously in *Journal of Archival Organization* (The Haworth Information Press, an imprint of The Haworth Press, Inc.) Vol. 4, No. 1/2, 2006, pp. 29-44; and: *Archives and the Digital Library* (ed: William E. Landis, and Robin L. Chandler) The Haworth Information Press, an imprint of The Haworth Press, Inc., 2006, pp. 29-44. Single or multiple copies of this article are available for a fee from The Haworth Document Delivery Service [1-800-HAWORTH, 9:00 a.m. - 5:00 p.m. (EST). E-mail address: docdelivery@haworthpress.com].

Available online at http://jao.haworthpress.com
© 2006 by The Haworth Press, Inc. All rights reserved.
doi:10.1300/J201v04n01_03

external experts into the design and execution of digitizing archival materials. doi:10.1300/J201v04n01_03 *[Article copies available for a fee from
The Haworth Document Delivery Service: 1-800-HAWORTH. E-mail address:
<docdelivery@haworthpress.com> Website: <http://www.HaworthPress.com>
© 2006 by The Haworth Press, Inc. All rights reserved.]*

KEYWORDS. Digital projects, TEI, Text Encoding Initiative, digital
libraries, digitized texts, collaborative projects

INTRODUCTION

In a grant-driven financial climate for archives and cultural institutions, digitization projects are a priority or, at minimum, a component in
requirements for many funding agencies. For many repositories, the
thought of preserving, migrating, and ensuring access to digital collections looms as a burden, not a solution. For archivists comfortable with
acid-free folders, mylar sleeves, finding aids, and indexes, the long-term
benefits of applying for digitization grants may not be immediately apparent when weighed against the short-term drawbacks of having to
scan digital images, create descriptive metadata, encode some kind of
standardized computer access, design a user-interface, and host the whole
thing on a server. The idea that precious climate-controlled shelf space
will be eaten up by rows of CD-ROMs filled with images that could be
produced for a fraction of the cost and take up a fraction of the space ten
years from now may cause one to question: Are digitization projects just
the microfilm of the new millennium? Is the rush to digitize simply a
reaction to the funding climate, or is there added value in creating digital instances of existing archival collections?

The difference between making a digitization project into a digital
surrogate that lingers as a preservation burden, and making a digital
product that enhances access to an archival collection, can be found at
the very beginning stages of a project, before documents are scanned,
before grant proposals are written. Identifying potential collaborators
and shared resources (both physical and intellectual) can mean the difference between putting together a project bound by the limits of a single repository and one that uses opportunities of affiliation and common
goals to create a product that is valuable to the institution as well as to its
users. An unlikely venture involving the Mark Twain Papers & Project,
the California Digital Library's eScholarship program, and the University

of California Press highlights a successful case of effective collaboration. Relying on expertise and input from each institution, the project ultimately produced an innovative outcome beyond the capabilities of any individual partner.

Digital projects are expensive largely because the required expertise and equipment are not generally found within a single institution. Programming, coding, scanning, and interface design often must be outsourced to high-priced vendors. Documents, photographs, and drawings must be carefully inventoried, packed, and shipped to a scanning lab, fingers crossed that a lab technician won't find transparent tape to be adequately archival in repairing an accidental tear in a page.[1] As just one of many steps in the process of converting an archival document to a digital object, the scanning process may be the simplest for many archivists to comprehend; an image of a physical item either looks like the real thing or it doesn't. Metadata and code, however, introduce complexity and require decisions to be made that are often not intuitive. Without a reliable employee with a background, aptitude or interest in computers, the archivist must look outside the archives to find another costly expert to move the digitization project along.

With so many hurdles, it is a wonder archivists apply for digitization grants at all. Nonetheless, there is ample grant money for digitization because users want digital access. Archivists are faced with what librarians have been dealing with for years: a demand for immediate, convenient, and free access to collections. As "Google" becomes a verb, the NUCMC[2] seems terribly archaic when compared with consortial Encoded Archival Description (EAD) finding aid ventures like the Online Archive of California (OAC)[3] or the Northwest Digital Archives.[4] With embedded images, links to external documents, full-text searching, and targeted metadata browsing for which EAD provides opportunities, a repository that is limited to paper finding aids and "by appointment only" research requests will quickly find itself unknown beyond the most local of researchers.

There is no question that the digital age is upon us, that repositories must accommodate it in some way, and that digital projects can represent a huge budgetary drain on institutions that generally have to struggle to pay staff and keep the air conditioning on. Whether digital projects are part of a grant proposal, a mandate from a board or university, or the next step in fulfilling a repository's mission statement, it is worth investing the time at the beginning stages of a project to try to imagine how, in an ideal world, an online presence would look and function. There is always room to scale back, but in imagining the possibilities of how technology can enhance access to collections, archivists may stumble upon opportunities for collaboration with groups outside their own institutions that can enable a digital project to become valuable beyond the parameters of the institution's funded capacity.

NEW TECHNOLOGIES AND ARCHIVAL COLLECTIONS: CAN'T WE ALL JUST GET ALONG?

Digital access to collections may be as simple as putting a document on a desktop scanner and e-mailing the image to a researcher: remote access at its most basic. This is akin to photocopying the same document and sending it through the mail, possibly with some better resolution and detail while simultaneously saving on postal expenses. However, this serves an individual user a single time. What if, instead of e-mailing the image, the archivist puts it on a Web site? The image becomes accessible to a larger audience, and is valuable if every researcher wants to see that single document. Making images available to an unknown audience also means that there needs to be some kind of contextual description that travels with the image–for example, repository name, collection title, item description–for it to have any meaning. Eventually, the progression of this argument leads to questions about metadata, standardization, archival-quality images, cross-institutional interoperability, user experience, and digital preservation.[5] The breadth of considerations can be overwhelming, but fortunately, if a repository doesn't happen to be part of an institution large enough to develop advancements in technologies and standards internally, other organizations are already engaged in this work and publishing their conclusions and recommendations on the Web. This doesn't eliminate the considerable amount of work necessary to create a successful digital project; it just means each archivist doesn't have to reinvent the wheel every time a new digital venture is undertaken.

Making digital copies of archival materials and preserving them along with the originals has merit in its own right. This may reduce handling of fragile materials, or allow collection materials to be accessed remotely, saving staff and researchers time and money. In addition, the harvested metadata may allow collections to become discoverable to a whole new group of scholars. What justifies many digital projects for archivists and funding agencies alike are legitimate benefits to archives and the scholarly community. Enhancements to how images are searched and accessed, how objects can be intellectually grouped together, how information is harvested and repurposed on the Internet, continue to make digital projects more relevant and valuable to content users and providers. Digitization of archival collections is finally coming into full bloom, making archival materials more accessible, desirable, and less visually clunky every day. As this new-millennium functionality and access is not only accepted, but expected of archival repositories, one may start to get comfortable with the idea of digitization enough to wonder whether new technologies will someday actually make collections better than they are now, not just simulating the experience of doing research in an archives, but enhancing the experience to the point where digital access creates a level of complex research unavailable in the original format.

THE CASE STUDY: WHICH CAME FIRST, THE THEORY OR THE PRACTICE?

Though not a traditional archives, the Mark Twain Papers & Project (MTP)[6] has an extensive collection of original letters, manuscripts, scrapbooks, photographs, and various other materials by and about Mark Twain.[7] These materials are supplemented with an even larger collection of photocopies and transcriptions of every extant Twain and Twain-related document, necessary in order for the MTP to create a *virtual* Twain collection that emphasizes completeness over ownership. Included in the photocopy collection are letters to and from Twain and his immediate family, along with literary manuscripts, photographs, and drawings.[8] Since the original deposit at Berkeley of Twain documents in 1949, the editors of the MTP have painstakingly researched and assembled this group of original and photocopied documents to produce comprehensive print editions of Twain's collected letters and notebooks as well as critical editions of his published works. In addition to the over 11,000 letters written by Twain and the 17,000 written to Twain that the MTP editors have collected, new letters surface at the rate of about one per week, making print editions of the letters outdated nearly as soon as they are published.

The MTP divides the cornucopia of Twain writings into three print series: *Works*, which includes the literary works published during Twain's lifetime; *Papers*, the unpublished papers such as letters and notebooks; and the *Library*, the popular editions of the works and papers. The University of California Press (UC Press),[9] the MTP's publisher, has printed more thanthirty volumes of the Works and Papers series since 1962, with an estimated forty additional volumes of material yet to be published.

Six full-time editors do the majority of the work at the MTP, applying over a century's worth of collective experience with the Twain papers to annotating every newly discovered letter or to creating the signature pieces of the project: the critical editions. Critical editions include the published version of a text, or the source text, with several added layers of historical, contextual, and analytical annotations, as well as original emendations by both Twain and his publishers. In addition to these strata, Twain used his own form of shorthand, critical to the understanding of his thought process yet requiring a glossary to interpret. The MTP has created a complicated and innovative way to transcribe these notes, illustrating the text with crossed-out phrases, shading, line-through deletions, inserting blank spaces where Twain intended to fill in text, and showing margin-note revisions. All of these graphic applications to the text appear on a single printed page, the interpretation of which can be found in other sections of the volume.

Many of the editorial components of critical editions are used as well in the Papers series, annotating letters and journal entries to explain historical context, inside jokes, and whom Twain is referencing in a sentence that starts with "I saw him at the theater...." In a reprint of a letter by Twain, the text may include a photo reproduction of the original manuscript, a transcription of the text, footnotes to contextualize, and various shaded and crossed out passages that correspond to ongoing emendations.

In the print versions of critical editions and the annotated Papers series, there is generally a lot of page flipping to all of the endnotes, glossaries, and historical and biographical explanations at the back of the book. The 362 pages of original *Adventures of Huckleberry Finn* text are supplemented by another 800 pages of annotation in the critical edition.

The MTP editors conceived of a digital version of these complicated and expensive texts that would seamlessly integrate the notes and emendations through links, pop-ups, and rollovers on a single screen, ultimately making the digital versions easier for researchers to use than the print versions. Hovering over a phrase like "I met him at the theater" may tell the reader who "him" is and what production Twain saw that night at the "theater." Clicking on a referenced name may take the reader to a list of all instances of that person in the document or in the series. Emendations could be referenced as pop-up boxes rather than interrupting the reading flow to scan pages at the end of the book.

But why would the MTP, with so many successfully published volumes and dozens more in the works, suddenly take on a massive, experimental digital project? It was a forced economic decision. Their largest and most consistent funding agency, the National Endowment for the Humanities (NEH), refused to fund any additional print volumes, directing instead that the project "go digital." Once the MTP editors accepted this directional shift, they realized that the new, digital system might actually improve their workflow and ability to serve researchers. Instead of print editions of the Papers series capturing only the Twain letters known and available at the time of printing, the digital edition would allow editors to add new material as it was discovered. The project could also make documents publicly accessible before all editorial annotations and publishing revisions had been made, accelerating the availability of materials to researchers.

Enter the Collaborators: UC Berkeley's Digital Publishing Group

The abrupt shift in priorities to a field in which none of the existing editors had expertise challenged the MTP editors to seek strategic partners from within the University of California to help them digitally articulate their vision. As a first step, the MTP solicited advice from UC Berkeley Library's Digital Publishing Group (DPG).[10] Together they formed a plan for the kinds of technology to use and the qualifications to look for when hiring people to manage and execute the project.

To best meet the needs of converting the complex print versions into some electronic format that made sense for how researchers might use the digital project, DPG directed the MTP towards Text Encoding Initiative (TEI).[11] TEI is an SGML-based encoding standard that has become the prevailing tool for archival conversion of textual documents. It is non-proprietary, international, and open source. Though an archival encoding standard, TEI addresses content and structure, but not display; a stylesheet must be applied to a TEI-encoded text in order to see anything other than unformatted text with a lot of tags and instructions meant for only computers to read. It is generally desirable to also integrate the stylesheet with an HTML-based (meaning pretty) user interface.

Why not go straight to HTML and skip TEI encoding altogether? There are several advantages of TEI over HTML for this type of project that relate to flexible search capabilities, long-term preservation and migration of the electronic files, and machine-readability–key to ensuring that files encoded for the project remains a library asset and not just a snapshot of a specific iteration of the work. With the advice of DPG and a survey of the existing landscape of undertakings by similar papers projects, the MTP editors were able to form a coherent concept for a grant proposal, leading to the first round of funding for the digital project. This digital series of TEI texts and the MTP's affiliated partners on the project came to be called collectively the Mark Twain Digital Project (MTDP).

Although the digital project was new for the MTP, the idea of digital editions of literary material was not new in the field. The MTP initially surveyed the existing landscape of literary projects, to purposefully direct the specific needs of their digital texts. Knowing they would be using TEI to encode the texts was merely a starting point for all of the decision-making that lay ahead. Much of the early consortial work in the area of TEI-based editions projects started in 1995 with the Model Editions Partnership (MEP), an NHPRC[12]-funded project based at the University of South Carolina.[13] The MEP set up TEI guidelines to meet the needs of primarily historical manuscript and document encoding projects. Though MEP was a model for how to encode text and an example of how to apply stylesheets, its standards for historical documents do not address many of the specialized editorial notes used for literary manuscripts. At the time of the original MTP grant proposal for the digital project in 2000, there were several projects working with the Institute for Advanced Technology in the Humanities (IATH) at the University of Virginia[14] that had goals and demands similar to the MTDP's.[15] These projects were started, though, at a time when fewer technological options and developments were available. The MTDP editors felt that they could create a more effective system by branching out on their own, enlisting, of course, assistance from specialized agencies within the University of California.

Enter eScholarship and the CDL

In an attempt to adopt an encoding standard that would not compromise the complexity of the critical editions, the MTDP editors opted to strive for the highest level of TEI encoding available to them.[16] MTDP's decision to apply a level of TEI encoding that was intricate and elaborate enough to accommodate the needs of the critical editions, led them to another strategic partner: the California Digital Library.

The California Digital Library (CDL)[17] is constituted as a University of California (UC) library, without the physical campus building or printed books, and serves the ten UC campuses as well as the affiliated laboratories and research centers. CDL provides leadership and resources for the development and implementation of digital services that any individual campus would be hard-pressed to develop on their own, benefiting libraries, faculty, students, and staff system wide. CDL is a partner in a UC-specific consortium leveraging the libraries and information resources of ten universities to explore and create innovative and diverse digital library technologies. At any given time CDL is hosting and developing a variety of technological and content-based projects. Additionally, CDL provides leadership within the broader academic digital library community.

The MTP editors initially approached the CDL for a basic set of TEI encoding guidelines, but with the complex nature of the critical editions project, the partners realized the existing guidelines would be insufficient. To address this unique project's needs, an MTP representative joined CDL's Structured Text Working Group (STWG)[18] in order to co-develop a set of encoding guidelines that would accommodate the MTDP requirements while retaining the ability to work within the CDL system structure. The STWG was formed at the CDL to establish guidelines for TEI encoding standards, preservation and institutional interoperability, intended for use primarily by content contributors to CDL projects, but freely available to projects outside of UC. The genre-based encoding guidelines developed by the STWG (for manuscripts, published books, etc.) were designed to give content contributors a series of basic TEI structures to use as foundations for encoding texts that will be standardized enough to be ingested into and displayed in the CDL system. These "best-practice" documents are intended to act as a preset agreement between the CDL and its contributors, where the CDL is essentially saying that if the contributor conforms to the guidelines, their material will be supported by the CDL's infrastructure and commitment to preservation. The STWG's work with the MTDP centered on expanding existing CDL TEI guidelines to meet the specific needs of the critical editions.

Rather than simply submitting their TEI texts to CDL's established Online Archive of Californial,[19] technically fulfilling the terms of their NEH grant, the MTDP opted to partner with another CDL project, eScholarship, to develop an infrastructure to create and publish the more complicated encoded critical editions. CDL's eScholarship program[20] was initiated in 1999 to explore experimental alternatives in scholarly publishing, with an eye to helping to address shrinking library budgets, growing material costs, and also to showcase the value of UC faculty's collective intellectual capital. After several pilot ventures, eScholarship split into two distinct projects: the eScholarship Repository and eScholarship Editions.[21] The repository functions as a publishing platform for generally article-length content produced by UC faculty and research units. It uses sophisticated software licensed from the Berkeley Electronic Press[22] to run what has become one of the most successful and innovative institutional repositories in the world. The Editions project supports TEI-encoded monographs published by university presses, about a third of which are available to the public for free and two-thirds of which are accessible only by the UC community.

With the publication of TEI-encoded texts at its heart, the eScholarship Editions project seemed a natural partner for the MTDP. But why would eScholarship want to invest time, money, and personnel into a project they didn't own, didn't initiate, and would not see revenues from? At the beginning of the partnership, the MTDP was only looking for guidance in TEI encoding standards from CDL. However, the MTDP and eScholarship realized their goals intersected, and the combined project would not only benefit both, but also create a much more usable and valuable tool for researchers. One of the benefits to eScholarship in taking on a complicated project, different than others already using TEI with the CDL, was to test the limits of the standards and guidelines the STWG had developed, additionally exploring what types of tools and workflows might be necessary to the production of encoded critical editions.

Collaboration has its drawbacks as well. Though working with the STWG and eScholarship provided the MTDP with technical expertise and input they would not have been able to develop or hire on their own, the project had to make compromises in order to accommodate the multi-institution needs of the CDL. Because of limited budgets and staff, the CDL is unable to produce custom solutions for a single client or contributor, but instead creates a framework of services that can be leveraged by all UC campuses to meet the needs of their specific communities. While MTDP editors were flexible enough in their project timeline to wait for the release of the next version of TEI, P5,[23] which would give them a few additional options to replicate some of the typesetting features used to mimic Twain's revision process, the CDL would not be ready to migrate its projects from the previous TEI release for at least a couple of years. In order to maintain their working relationship with eScholarship and CDL, the MTDP elected to work within the confines of the current TEI version. The MTP editors recognized the overall greater benefit in their partnered efforts with CDL and eScholarship than in the cutting-edge potential of their ideal project manifestations, likely usable only by the MTDP.

For CDL, working with the MTDP's ongoing project provided a way to develop and test technology, best practices, and a framework of standards to create a better service for all their users. Without the MTDP as an example, the STWG would not have been driven to create best practices for these complex types of documents. However, now that the encoding guidelines have been established, other repositories with similar materials have a tool to guide their encoding projects. These sorts of tools and guidelines eliminate the need for other projects to go through the years of research and obstacles the MTDP editors endured to get to a point where they could *begin* the encoding process. Ultimately, by gaining access to technologists already expert in a field the MTDP would have otherwise had to explore on its own, MTDP's 2004 partnership with CDL proved both economical and efficient.

Planning for People: Enter the Information Architect

Once encoding guidelines and strategies were developed, the MTDP had to start thinking about how the Web siteWeb site would technically function with the encoded texts, providing a searchable and coherent interface. CDL had already developed the eXtensible Text Framework (XTF)[24] that would act as an indexing and search tool for the encoded texts, as well as a basic text stylesheet. To enable a system-integrated, user-friendly, and elegant site for these encoded materials, eScholarship additionally contributed an information architect,[25] hired to make the subsequent creation of the user interface more logically and effectively navigable. Information architecture focuses on organizing content from the perspective of someone who will be using the Web site, and in the case of the MTDP site, the variety and complex layering of the content required a rather elaborate architectural plan. Learning from functional interfaces of other similar projects, like the established Walt Whitman and William Blake digital projects, the MTDP was able to use these examples as a base for establishing their own criteria for user experience. Taking direction from similar sites was a starting point, but the editors wanted to incorporate cues from unrelated, commercial sites like Amazon.com or the *New York Times*, where functionality was not only more effective, but more familiar to regular Internet users. Search boxes and results pages, navigation bars, and general layout of commercial sites are recognizable features from which Web designers of not-for-profit sites can learn, establishing a base of common Web knowledge that can help to more intuitively guide users through an unknown site.

Complicating the requirements of the MTDP site was the diversity of materials being presented therein, the Works and Papers series having very distinct encoding standards and interface needs. The information architect was able to plan for how the various sections of the project should function together, as well as how they could be found independently as series or documents, by establishing clear navigation goals before the site was actually built. With the information architect, MTDP editors developed a genre-based taxonomic categorization of Twain's writings to inform the site navigation. The modularity contributed to a plan to be able to provide easy access to content for casual researchers, hiding the deeper layers of annotation and explanation until the more serious researcher chose to surface them. For example, the wealth of editorial knowledge is seamlessly available in the digital editions, but the annotated view is an optional selection for users who want that level of information, concealed in another view so as not to distract from the general reading experience.

Enter the TEI Expert

With its goals and standards established, the project was ready to move to the transcription and encoding phase, which they quickly realized could not be economically or practically managed in-house. A TEI expert was hired, with the primary purpose of writing a series of Requests for Proposals (RFP) and encoding guidelines to subcontract the encoding and conversion of the thousands of pages of text. With the unusual nature of the project and its distinct encoding requirements, multiple sets of guidelines had to be written to address distinct types of documents. One set of encoding guidelines dealt exclusively with converting already published texts to TEI, another with encoding new material, but each ended up as a document of roughly 100 pages. The RFP itself, merely describing the project and giving instructions on how to interpret and carry out the guidelines, was near twenty-five pages. These elaborate guidelines and RFP are indicators of how this simple digitization project has developed into a plan to change how the MTP functions as an editorial organization and transform the way critical editions are used in the digital age. Bringing eScholarship, an information architect, and a TEI expert into the mix has elevated the MTDP from a straightforward TEI-based digitization project to an innovative model for using technology to enhance a researcher's ability to use the collection in new and more effective ways.

Can We Make Money Off of This? Enter UC Press

With a partnership between the University of California Press and the MTP already in place, dating from their decades-long print publishing relationship, the MTDP looked to UC Press for advice on a business plan. eScholarship additionally had a long-standing working relationship with the press, having collaborated on several eScholarship Repository publishing experiments as well as on encoding nearly two thousand UC Press books for the eScholarship Editions project. Since marketing strategies and product development fell within the expertise of neither the Twain editors, nor CDL's eScholarship staff, UC Press was a natural partner to lead the effort. Both the MTDP and UC Press felt that with the success of the print editions of the works and papers series, a business model for the digital series was worth investigating. Though the partnered organizations worked on several scenarios for charging for the use of the service and/or technology, they eventually came to the conclusion that the MTDP didn't have the personnel or resources to manage the demands of commercializing the venture, particularly when compared with the anticipated nominal financial returns.

In short, the answer was no, they couldn't make much money off of a project like this; accommodating subscription services and support would ultimately divert the project from its mission. Free digital access, however, could end up creating a new audience for the print editions, as well as attracting support and funding opportunities resulting from the increase in collection use via the digital site.

SO . . . HOW DOES THIS RELATE TO OTHER ARCHIVAL DIGITIZATION PROJECTS?

So many aspects of the MTDP are unique that it is difficult to translate the effectiveness of the example to understand how other archives can benefit from their experience. The collection itself is not traditional in the archival-collection sense, in that much of it is assembled from documents that the repository doesn't own. The function of the repository is aimed at adding value to original source material through editorial annotations and interpretation, again distinguishing the project from traditional archives. The mission of the organization is to serve its patrons largely through active publishing of the critical editions and papers series, in contrast to more traditional archives with preservation and access goals. And the ten-campus structure of the University of California provides a uniquely established consortium of available skills and resources. Nonetheless, the important lesson for archivists to learn from the Twain example is how MTP actively recruited resources in partner organizations to make an adequate project that was within their funding means into an innovative, mutually beneficial collaborative venture that will ultimately serve the larger scholarly, archival, and historical communities.

The success of the digital project, scheduled to go online (at writing) in 2006, ultimately depended on finding appropriate partners, in terms of both collaborators willing to contribute resources and paid contractors. The MTP editors had to acknowledge the need to look outside their own organization for experts to fulfill the goals of the digital project they had undertaken, compromising their control over the project by not doing everything in-house. Though the MTDP settled on TEI guidelines that didn't match their ideal setup, their willingness to make concessions in developing encoding standards to accommodate the broader CDL user community allowed them to create a better, more usable product than if they had not cooperated with the CDL at all. The resources and expertise that the CDL contributed to the project provided an opportunity to explore the limits of the technologies and standards developed for their broader community, beneficial both within UC and to the greater academic digital library community.

These collaborative efforts, though, are merely a backdrop for the project's real accomplishments: creating new uses for technology that enable enhanced, and ultimately superior, access to the collection materials when compared with their analog alternatives. Materials can be made available while in process, without waiting for each annotation and editorial review.[26] Layered information can be seen on a single screen, limiting the need for tangential interruptions characterized by page flipping in the print versions. Cross collection and intra-document searching creates indexing possibilities unavailable in the confines of a printed publication. New documents and manuscripts can be added to the digital collection as they are discovered, giving researchers access to the complete body of work rather than merely the works known at the time of printing. These features, however, would not have been technically viable even five years ago.

So how is an archivist or historian supposed to keep on top of all the digital advantages that could enhance access to their collections? They're not. The MTP editors could not have cooked up this scheme on their own; they wisely sought the help of people who could make up for the gaps in their technical experience, leading the project direction while knowing when to be willing to negotiate their goals. The editors, to fulfill the requirements of their grant funding, could have easily hired a single expert or technician to complete the TEI encoding at a basic level, but instead opted to take on a more elaborate, complicated, and cooperative project that will revolutionize the way their collections are used. Embracing technology has turned this successful, yet academically traditional institution into a leader in its field, establishing tools for smaller projects to adopt and acting as a model of innovation for other archival institutions to follow suit.

NOTES

1. One archivist relayed a story to the author of sending an important collection to a microfilm vendor, whereupon ripping a trace drawing cleanly in half, a technician decided the most helpful solution would be to tape the drawing back together, microfilm it, and send it back without informing the repository of the incident. An insurance claim and conservator later, the vendor learned an expensive materials handling lesson.

2. Information about the National Union Catalog of Manuscript Collections can be found at http://www.loc.gov/coll/nucmc/nucmc.html. Accessed 2005-11-28.

3. The Online Archive of California, a project of the University of California's California Digital Library, can be accessed at http://www.oac.cdlib.org/. Information about Encoded Archival Description can be found at http://www.loc.gov/ead/. Accessed 2005-11-28.

4. The Northwest Digital Archives includes encoded finding aids from archival collections in Washington, Oregon, Idaho, and Montana. See http://nwda-db.wsulibs.wsu.edu/ search/index.asp. Accessed 2005-11-28.

5. There are plenty of great books and articles about digital preservation and digital projects that make the case for putting efforts into these project components–metadata, standards, user experience, etc. Rather than trying to summarize the dense justifications here, see for example: Anne R. Kenneyand Oya Y. Rieger, *Moving Theory Into Practice: Digital Imaging for Libraries and Archives* (Cornell University Library, 2000); Maxine K. Sitts,. ed., *Handbook for Digital Projects: A Management Tool For Preservation and Access,* (Northeast Documents Conservation Center, 2000); and *The NINCH Guide to Good Practice in the Digital Representation and Management of Cultural Heritage Materials* (National Initiative for a Networked Cultural Heritage, 2002), available at http://www.nyu.edu/its/humanities/ninchguide/. Accessed 2005-11-28.

6. The MTP Web site is available at http://bancroft.berkeley.edu/MTP/. Accessed 2005-11-29.

7. Mark Twain is the pen name for Samuel Langhorne Clemens. The repository is called the Mark Twain Papers & Project, though editors sometimes refer to the author as Clemens. For consistency in this article, I refer to Clemens only as Mark Twain.

8. See the MTP Web site for more information about specific holdings: http://bancroft.berkeley.edu/MTP/about.html. Accessed 2005-11-28.

9. For more information about UC Press, see http://www.ucpress.edu/. Accessed 2005-11-28.

10. Information about the Digital Publishing Group at UC Berkeley can be found at http://www.lib.berkeley.edu/digicoll/planning/. Accessed 2005-11-28.

11. See http://www.tei-c.org/ for more information about TEI and the TEI Consortium. Accessed 2005-11-28.

12. "The National Historical Publications and Records Commission (NHPRC) is the outreach arm of the National Archives and makes plans for and studies issues related to the preservation, use and publication of historical documents." See http://www.archives.gov/grants/ for more information. Accessed 2005-11-28.

13. See http://mep.cla.sc.edu/ for more information on the Model Editions Partnership. Accessed 2005-11-28.

14. See http://www.iath.virginia.edu/ for more information on the IATH at the University of Virginia. Accessed 2005-11-28.

15. See, for example, the William Blake Archive, http://www.blakearchive.org/main.html, and the Walt Whitman Archive, http://www.whitmanarchive.org/. Accessed 2005-11-28.

16. TEI levels refer to "levels of encoding," where Level 1 requires only the most basic encoding and Level 5 uses the more complex TEI components to encode every part of a document. The same document could be encoded at any level, depending on how much effort an organization is willing to devote and what level of access is desired for the content. These levels are primarily used by the digital library community.

17. See http://www.cdlib.org/ for information on the California Digital Library. Accessed 2005-11-28.

18. The STWG maintains an information page at http://www.cdlib.org/inside/groups/stwg/. Accessed 2005-11-29.

19. The OAC provides technical infrastructure to support and display TEI-encoded texts, see http://www.oac.cdlib.org/texts/. The texts are generally transcriptions of archival materials and the OAC requirements for submission are based on a basic TEI structure, simple enough to be accessible to projects with limited budgets and expandable to meet the needs of experienced encoders. Accessed 2005-11-28.

20. See http://www.cdlib.org/programs/escholarship.html for more information on the eScholarship initiative and program. Accessed 2005-11-28.

21. The eScholarship Repository is available at http://repositories.cdlib.org/escholarship/, and eScholarship Editions at http://content.cdlib.org/escholarship/. Accessed 2005-11-28.

22. See http://www.bepress.com/ for more information about the Berkeley Electronic Press. Accessed 2005-11-28.

23. TEI "P" numbers refer to the progressive releases of the guidelines, P1 being the first release and P5 being the most recent. The next release will be P6, then P7, and so on. The primary difference between P4 and P5 is that P4 is DTD (document type definition)-based and P5 is XML schema-based.

24. See http://www.cdlib.org/inside/projects/xtf/ for more information about XTF. Accessed 2005-11-28.

25. The Information Architecture Institute provides a good explanation of information architecture on their Web site at http://iainstitute.org/pg/about_us.php. Access 2005-11-29.

26. This is a controversial endeavor. What will it mean for users to see non-authoritative versions of material? Scholars and users will have to start thinking differently in the near future about source materials, as they increasingly become available electronically.

doi:10.1300/J201v04n01_03

California Cultures:
Implementing a Model
for Virtual Collections

Genie Guerard
Robin L. Chandler

SUMMARY. This article highlights the California Cultures Project as a case study examining the architecture and framework required to support the deployment of digital objects as virtual collections at the California Digital Library. Chronologically arranged, it describes the Online Archive of California (OAC) Working Group's functional requirements for access to digital objects independent of parent finding aids, and the development and implementation of infrastructures supporting this vision. Discussion includes project organization and content selection

Genie Guerard, BFA, MLIS, is Head of Manuscripts Division, UCLA Library, Department of Special Collections, and Manuscripts/Digital Manuscripts Librarian, A1713 Charles E. Young Research Library, Box 951575, Los Angeles, CA 90095-1575 (E-mail: gguerard@library.ucla.edu).

Robin L. Chandler, MA, MLIS, is Director of Built Content, California Digital Library (CDL), University of California Office of the President, 415 20th Street, 4th Floor, Oakland, CA 94612 (E-mail: robin.chandler@ucop.edu).

The authors would like to thank Bill Landis and Bradley Westbrook for the inspiration provided by their articles published in the first issue of the *Journal of Archival Organization*, and Bill Landis specifically for reviewing and commenting on early drafts of the article.

[Haworth co-indexing entry note]: "California Cultures: Implementing a Model for Virtual Collections." Guerard, Genie, and Robin L. Chandler. Co-published simultaneously in *Journal of Archival Organization* (The Haworth Information Press, an imprint of The Haworth Press, Inc.) Vol. 4, No.1/2, 2006, pp. 45-67; and: *Archives and the Digital Library* (ed: William E. Landis, and Robin L. Chandler) The Haworth Information Press, an imprint of The Haworth Press, Inc., 2006, pp. 45-67. Single or multiple copies of this article are available for a fee from The Haworth Document Delivery Service [1-800-HAWORTH, 9:00 a.m. - 5:00 p.m. (EST). E-mail address: docdelivery@haworthpress.com].

Available online at http://jao.haworthpress.com
© 2006 by The Haworth Press, Inc. All rights reserved.
doi:10.1300/J201v04n01_04

for digitization, Web site service vision for K-12 teacher target audience, best practices for encoding, data standards, lesson plans, metadata requirements, METS creation tools, project manuals, repositories, search engines, tools enabling customizable interfaces, user assessment, and usability testing. doi:10.1300/J201v04n01_04 *[Article copies available for a fee from The Haworth Document Delivery Service: 1-800-HAWORTH. E-mail address: <docdelivery@haworthpress.com> Website: <http://www.HaworthPress.com> © 2006 by The Haworth Press, Inc. All rights reserved.]*

KEYWORDS. California Cultures, California Digital Library (CDL), Calisphere, eXtensible Text Framework (XTF), Interface Customization Toolkit, K-12 teachers, lesson plans, Metadata Encoding Transmission Standard (METS), Online Archive of California (OAC), UCLA Institute on Primary Resources (IPR), WebGenDB

VIRTUAL COLLECTIONS AND CALIFORNIA CULTURES

In a series of articles published in 2002, Brad Westbrook, Bill Landis, and Robin Chandler articulated a model for user-defined virtual collections that "can change dramatically from one iteration to the next, as more digital objects[1] are made available."[2] Analyzing the results of user assessment studies for the Online Archive of California (OAC),[3] these archivists/digital librarians concluded that a majority of online users preferred accessing digital objects directly and found drilling through online finding aids in order to surface digital content cumbersome. To enable research and development at the California Digital Library (CDL),[4] they sketched a vision for a new online environment for the OAC database of finding aids and digital objects.

Westbrook articulated the model's vision as a "wake-up call" for archivists contributing finding aids and digital objects to online consortia or databases.

First, producing meaningful virtual collections requires [establishing] ... standardized control over the digital collections and objects we administer. Second ... not all end users come to our collections with the same need. [Thus, not all users] want to invest significant time drilling into a collection-level description such as a finding aid encoded using [Encoded Archival Description (EAD)],[5] learning how to navigate the EAD interface, and how to interpret the arrangement of the collection materials.... Let us allow users to access digital objects independent of finding aids ... [and] to access those digital objects in association with other digital objects.[6]

An environment where digital objects can be accessed–browsed, searched, repackaged–independently of finding aids requires a clear articulation of specifications and requirements. Landis described access in this environment as a

> mechanism that might allow end users interested specifically in finding digital objects to search the OAC directly for those objects, bypassing [the] ... context-providing metadata of our finding aids and guides completely. Digital objects searched and retrieved in this manner would certainly retain links back to the descriptions of the collections to which they belong, though the end user would not be forced to wade through those descriptions in order to access the digital objects.[7]

Landis further articulated the key role of archival description in supporting user access in an online environment, noting "... archivists are and always have been responsible for the core descriptive data that we assemble regarding our collections. In the world before the web, we may not have had compelling reasons to put that descriptive-data house in order. As we move into the world of the digital and the digitized, however, this task is both a fundamental responsibility and challenge to us as professionals."[8] Landis argues persuasively that a stable set of data elements will form the basis for future access portals for users.

In February 2001, the OAC Working Group (OAC WG)[9] developed a list of functional requirements for an infrastructure enabling the "creation of virtual collections by users."[10] According to Chandler, the new OAC infrastructure must provide multiple views of finding aids, including repository, subject, and project; enable zone searching (limit searching to specific tag sets); allow for different options for displaying retrieved lists of finding aids; support search and retrieval of attached digital objects in isolation from the finding aid and amidst other unrelated digital objects; and permit the searching of EAD data with other metadata such as Text Encoding Initiative (TEI)-encoded texts and Dublin Core. However, Chandler cautioned that a sophisticated technical system would always be limited by the quality of the metadata. "While best practices can go a long way towards standardizing encoding and creating digital collections, they cannot resolve inconsistent descriptive practices.... It would be prudent to see the OAC serve as a testbed for demonstrating the impact of implementing good descriptive practices ... coupled with the consistent use of controlled access systems."[11]

Through several projects the CDL has taken steps to build a framework of tools and services enabling the configuration of digital objects to meet the needs of multiple user communities. These efforts have been made in support of the general vision for facilitating the flexible creation of virtual collections defined in the articles by Westbrook, Landis, and Chandler cited above. This case study of one of those projects, California Cultures,[12] will describe the development process through which this new online environment was implemented. With California Cultures, the OAC is coordinating the creation of a virtual collection from materials in the University of California's rich special collections repositories documenting four primary ethnic groups in the state of California: African Americans, Asian Americans, Hispanic Americans, and Native Americans. The project's goal is to make these digital surrogates readily available through a specialized portal to students, teachers, scholars, and the general public to serve as a resource for historical study, analysis, and interpretation.

OAC DEVELOPMENT AND THE CALIFORNIA CULTURES PROJECT

On November 9, 2001, the California Cultures Editorial Board–comprising History and American Studies faculty, subject bibliographers, and special collections curators–met to select materials from University of California libraries for inclusion in a virtual collection of primary resources documenting ethnic groups throughout the state. With an eye to future use, the Editorial Board chose the framework articulated in *California: A Changing State*, the official state educational guidelines for teaching California history and social studies,[13] as a basis for collection development, and identified K-12 teachers as the primary audience.

Funded by the Library of Congress American Memory project, California Cultures provided a timely and opportune testbed mechanism for the OAC. With a control group of content contributors, the OAC could use this opportunity to create metadata according to best practices and consciously build a service framework leveraging standardized digital object description. An access system built upon metadata knowingly created with users in mind and not solely for mediated use in libraries or archives, and an infrastructure supporting reconfigurable interfaces were reachable goals for the first time for the OAC. Multiple content pathways could be realized to provide access for different user communities independent of finding aids. These pathways include theme-based collections, lesson plans, and browsing structures providing access by topic, date, genre, or location. The implementation of access environments configurable for user communities will be explained through subsequent discussions of metadata creation and the development of an infrastructure capable of supporting customizable interfaces.

The model described in the previously cited *JAO* articles reflected an ongoing desire within the OAC community to achieve standardized control of its digital resources, including finding aids, image-based digital objects, and electronic texts. In 2001, subgroups of the OAC Working Group developed functional specifications for a new OAC infrastructure that would facilitate the discovery of digital objects through multiple searching and navigational routes, and best practices guidelines for encoding digital object metadata. OAC infrastructure issues will be discussed later in this article. What follows is a consideration of several themes relating to metadata best practices, and the development of tools that support their usage by libraries and archives to produce high-quality metadata as a component of digital objects encoded and managed in an access repository using the Metadata Encoding and Transmission Standard (METS).[14] Developing these best practices and experimenting with METS-generating tools proved to be an important factor in the success of the California Cultures project, and a jump-start for more sophisticated access interfaces for digital objects created by partners in the OAC.

OAC Best Practices Guidelines for Digital Objects

Digitized surrogates of collection materials began appearing in the OAC fairly early in its history,[15] attached to finding aids using links created with EAD's Digital Archival Object (<dao>) element.[16] Reflecting on the access experience utilizing this model, the OAC WG recognized the need for a clear, well-articulated rationale for providing a robust, stand-alone object description that could exist in a digital repository independent of the multi-level, inheritance-savvy data found in traditional descriptions of collections of archival materials. As such the group sought to:

- Develop best practices for simple and complex digital objects at lower, more detailed levels of archival description than traditionally appear in finding aids

- Identify possible standards and develop guidelines for incorporating non-EAD descriptive metadata into OAC.

In formulating best practices guidelines for describing digital objects, working group members reviewed existing CDL standards and METS documentation.[17]

The group benchmarked its emerging guidelines using various desired functions for digital object discovery, interpretation, and management in the OAC, with a goal of defining standards for metadata that would enable the discovery, use, storage, and migration of digital objects. Throughout its deliberations the group remained cognizant of the paucity of resources for creating item-level metadata available at many OAC repositories, which range from small historical societies to large universities and state repositories. An important aim of these initial guidelines was to articulate clearly the minimum amount of metadata necessary for discovery and identification. Additional goals were to identify relevant standards and thesauri useful for formulating data content for specific fields, and to address the "requiredness" of specific metadata fields from a functional OAC perspective. The resulting OAC Best Practice Guidelines for Digital Objects (OAC BPG DO) Version 1.0[18] was first published in January 2003.

Metadata Lessons Learned from Early OAC Digitization Projects

Early digital projects provided models within the OAC for implementing standards for descriptive metadata at the item level to accompany digital surrogates, though as previously noted, these projects focused on encoding object descriptions within the broader context of an EAD-encoded collection description. Nonetheless, these early efforts allowed the OAC to explore using descriptive standards as underpinnings for developing user-friendly digital content interfaces. An overview of the Museums in the Online Archive of California (MOAC) and Japanese American Relocation Digital Archive (JARDA) projects[19] provides some insight into how these early projects informed the creation of the OAC BPG DO and the subsequent development of tools for creating METS-encoded digital objects.

Funded by the Institute for Museum Library Services (IMLS) in 1999, MOAC sought to integrate collections of art, historical artifacts, photography, and manuscripts across institution types (libraries, archives, and museums) by applying EAD encoding to descriptions of museum collections. Most importantly, the MOAC project tested the integration of rich item-level description for digital content with collection-level description. For the MOAC project, the descriptive structure of EAD and established delivery mechanisms of the OAC provided a bridge across the disparate descriptive practices of museums, libraries and archives, and offered the promise of integration, from an end-user perspective, of museum collection information with those of other repositories.

Because of their core mission to interpret objects, museums emphasize description of the artifact, a descriptive tradition quite different from the higher levels of description on which archivists typically focus. Through the MOAC project, museums provided leadership to collection-minded archivists on strategies for describing individual digital objects. MOAC focused on the Record Export for Art and Cultural Heritage (REACH) elements,[20] a base set of twenty elements considered essential for describing museum objects. The MOAC Technical Specifications mapped fourteen of these REACH elements to EAD, and provided a generic framework for extracting metadata from museums' collection management systems to share with disparate end users as part of the OAC. While the fields identified as essential to describing works of art in EAD by MOAC[21] do not all apply to the description of archival materials, this set of descriptive elements did provide a starting point for evaluating the notion of universally applicable data elements that might be present across all types of OAC digital content.

JARDA, a digital thematic collection documenting the experience of Japanese Americans in World War II internment camps, served as a testbed for the development of the Making of America II (MOA2)[22] encoding standard for digital library objects, A Digital Library Federation[23] initiative, MOA2 provided a vehicle for communicating technical, structural and administrative metadata, a need not met by the description-focused Dublin Core metadata standard.[24] MOA2 promoted the need for interoperability, scalability, and preservation of library digital objects, and later served as the basis for the development of the METS transmission standard.

WebGenDB: DEVELOPMENT OF A WEB-ACCESSIBLE METS-ENCODING TOOL

The WebGenDB digital object tool[25] supports the gathering of descriptive, administrative, and structural metadata for digitized content and the export of METS objects. The Metadata Object Description Schema (MODS)[26] is the companion schema in which WebGenDB exports descriptive metadata. WebGenDB represents a significant enhancement of GenDB, a Microsoft Access-based metadata capture tool initially developed by the Library Systems Office (LSO) at the University of California, Berkeley[27] in conjunction with the DLF MOA2 project. GenDB, like its successor WebGenDB, supported the creation of descriptive, administrative, structural, and technical metadata regarding digital objects, and an auxiliary Java program produced these objects as files conforming to the MOA2 DTD. Archivists at the Bancroft Library[28] collaborated with the LSO to define GenDB's relational database table structure and constituent data element sets. Most of this structure has been carried forward into WebGenDB as developed for use in the California Cultures project.

GenDB was "generic" intwo senses. First, it did not privilege any single descriptive metadata-encoding standard, and supported output in Categories for Descriptions of Works of Art (CDWA), Visual Resources Association (VRA) Core, REACH, and Machine-Readable Cataloging (MARC), among others. Second, it could readily be adapted for localized use on any digital content project. During the JARDA project, for example, copies of the GenDB database were distributed to participating institutions, where descriptive, structural, and portions of the administrative metadata were input. Once project-based inputting was complete, institutions returned databases to the LSO, where datasets were merged. Technical metadata was imported into the GenDB from scanning equipment as available. This distributed database approach for multi-institutional projects, while productive, proved cumbersome and difficult to scale, inviting synchronization problems. Further, users found the GenDB interface unintuitive, and it could not easily be configured to meet the needs of individual inputting institutions. Accurate capture of the hierarchical levels of a digital object's structure also proved to be a challenge. The advent of the California Cultures collaboration proved to be a catalyst for the LSO to develop WebGenDB, address many issues relating to GenDB, and ultimately upgrade the output of digital object files to METS.

With LSO engaging in technical development work, California Cultures project staff advised on interface operability and best practices for describing digital objects, both important elements directly informing the construction and functionality of the database.[29] Descriptive fields articulated in the OAC BPG DO version 1.0, then under development, were aligned with the WebGenDB database structure and project goals, providing a valuable opportunity to test the interaction between articulated metadata standards, a metadata capture tool, and the project-driven production of new digital surrogates for cultural heritage materials selected and described with usage by a targeted audience in mind.

California Cultures project staff analyzed each of the OAC BPG DO metadata guidelines for their application to the project's specific goals and audience. This resulted in the specification of additional metadata requirements for project participants in order to provide predictable interface hooks to support discovery and use of the content created in the course of the project. Examples of these include:

- A "required when applicable" topical term representing the ethnic group relevant to the resource in order to support an "browse by ethnic group" functionality.
- A metadata element containing a standardized name of the virtual collection created by the project to support use of CDL's Interface Customization tools[30] to isolate only California Cultures project content from the broader pool of OAC digital objects for presentation in the project's public interface.

This process facilitated the creation of a WebGenDB interface that accommodated both OAC BPG DO-stipulated metadata requirements and those specified specifically for the project.

For the CDL/OAC, the opportunity to contribute through the California Cultures project to the LSO's creation of a WebGenDB metadata-encoding and METS-creation tool supported a longer-term goal of exploring user-friendly tools that might be used by affiliated institutions for creating and describing digital objects. CDL's specific goals in this effort included providing OAC affiliated institutions with

- A manageable, practical set of structural, descriptive and administrative metadata fields to enable the production of rich digital objects in a variety of formats conforming to the METS, MODS, and MIX schemas.
- A user-friendly means of expressing the structure of multipart, multilevel documents (e.g., multipaged letters, manuscripts and pamphlets, photo albums, scrapbooks).
- A means of outputting work orders for digitization services, whether done internally within an institution or outsourced to external vendors.
- A flexible interface that was reconfigurable to accommodate the needs of particular repositories and projects.

The Web interface developed for WebGenDB is very intuitive, and implements a structural approach to metadata input. A "table of contents" for the object being created, corresponding to the object's structural metadata, is always visible. Users can easily expand this structural map, and navigate through the object by means of it. The input fields that appear and the way that these fields are tagged are completely configurable for each type of material being digitized. Each institution involved in a digitization project can configure the input screens to meet its needs.

The technical architecture for the WebGenDB system consists of three layers: a relational database; a server program written in Java that mediates between the database and the user interface; and a Java servlet-driven Web interface. The database that underlies WebGenDB is SQL running on a Windows2000 server. The Java server program that mediates between the database and the user interface uses Java Database Connectivity (JDBC) to extract data from and commit data to the SQL database. It transforms the data between database-centric and user-centric views, and shields the user from the underlying table structure. The Java servlet-driven Web interface program communicates with the server program using Java's Remote Method Invocation (RMI) protocol. The servlet, of course, uses standard HTML enhanced with JavaScript for presenting data to the end user via a Web browser.[31]

LINKING FINDING AIDS TO DIGITAL OBJECTS

While the discussion thus far has focused on providing access to digital objects independent of their associated EAD finding aids, there remains intrinsic value in providing access to digital surrogates of archival and manuscript materials within the context of the intellectual organization of the collections with which they are associated. EAD finding aids describe discrete collections of materials that have been organized according to long-standing archival principals, including that of maintaining, whenever possible, the original, organic order in which the materials in an archival collection were created, maintain, and used by the individual or organization responsible for the creation of that collection. The archival principle of provenance, or *respect des fonds*[32] has long been maintained in part to allow researchers–by examining evidence found in primary source documents–to discover, connect, and derive meaning from a person's or organization's associated activities or creative processes. Put another way, the context inherent in an archival collection formed around the basis of the principle of provenance provides one important component in the use of information content to interpret historic events.

As Westbrook argues in his previously cited article, one value in constructing virtual collections of digital materials, reformatted and born-digital, is to create access portals focused on meeting the needs of specified groups or types of end users.[33] Nonetheless, the evidentiary value of the digital object is maintained through linkage to information about the archival collection to which it belongs, as described in the finding aid. Taking advantage of the ability of a METS-encoded object to point to external collection-level description from within any number of hierarchically arranged descriptive metadata sections (the METS <dmdSec>), Web GenDB provides a practical means for embedding links from OAC digital objects to their associated finding aids. Links can be input from digital object descriptions to collection-level descriptions, which allows institutions to control the retrieval of external metadata associated with a given object. This can be done at any level of granularity that the institution feels is appropriate for the object: collection-, series-, subseries-, file-, or item-level. Object groups or individual objects may be linked to the highest descriptive levels within the finding aid, or to specific component levels (within an EAD file, this is the equivalent of, for example, a <c03 level = "file"> tag). On a case-by-case basis, institutions are free to determine the level of descriptive granularity and to choose the approach best afforded by their resources.

THE CALIFORNIA CULTURES PROJECT MANUAL: BRINGING TOGETHER *WebGenDB* AND BEST PRACTICES

The various threads of planning and development efforts came together in the form of an online manual to assist participants in the California Cultures Project with using the new WebGenDB tool effectively in applying the OAC BPG DO to content created for the project. The *California Cultures Project Manual*[34] formed the basis for a two-day workshop for project participants, held in August 2002 at UCLA. The manual provides step-by-step instruction in the functionality of the WebGenDB tool itself, including inputting metadata, outputting work orders to accompany materials for reformatting, and procedures for workflow and communication. The workshop also supplied instruction on allied descriptive standards that are available for use with item-level metadata creation. The LSO continued to enhance and add functionality to the WebGenDB tool over the course of the project, so input from project participants proved crucial to this refinement process. When the California Cultures Project ends in 2006, the manual will be officially handed over by CDL to the LSO to be maintained as they see fit in conjunction with anticipated ongoing WebGenDB use and development.

WebGenDB Workflow Overview

The WebGenDB interface facilitates the input of descriptive metadata for digital objects, and displays graphically the navigational path through an individual object. The workflow for this tool comprises four major steps:

1. Input structural and descriptive metadata for an object to be digitized.
2. Generate digitization work order for each object and send with original materials to the digitization vendor.
3. Import pertinent technical metadata received from vendor along with original materials and digital files.
4. Generate METS file for the completed digital object.

Figure 1 below represents a complex digital object entered into the WebGenDB interface. The main screen of the WebGenDB interface is

FIGURE 1. A Typical "Main Screen" of a Record for a Complex Digital Object

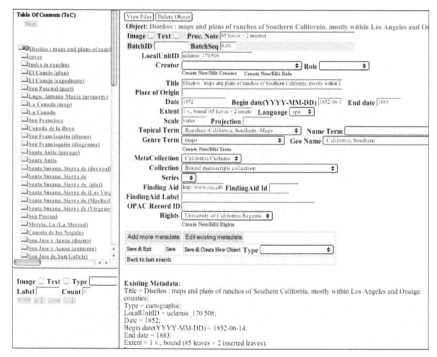

Courtesy of University of California, Berkeley Library. Used with permission.

configured to display the fields related to a selected digital object type, in this case "cartographic." The fields displayed for each object type are aligned with the MODS, a widely used, highly granular schema modeled on the MARC data structure standard, and also endorsed as an extension schema by the METS Editorial Board.[35] In terms of the interface, utilizing the MODS and MARC as an underlying data structure proved to be a logical basis upon which to configure and vary the tool's input screens. For example, the input screen for a "still image" type of digital object includes a field for a caption, while the input screen for a "cartographic" type of object includes fields for projection and scale.

INTERFACE CUSTOMIZATION AT CDL

At the same time that the California Cultures project members were focusing on the creation of quality metadata, the CDL was engaging in the long-term development of an infrastructure that would contribute to realizing an unlimited number of user-focused virtual collections. These access portals, it was envisioned, could easily be layered over the same content to provide a different access look, and could serve to focus access by end users to specifically selected content from a larger digital repository. In October 2003 the CDL released the Interface Customization Tools (ICT), known internally and affectionately as the "skin and slice toolkit." This service provides a mechanism that allows institutions contributing METS-encoded digital objects to a CDL-hosted access repository to develop customizable views of content tailored to the needs of specific communities of users. These interfaces are also referred to as portals.[36] Examples of portals rendered using the ICT include those for the previously mentioned JARDA and MOAC projects. The service is based on a specific eXtensible Stylesheet Language Transformations (XSLT)[37] parameter, for example XSLT = jarda, used within the URL to render digital object search results (a slice or metadata subset) with a predefined brand (a skin providing a desired look and feel for search results). In other words, a search launched from a virtual collection portal can be scoped only to object records identified by a standardized virtual-collection "relation" metadata element in those records; an XSLT parameter set for that virtual collection in the returned set of search results brands the display of those results with that virtual collection's look and feel.

Use of the ICT requires a working knowledge of Web development standards and procedures. This includes familiarity with XSLT programming and an institution-based Web server that can host an HTML search form, and files enabling the customization of search results and object displays (XSLT, HTML, and Cascading Stylesheets [CSS][38]). This system of stylesheets that render a specific look and feel for a subset of digital objects uses an infrastructure implemented by CDL, which includes METS objects and profiles, the Content Management System (CMS), and the eXtensible Text Framework (XTF, an open source, cross-collection indexing and querying tool), all of which continue to be enhanced and upgraded to meet the evolving needs of users.[39]

TRANSITIONING TO A METS-BASED REPOSITORY INFRASTRUCTURE AT CDL

At the Digital Library Federation (DLF) spring forum held in San Francisco in April 2001, Jerome McDonough presented a session paper proposing a new schema, the Metadata Encoding and Transmission Standard (METS). McDonough's proposed METS schema intrigued the CDL Content Management Infrastructure Group (CMIG), which was simultaneously evaluating platforms for delivering encoded finding aids and digital objects independently of one another, motivated in part by functional requirements for such a system promulgated by the OAC WG. CMIG evaluated two XML software packages: New Zealand Digital Library's Greenstone[40] and the University of Michigan's Digital Library eXtenstion Service (DLXS).[41] While no existing open source or off-the-shelf software met all of CDL's needs, DLXS was chosen to serve as a stable and well supported environment in which to manage the EAD finding aids. CMIG envisioned DLXS as a transition software, part of a multiphase plan to design and build CDL's eXtensible Text Framework to meet needs identified across a wide array of CDL non-licensed content development programs.[42] CDL also committed at the time to building the previously mentioned Content Management System (CMS) as a testbed to demonstrate and implement the use of METS and Archival Resource Keys (ARKs)[43] as standards for digital object management, access, and unique identification.

Once developed, it was necessary to populate the CMS with METS objects in order to successfully test it. This proved to be somewhat of a challenge in 2001/2002, when there were no readily available tools that could be used to create METS objects. As noted earlier, the GenDB used in early OAC imaging projects created MOA2-encoded objects (which did not contain descriptive metadata), but it had not been upgraded to produce METS. At the time there were thousands of digital images in the OAC, but their limited descriptive metadata was embedded in EAD finding aids. Lacking robust item-level descriptions, most of these images relied upon the hierarchical nature of EAD-encoded finding aids to provide key contextual information. As a short-term solution, CDL implemented a script designed to grab relatively generic title information from hierarchical <c0x> component elements above the Digital Archival Object <dao> tags used in EAD to encode references to digital objects. This information was used to automate the creation of METS files for the OAC's MOA2-encoded objects. This solution could be applied upon ingest to any EAD-encoded finding aids that included <dao> encoding. These simple, automatically generated METS objects had no administrative, structural, or behavioral metadata, but they served to link some relatively specific descriptive metadata with pointers to content files, including links to each object's parent finding aid. They also allowed the OAC to move forward with planning the incorporation of newly encoded METS objects into the CMS without forcing affiliates to re-describe and re-encode thousands of existing digital image surrogates.[44]

The new DLXS-supported, CMS-driven finding aid interface–OAC version 2.0–was released in July 2002 with new functionality, including targeting searches to specific sections of finding aids, limiting searches to finding aids that include online images, and browsing by institution or collection titles. OAC 2.0 also gave end users the option of displaying finding aids with highlighted keywords-in-context, in an outline view, or in a printable full-text view. Three months later, the OAC version 2.5 release featured image search and browse functionality. Collaborating with the Pacific Bell/UCLA Initiative for 21st Century Literacies project, led by Professor Howard Besser at the UCLA Graduate School of Education and Information Science (GSEIS), the OAC surfaced a system of hierarchical topical terms to facilitate subject browsing by users.[45] For the first time in OAC history, "METsified" digital objects were keyword searchable and topically browsable independent of their parent EAD finding aids.

By December 2004, CDL had readied the previously mentioned XTF indexing and querying tool for use with the OAC, which was incrementally migrated off of DLXS software between December 2004 (finding aids and TEI-encoded texts) and October 2005 (METS objects managed by the CMS). As of this latter date, all OAC formats (EAD finding aids, TEI documents, and image files) and other CDL non-licensed content services (including eScholarship Editions) now use the same architecture: METS and ARKs for digital object description and identification, XSLT 2.0 servlets as an interface platform, XTF/Lucene as the search engine platform, and a common file system for the master repository. There are plans to migrate components of Counting California, a CDL managed statewide statistics resource, to XTF in 2006. CDL technology staff has plans to migrate the XTF file system into the CDL repository service layer (known as the Common Framework) used to support the UC Libraries Digital Preservation Repository sometime in 2006.[46]

XTF currently supports a broad range of functions: Boolean operators, proximity searching, wildcards, structure-aware searching, metadata-based queries, relevance ranking, collection-dependent queries, searching within results, multicollection searching, full-text searching, and customizable results display. Future enhancements will include the ability to integrate external systems such as spell checkers, recommender systems, and thesauri; e-mail, or save and export search results; and support for stemmed searches.

With the full migration to XTF for all OAC content, Interface Customization branding can now be applied at the item level for both digital objects and finding aids. Grouping by specified metadata element tag is now supported, which will permit a "curatorial view" of ingested digital objects, enabling analysis of specified objects across a variety of metadata fields including subject headings, geographic locations, and rights statements. In future developments, it is anticipated that this feature will facilitate metadata normalization and enrichment services that OAC contributors can apply when customizing portals for specific user communities. Universal application of XTF across CDL collections will streamline use of the Interface Customization Toolkit and support design application at the item level. Several University of California libraries are currently using the tool to develop customized content portals, or virtual collections, and the toolkit will form the basis of the California Cultures interface when it is released later in 2006.[47]

SERVICE VISION FOR CALIFORNIA CULTURES

Between the years 2001 and 2002, a range of user assessment studies pertaining to OAC interfaces and digital objects were conducted by CDL to determine interface usability and desired functionality, and to identify needed services. These studies confirmed users' preferences for clearly marked image access and the added value of content interpretation such as historical essays and lesson plans. Users "did not notice links to 'virtual archive' and 'electronic texts'" in part because labels did not clearly indicate the availability of primary resources. Participants also commented that "it would have been helpful if there was some indication that [the finding aid] contained images"[48] and suggested image searches should not be buried on the advanced search page. User interviews conducted in 2004 for CDL's Documenting the American West Project confirmed that K-12 teachers, media specialists, public librarians, academic librarians, faculty, and graduate students "placed a high value on access to primary source materials, especially images."[49] High school social studies teachers indicated "digital collections need contextual introduction" for successful use in classrooms. Assessment also revealed that "distillation and informed selection are essential"[50] to teachers. The abundance of materials available on the Internet makes the curation of materials an issue of the highest importance to teachers.

CDL assessment activities have directly informed the development of the California Cultures portal. A component of Calisphere, CDL's public access gateway to University of California content, the California Cultures Web site will be released in Summer 2006. The California Cultures portal helps K-12 teachers and students access digital resources within the context of the historic eras, people, and places they study. Constructed with the Interface Customization Toolkit, the Web site provides multiple pathways into the content leveraging the uniformly described digital objects. The pathways include historical essays tied to the California state framework for teaching history; subject browsing structures pertaining to ethnicities; and lesson plans based on significant events in California's history such as the Chicano movement, Chavez Ravine, and Japanese American internment camps.

As part of the California Cultures project, eight experienced teachers, well versed in teaching with primary resources, were called upon to develop lesson plans for classroom use within the fourth through twelfth grades. Enrolled in UCLA's Institute on Primary Resources (IPR),[51] the teachers visited the special collections libraries at many of the UC campuses participating in California Cultures, conducted in-depth research across the collections selected for the project, and developed lesson plans featuring selected primary resources. The teachers chose primary resources aligned with the California State History and Social Sciences K-12 curriculum. In many instances, archivists and manuscript curators were in the process of making final selections regarding materials to be digitally reformatted at the same time IPR teachers were working with curators in selecting materials appropriate for the project and relevant to the lesson plans. The California Cultures project underscores the importance of collaboration between archivists, manuscripts curators, and K-12 teachers in identifying particular resources for digitization, maximizing the possibilities of developing useful digital resources for a variety of users.

CONTINUING RESEARCH

In a few short years, the OAC consortium has taken significant steps fostering the creation of quality metadata and providing tools enabling the customization of portals for user communities. Each step forward provides another opportunity to reflect, refine, and redirect our efforts towards improvement. Reflecting upon the California Cultures project raises significant questions about sustainability. As a service provider, CDL has invested in the building of an Interface Customization Toolkit to leverage the exposure of high-quality metadata. Supported by temporary grant funds, California Cultures content contributors invested significant amounts of staff time in the creation of high-quality metadata describing their digital objects. Significant questions remain regarding the future sustainability of this level of effort for future digital object creation. Can libraries afford to allocate staffing resources to the creation of high-quality digital objects beyond the scope of grant-funded projects? Further research and discussion are required to understand how users interact with high-quality metadata for digital objects, and to assess the level of operational commitment and resource expenditures needed to support the creation of useful metadata.

At a recent Calisphere Advisory Board meeting, K-12 teachers expressed a desire for associating state curriculum standards with digital object metadata to encourage classroom utility. In their effort to create high-quality metadata, California Cultures content contributors diligently supplied Library of Congress Subject Headings (LCSH) as controlled vocabulary. The LCSH scheme serves the internal needs of librarians and archivists when mediating access to online content, but is neither easily grasped nor reliably useful for many user communities, especially teachers seeking relevant resources for classroom activities. It is clear that metadata requirements are likely to shift and expand as we understand our user communities better. Who is in the best position to respond to these evolving metadata requirements? Are content contributors, or service providers like CDL in the best position to create metadata accommodating these new user vocabularies? Or can tools be provided to users to support and manage infrastructures for meaningful access to content for their communities?

Research in these areas has started at CDL. In the Documenting the American West Project,[52] CDL is exploring strategies to automate or semiautomate the creation of high-quality metadata. CDL staff members are aggregating OAI-harvested metadata[53] from eight major research libraries and consortia, and developing tools and strategies to normalize dates and geographic locations, as well as adding consistent, meaningful topics to existing metadata. The harvested metadata was created according to multiple descriptive standards for disparate audiences and varies in levels of quality. The American West Project is providing an opportunity to analyze metadata from multiple repositories, test the effectiveness of tools built to enrich and normalize this metadata, and assess the value of this enhanced metadata to users in faceted hierarchical browse interfaces.[54] Formal user assessment for the American West portal will begin in fall 2006. CDL is also beginning to consider the effectiveness of implementing recommender systems where users supply meaning to aggregate collections supporting teaching and research. Felicia Poe, CDL Assessment Coordinator, states that "collaborative categorization tools, such as the social bookmark manager *del.icio.us* and the photo-sharing site *Flickr*, demonstrate that some users are interested in contributing to the categorization of web content."[55]

California Cultures is a valuable educational resource and the project did provide a timely and opportune testbed mechanism for the OAC. With a control group of content contributors, the OAC leveraged an opportunity to create metadata according to best practices and to build consciously a user-focused interface that takes advantage of standardized digital object descriptions. Perhaps most significantly, California Cultures was an opportunity to reflect upon our motives and mechanisms for creating meaning for users, and to explore new avenues for enhancing access to archival collection materials.

NOTES

1. The following definitions are from the California Digital Library's online glossary, available at http://www.cdlib.org/inside/diglib/glossary/. Accessed 2006-03-20. *Digital object*: an entity in which one or more content files and their corresponding metadata are united physically and/or logically, through the use of a digital wrapper. *Content file*: A file that is either born digitally or produced using various kinds of capture application software. Audio, image, text, and video are the basic kinds of content files. Versions of a content file may be dispersed across several file formats. For example, an image may be scanned into a TIFF file and then JPEG and GIF files may be created from the TIFF file to increase delivery speeds and protect property rights.

Metadata: Structured information about an object, a collection of objects, or a constituent part of an object such as an individual content file. *Digital wrapper*: A structured text file that binds digital object content files and their associated metadata together and that specifies the logical relationship of the content files.

2. Bradley D. Westbrook, "Prospecting Virtual Collections," *Journal of Archival Organization* 1:1 (2002), 77.

3. The Online Archive of California is a statewide consortium of cultural heritage repositories providing access to online finding aids and digital surrogates of collection materials. More information is available at http://www.oac.cdlib.org/. Accessed 2006-03-20.

4. The California Digital Library, which manages the OAC, provides digital library resources, services, tools, and infrastructure in partnership with the libraries of the University of California system. More information is available at http://www.cdlib.org/. Accessed 2006-03-20.

5. EAD is an encoding standard for encoding the hierarchy and designating the content of finding aids for archival holdings. It enables Internet delivery of these finding aids and also ensures their permanence by providing a stable, nonproprietary encoding format, which is maintained by the Society of American Archivists. EAD has been adopted by a wide variety of archives, libraries, and other cultural heritage institutions worldwide. For more information see http://www.loc.gov/ead/ead.html. Accessed 2006-03-20.

6. Westbrook, "Prospecting Virtual Collections," 79.

7. William E. Landis, "Nuts and Bolts: Implementing Descriptive Standards to Enable Virtual Collection," *Journal of Archival Organization* 1, no. 1 (2002), 89.

8. Landis, "Nuts and Bolts," 90.

9. The OAC Working Group advises the CDL on issues relating to the OAC; for more information see http://www.cdlib.org/inside/projects/oac/admin.html. Accessed 2006-03-27.

10. Robin L. Chandler, "Building Digital Collections at the OAC: Current Strategies with a View to Future Uses," *Journal of Archival Organization* 1, no. 1 (2002), 100.

11. Chandler, "Building Digital Collections at the OAC," 99.

12. California Cultures is funded by a Library of Congress American Memory Project grant, and will be made publicly available during 2006. The project Web site is available at http://calcultures.cdlib.org/. Accessed 2006-03-20.

13. Information regarding *California: A Changing State* is available online at http://www.cde.ca.gov/be/st/ss/hstgrade4.asp. The entire California State History-Social Science standards are available at http://www.cde.ca.gov/be/st/ss/hstmain.asp. All URLs accessed 2006-05-24.

14. METS is an XML-based standard for wrapping digital library materials. All of the content files and corresponding metadata can be stored within the wrapper (embedding, or physical wrapping), or stored independently and referred to by file pointers from within the wrapper (referencing, or logical wrapping). Wrapping strategies can be implemented concurrently within the same METS file. For more information on METS, see http://www.loc.gov/standards/mets/. Accessed 2006-03-20.

15. For a concise OAC timeline, see http://www.cdlib.org/inside/projects/oac/history.html. Accessed 2006-03-27.

16. Specifications regarding the usage of this element are supplied in *Encoded Archival Description Tag Library, Version 2002*, Chicago: Society of American

Archivists, 2002, available online at http://www.loc.gov/ead/tglib/elements/dao.html. Accessed 2006-04-02.

17. CDL documentation reviewed included *CDL Digital Image Format Standards* and *CDL Digital Image Collection Standards*, earlier versions of which have been significantly updated. See http://www.cdlib.org/inside/diglib/ for current versions of CDL guidelines and best practices relating to digital objects. The OAC WG also consulted the *MOAC Technical Specifications*, available at http://www.bampfa.berkeley. edu/moac/moacfullspecs.html. See http://www.loc.gov/standards/mets/ for METS documentation. All URLs accessed 2006-03-27.

18. OAC BPG DO Version 1.0 was incorporated into the California Digital Library's Guidelines for Digital Objects available at http://www.cdlib.org/inside/diglib/guidelines/. Version 1.0 of the OAC BPG DO is available via the Internet Archive's Wayback Machine at http://web.archive.org/web/20030713032451/oac.cdlib.org/oac-bpgdo/ OAC-BPGDO-md1a.html. URLs accessed 2006-03-27.

19. For further information about MOAC, see http://www.bampfa.berkeley.edu/ moac/, and for JARDA see http://jarda.cdlib.org/. URLs accessed 2006-03-27.

20. More information on RLG's REACH element set is available at http://www. rlg.org/en/page.php?Page_ID=432. Accessed 2006-03-29.

21. For additional information on MOAC, see Guenter Waibel, "MOAC Standards and Specifications," 2003, available at http://www.bampfa.berkeley.edu/moac/classic/ bpg.html. Accessed 2006-03-29.

22. Additional information is available at http://sunsite3.berkeley.edu/moa2/. Accessed 2006-03-29.

23. See http://www.diglib.org/ for additional information on the DLF. Accessed 2006-04-03.

24. The MOA2 project developed an XML DTD (eXtensible Markup Language Document Type Definition) as a means of "wrapping" this additional metadata relating to digital objects so that it could be exchanged between systems. For more information on this DTD, see http://sunsite.berkeley.edu/moa2/papers/dtdtutorial2.htm. For information on the Dublin Core Metadata Initiative see http://www.dublincore.org/. URLs accessed 2006-03-29.

25. A brief overview of WebGenDB is available at http://sunsite.berkeley.edu/ ~rbeaubie/uccsc/. Chapter 3 of the *California Cultures Project Manual*, available at http://calcultures.cdlib.org/project_manual/chapter3.html, provides a good introduction and illustration of how WebGenDB works and was utilized in this project. URLs accessed 2006-03-29.

26. Information on MODS is available at http://www.loc.gov/standards/mods/. Accessed 2006-03-30.

27. Information about the UC Berkeley LSO is available at http://www.lib.berkeley. edu/ LSO/. Accessed 2006-03-30.

28. Information about The Bancroft Library is available at http://bancroft.berkeley. edu/. Accessed 2006-03-30.

29. Rick Beaubien (lead software engineer at LSO), Genie Guerard (California Cultures project manager), and Bradley Westbrook (OAC Metadata Standards Subcommittee chair) were instrumental in coordinating this effort, which occurred early in 2002.

30. Additional information about the Interface Customization tools available for use with the CDL METS repository is can be found at http://www.cdlib.org/inside/diglib/ repository/customize/. Accessed 2006-04-02.

31. For those interested, the following are readily available sources for additional information on the technologies discussed: SQL databases, http://www.sql.org/; Java technologies, http://java.sun.com/; JDBC (Java Database Connectivity), http://java.sun.com/products/jdbc/; Java RMI (Remote Method Invocation), http://java.sun.com/products/jdk/rmi/; JavaScript, http://javascript.internet.com/. URLs accessed 2006-04-02.

32. See the definition in Richard Pearce-Moses, *A Glossary of Archival and Records Terminology*, Chicago: Society of American Archivists, 2005, also available online at http://www.archivists.org/glossary/term_details.asp?DefinitionKey=196. Accessed 2006-04-02.

33. Westbrook, "Prospecting Virtual Collections," 75-76.

34. The project manual is available at http://calcultures.cdlib.org/project_manual/chapter1.html. Accessed 2006-04-02.

35. For additional information about METS extension schemas, see http://www.loc.gov/standards/mets/mets-extenders.html. For additional information about the MARC 21 format, see http://www.loc.gov/marc/. URLs accessed 2006-04-02.

36. For a more detailed discussion of this concept, see the Wikipedia entry on web portals at http://en.wikipedia.org/wiki/Portals. Accessed 2006-04-02.

37. XSLT can be used to transform an XML document into another form such as PDF, HTML, or even Braille. XSLT stylesheets work as a series of templates that produce the desired formatting effect each time a given element is encountered. One of the most common uses of XSLT is to apply presentational markup to a document based on rules relating to the structural markup. For example, each time a "title" appears in the structural markup, the text within the element could be put into italics. XSLT can also control the order in which elements and attributes are displayed. This means that tables of contents or indexes can be generated automatically on the basis of the content of a document. For additional information consult the World Wide Web Consortium's XSLT page at http://www.w3.org/TR/xslt. Accessed 2006-04-02.

38. Cascading Style Sheets (CSS) represent a breakthrough in Web design because they allow developers to control the style and layout of multiple Web pages all at once. Before Cascading Style Sheets, changing an element that appeared on many pages required changing it on each individual page. Cascading Style Sheets work like a template, allowing Web developers to define a style for an HTML element and then apply it to as many Web pages as they like. Making a change to all relevant pages on a web site simply involves change the style. For additional information see the Cascading Style Sheets homepage, maintained by the World Wide Web Consortium at http://www.w3.org/Style/CSS/. Accessed 2006-04-02.

39. Additional information on the CDL METS Repository is available at http://www.cdlib.org/inside/diglib/repository/, and on XTF at http://www.cdlib.org/inside/projects/xtf/. URLs accessed 2006-04-03.

40. Greenstone is a suite of open source tools for building and distributing digital library collections on the Internet, and for exporting records according to the Open Archives Initiative Protocol for Metadata Harvesting (OAI PMH) and METS standards. For more information see http://www.greenstone.org/cgi-bin/library. Accessed 2006-04-03.

41. DLXS is a suite of tools including a powerful search engine, XPAT, and an array of class-based middleware (text class, image class, bib class, finding aid class) that support development and management of digital library collections. For more information see http://www.dlxs.org/. Accessed 2006-04-03.

42. These programs include the OAC, eScholarship editions (http://content.cdlib. org/escholarship/), and the eScholarship repository (http://repositories.cdlib.org/ escholarship/). URLs accessed 2006-04-03.

43. The Archival Resource Key (ARK) is a naming scheme for persistent identifiers ensuring access to digital objects. It has been implemented at CDL and a variety of other digital library programs. For more information see http://www.cdlib.org/inside/ diglib/ark/. Accessed 2006-04-03.

44. For more information about this process see the METS Profile Schema Version 1.2 at http://www.loc.gov/standards/mets/profile_docs/mets.profile.v1-2.xsd, and Brian Tingle, *Managing Content Diversity with METS Profiles* (2004) at http://www. loc.gov/standards/mets/presentations/od2/tingle.pdf. URLs accessed 2006-05-24.

45. Additional information about this effort is available in the OAC WG meeting minutes for November 22, 2002, available at http://www.cdlib.org/inside/groups/ oacwg/minutes.2002.11.22.rtf. Additional information on Pacific Bell/UCLA Initiative for 21st Century Literacies is available at http://www.newliteracies.gseis.ucla.edu/. URLs accessed 2006-04-03.

46. For more information see http://www.cdlib.org/inside/projects/preservation/ dpr/ (DPR) and http://www.cdlib.org/inside/projects/common_framework/index.html (Common Framework architecture). URLs accessed 2006-04-03.

47. See, for example, the Bancroft Library's San Francisco Earthquake and Fire portal at http://bancroft.berkeley.edu/collections/earthquakeandfire/index2.html, which is built on top of digital objects housed in the OAC. Accessed 2006-04-03.

48. For more information see *OAC Usability Test Summary* (2001) at http:// www.cdlib.org/inside/assess/evaluation_activities/oac_usabilitytest2001_summary.pdf. Accessed 2006-05-24.

49. For more information see *Documenting the American West: User Interviews, Final Report* (2004), 3, available at http://www.cdlib.org/inside/projects/amwest/ americanwest_assessmentfindings.pdf. Accessed 2006-05-24.

50. Additional information about this effort is available at *High School Social Studies Teachers: The Use of Digital Objects in Teaching Practices* (2005), 13, available at http://www.cdlib.org/inside/projects/amwest/AmWestAssessment-2005-0202.pdf. Accessed 2006-05-24.

51. Detailed information about the UCLA IPR is available at http://ipr.ues.gseis. ucla.edu/index.html. Accessed 2006-05-24.

52. For more information see http://www.cdlib.org/inside/projects/amwest/. Accessed 2006-05-24.

53. For more information about the Open Archive Initiative Protocol for Metadata Harvesting (OAI-PMH) see http://www.openarchives.org/. Accessed 2006-05-24.

54. For an overview of the role of faceted metadata in browse infrastructures see Ka-Ping Yee et al., "Faceted Metadata for Image Search and Browsing" (2003), available online at http://bailando.sims.berkeley.edu/papers/flamenco-chi03.pdf. For more information generally on faceted browsing see the Flamenco Project Web site at http://flamenco.sims.berkeley.edu/. URLs accessed 2006-05-24.

55. Felicia Poe, *Do You Have Any Recommendations?: An Introduction to Recommender Systems* (2005), 1, available at http://www.cdlib.org/inside/assess/evaluation_ activities/docs/2005/recSystemIntro_2005.pdf. Accessed 2006-05-24.

doi:10.1300/J201v04n01_04

The Importance of User-Centered Design:
Exploring Findings and Methods

Rosalie Lack

SUMMARY. Given the rising number of information resources available, it is increasingly important for digital libraries and archives to create usable services that meet their users' needs. Seeking input from users at all stages of development can help achieve this goal. This article briefly defines four methodologies for gathering user input: focus groups, interviews, questionnaires, and usability testing. In addition, it presents the "top ten" themes that emerged from over four years of assessment and evaluation activities at the California Digital Library. doi:10.1300/J201v04n01_05 *[Article copies available for a fee from The Haworth Document Delivery Service: 1-800-HAWORTH. E-mail address: <docdelivery@haworthpress.com> Website: <http://www.HaworthPress.com> © 2006 by The Haworth Press, Inc. All rights reserved.]*

Rosalie Lack, MIMS, is Public Content Manager, California Digital Library, University of California, Oakland, CA 94612 (E-mail: lack@ucop.edu).

[Haworth co-indexing entry note]: "The Importance of User-Centered Design: Exploring Findings and Methods." Lack, Rosalie. Co-published simultaneously in *Journal of Archival Organization* (The Haworth Information Press, an imprint of The Haworth Press, Inc.) Vol. 4, No.1/2, 2006, pp. 69-86; and: *Archives and the Digital Library* (ed: William E. Landis, and Robin L. Chandler) The Haworth Information Press, an imprint of The Haworth Press, Inc., 2006, pp. 69-86. Single or multiple copies of this article are available for a fee from The Haworth Document Delivery Service [1-800-HAWORTH, 9:00 a.m. - 5:00 p.m. (EST). E-mail address: docdelivery@haworthpress.com].

Available online at http://jao.haworthpress.com
© 2006 by The Haworth Press, Inc. All rights reserved.
doi:10.1300/J201v04n01_05

KEYWORDS. Assessment, digital libraries, evaluation, focus groups, interviews, methodology, questionnaires, usability testing, user-centered design

INTRODUCTION

One of the biggest challenges facing digital librarians and archivists today is creating useful, easy-to-use services. It is not enough to provide access to information in a digital format. Patrons have more information resource choices than ever before; therefore it is increasingly important for libraries and archives to provide easy-to-use sites and services aligned to their patrons' needs. Pointing out the difficulty of this goal, Christine Borgman notes that those who want a digital library to be as easy as an ATM (automatic teller machine) are not taking into consideration that ATMs support a relatively small number of actions. Complex information technology systems such as digital libraries, on the other hand, offer a multiplicity of features and functions.[1] As difficult as it is, libraries and archives must cut through the complexity of information systems, or at least make the complexity transparent to patrons, in order to provide the best possible services.

This challenge is twofold: digital librarians and archivists must (1) address issues of usefulness for patrons, and (2) ensure ease of use, frequently referred to as usability. Prior to designing usable interfaces, it is necessary to first define the target audiences and develop a deep understanding of their goals, environment, and technical skill level. Borgman states, "design must be driven by questions of who will use your content, how and why." [2]

USER-CENTERED DESIGN

User-Centered Design (UCD) is a philosophy and a methodology that advocates user involvement at all stages of product development–before, during, and afterwards.[3] UCD has roots in a variety of fields, including cognitive psychology, anthropology, computer science and engineering, and information management. By actively following good UCD methods, sites can be planned properly, shifted accordingly during construction, and revised as needed after implementation.

The following steps outline a product development model that supports the UCD principle of user involvement at all stages:

1. Talk to or observe your target audience to understand their current environment–their needs, behaviors and goals;
2. Create a prototype service that meets those goals;
3. Iteratively design the service using methods that directly involve users, such as usability testing;
4. Follow up after release to learn if their needs have been met.

The California Digital Library (CDL)[4] strives to meet the ideal of this UCD model through close collaboration between the Assessment and Evaluation Program and the Interface Design Team. By incorporating UCD methods throughout the planning and development process, CDL builds user interface services closely aligned with identified user needs. The CDL Assessment and Evaluation Program, described below, is a key component of the CDL development process.

DESCRIPTION OF CDL'S ASSESSMENT AND EVALUATION PROGRAM

Established in 1997, the California Digital Library is a University of California systemwide digital library. Through the use of technology and innovation, CDL supports the University of California libraries and the communities they serve. From 1999 to 2003, the CDL Assessment and Evaluation Program consisted primarily of one full-time staff member dedicating 50 percent time to evaluation activities. The program has since expanded to two positions–a full-time manager dedicated exclusively to assessment and evaluation and a two-year grant-funded analyst. In addition, on each of the ten UC campuses, two to three library staff are designated as Evaluation Liaisons; they work collaboratively with CDL staff to conduct evaluation activities on their campuses. As part of this program, CDL sponsors training sessions for Evaluation Liaisons and other campus staff covering topics such as focus group and usability testing methodologies.[5]

Over four years, CDL staff and Evaluation Liaisons have used a variety of methods to gather user needs information. CDL has conducted more than fifteen focus group sessions, with approximately 150 participants; sixteen structured interviews; more than 150 usability testing sessions; and approximately twenty-five questionnaires. There is also ongoing analysis of usage logs and user feedback. Evaluation activities have been conducted with a variety of audiences. Resources that have been the focus of evaluation activities include ebooks (eScholarship editions), an archival finding aids site (Online Archive of California), a personalized library portal (MyLibrary), a California statistics site (Counting California), a metasearch tool (SearchLight), an online catalog (Melvyl Catalog), a digital images delivery system (Luna Insight) and library information Web pages.[6]

METHODS

This section provides a broad overview of the methods CDL uses for collecting user feedback, with concrete examples of their application. CDL typically chooses methods based on the stage of development and objectives. In general, focus groups and interviews are primarily used during the initial stages of development. Usability testing is used during the design phase, and questionnaires are used across all phases. There are many other methods that are not discussed here.[7] Regardless of the methods chosen, it is important to develop a systematic approach based on one or more methodologies that best match an institution's available resources.

Focus Groups: The Group Dynamic Generates Ideas

Focus group sessions are moderated discussions designed to obtain participants' perceptions and opinions about a particular area of interest. A moderator, whose role it is to encourage meaningful conversation and interaction among the participants, runs these sessions. The give and take of focus group conversations is useful for learning what participants think about a particular topic and for uncovering why they think as they do. A session usually includes eight to ten participants who share certain characteristics (e.g., humanities faculty, science and engineering graduate students).[8]

Most useful at the early stages of development, focus groups provide insight into the user's current environment–what works well or not with their current system and what are the glaring omissions. In addition to providing a good tool for gathering feedback about a service currently in use, focus groups can also reveal user expectations regarding new services.

Focus groups were used to gather user information for two CDL services, MyLibrary and SearchLight. MyLibrary is a prototype service that allows users to create a personalized Web site of library resources such as ejournals and databases, along with links to non-library resources. SearchLight was a metasearch tool allowing users to search across more than 100 journal article databases, book catalogs, and other library resources.[9]

For MyLibrary and SearchLight, focus groups were used at different stages of product development to provide valuable information. For MyLibrary, focus groups were used to investigate continuing development after existing open source code was used to rapidly create a prototype. SearchLight, on the other hand, was an existing service, and focus groups were used to help determine changes and potential improvements to the underlying technology. In both cases the focus group objectives were to learn from users how they were currently performing tasks that these services offered–organizing online library resources and researching new topics, respectively–and to gather broad user input about both interfaces.

A similar format was used for conducting focus groups for both services. The sessions were divided into two parts; they began with a general discussion regarding participants' current practices, and then participants were shown screen shots of the services to elicit reaction. This format provided an understanding of the tools users currently employ and uncovered their "points of pain" (i.e., what wasn't working for them). In addition, showing screen shots helped to concretize the proposed services and resulted in general feedback about look, feel and functionality.[10]

Interviews: One-on-One Feedback

Structured interviews are similar to focus groups in the use of a predefined set of questions and discussion points. However, interviews vary in that they are conducted with one to two participants, rather than eight- to ten-member focus groups. In addition, interviews do not benefit from the group dynamic of focus groups in which lively discussion can potentially lead to new and different ideas. Interviews can also take longer because of the time needed to schedule and conduct sessions as well as the additional time necessary to analyze results. The primary benefit of interviews is that one-on-one time allows for probing more deeply into issues; since interviews are more controlled than focus groups it is easier to pursue leads or adjust the interview based on the individual.[11]

Interviews were used for the CDL Image Demonstrator project, a development initiative exploring the viability of using the Luna Insight software to build an online digital image service. Interviews were chosen over focus groups because the objective was to gather detailed feedback on the Luna Insight interface and functionality. The interviews also had the additional objectives of seeking to understand the user's current environment with regard to digital images and learning about their perception of the value or potential usefulness of digital images in research and teaching.

Sixteen interviews were conducted with UC faculty and graduate students. Similar to the focus group format discussed above, the first half of the sessions was spent in discussion where participants were asked questions about how and why they currently used digital images. If they didn't use digital images, they were asked to elaborate on the usage barriers. Participants were then asked to complete a set of tasks using the Luna Insight software. In a larger focus group session, it would not have been as effective for participants to do this type of hands-on work, but with one or two participants per interview session, it was a highly effective and informative methodology.[12]

Questionnaires: Input from Many

Like interviews, questionnaires consist of a pre-defined set of questions. One key advantage of questionnaires, however, is that they allow the participant to answer the questions on their own rather than in a small "live" setting. This provides an excellent means of gathering input from a large number of people. In addition, questionnaires can be done relatively quickly in comparison to interviews. One risk associated with questionnaires is that respondents may misinterpret questions or not fully answer them.[13]

CDL has administered more than twenty-five online questionnaires. Questionnaires have been used for gathering input to prioritize features and functionality, for helping to make key interface design decisions and for measuring user satisfaction. During the migration of the Melvyl Union Catalog to a new vendor system, faculty, students, and university staff members answered questionnaires to provide information about what current features and functionality they liked (as well as what they didn't like) and what new features they would like to see implemented. A separate "Hidden Uses Questionnaire" was also created for library staff, designed to unearth information about nontraditional catalog usage in order to ensure continued support for those features.

A questionnaire was also used during the redesign of CDL's administrative library staff Web pages (see Figure 1). For that site, a Yahoo-like directory structure was envisioned for the home page, and a questionnaire was used to determine if the selected category headings were intuitive. Consisting of ten tasks users might accomplish by using the site, this questionnaire asked respondents to choose the category heading from the supplied list that best matched the task. For example, a task might be "Find a list of licensed databases"; the user would then select the category heading best suited to answer this question. This method

FIGURE 1. This is an example question in a questionnaire created to determine whether top-level category headings were intuitive or not.

1) You would like to find a list of all databases that CDL has licensed. Which category will you choose to find this information?

    ○ **Projects and Programs**
       eScholarship, Melvyl, Shared Cataloging Program, ...
    ○ **Shared Acquisitions**
       Selection criteria, JSC surveys, status of negotiations, ...
    ○ **Licensing Toolkit**
       Model license, sample language, negotiating a license, ...
    ○ **Licensed Resources**
       Usage statistics, ILL terms, instructional materials, ...
    ○ **Digital Library Building Blocks**
       Standards, best practices, usability testing, ...
    ○ **Committees, Groups, and Liaisons**
       CDL advisory structure, JSC, Resource Liaisons, Users Council, ...
    ○ **News and Events**
       CDLINFO newsletter, LISTSERVs, workshops, ...
    ○ **Report a Problem**
       System status, planned outages, troubleshooting, ...
    ○ **Contact CDL**
       Who does what, email, phone numbers, ...
    ○ **Suggest a different category heading**

Enter your suggested category heading:

proved to be an effective way of gathering quantitative information about which category headings were clear and which were not.

Online questionnaires can also be used to gauge user satisfaction for both newly created and existing services. Questions can cover overall satisfaction as well as dealing with specific features. The feature questions force users to give thoughtful and detailed input and not just blanket statements of whether they were satisfied or not.

Usability Testing: Watch and Learn

Usability testing consists of one-on-one sessions in which participants are asked to complete a set of tasks related to a specific software product or Web site. Observers watch (and do not intervene) while participants are encouraged to "think aloud" (i.e., verbalize their thoughts) as they complete each task. Usually there is one experimenter who runs the tests and one or two recorders.[14]

Usability testing is an essential part of an iterative design process. The first step of the process consists of creating a prototype interface, and then conducting an initial round of usability tests. Based on feedback, changes are made to the interface that address the user concerns, and then another round of testing is conducted. This iterative process continues until the resulting interface is one that users find easy to navigate and use. Each round should include at minimum four two six participants and there should be a minimum of two rounds.

Before creating a new interface, usability testing can be conducted on the existing site and on other similar sites as a comparative analysis to learn what users like or don't like. For example, when the Online Archive of California (OAC) finding aids site was migrating to a new delivery mechanism (from Dynaweb to DLXS[15]), usability testing was conducted on the then-current OAC site[16] and on an implementation of DLXS at the University of Michigan's Bentley Historical Library.[17] Usability testing proved to be beneficial for learning which features to keep in the current interface, which features users liked in the new interface, and which features they found confusing.

In all, more than 150 usability sessions have been conducted with faculty, library staff, and graduate and undergraduate students for a wide variety of CDL tools and services. Usability testing provided valuable information that helped CDL to find and solve usability problems for each of these services. Nonetheless, it is important to recognize the limitations of usability testing. It should be used to help create intuitive, usable sites, not to test the need for or usefulness of a new service. It is certainly possible to create an extremely usable site that is not useful. To guard against such a scenario, it is important that the first step in new service creation, or when modifying existing services, is to employ methods such as focus groups or interviews in order to understand the target audiences' needs and goals.

Top Ten Themes

At CDL, a number of themes became evident after conducting evaluation and analyses across a wide spectrum of digital library tools and services. Overall, the findings related to interface design were in alignment with other studies and good design principles.[18] CDL findings are uniquely interesting in that they take into consideration such a varied cross-set of resource types.

1. Integration: One-Stop Shopping

The concept of "one-stop shopping" is an expectation that has been fueled by the Internet, which now makes it possible for users to access, from one Web site, information distributed across multiple storage resources. In addition, the traditional physical division of library resources by formats (e.g., books on one floor and videos on another) is not acceptable in the digital world. Users want to go to one place to find texts, images, and videos. They quickly become frustrated with most current online library resources because they are forced to go to multiple places to find what they need. At times it also becomes necessary to consult multiple services for related resources; for example, journals are located in the library catalog, but journal articles are spread across many vendor-supplied abstracting and indexing databases.

In addition to wanting integration within library services, users also expressed interest in the integration of library services with other campus services. For example, respondents surveyed about CDL's MyLibrary wanted integration between MyLibrary and broader campus services such as class registration.

2. Research: Google May Be the First Step, But It's Not the Last

Across CDL user groups studied (faculty, graduate, and undergraduate students), all used Google, even for image searches. Most cited it as a place to start when researching a new topic. However, all of the respondents also said they did not use Google exclusively. They felt the library was the place to find trusted information. Google provides a basic understanding of a topic, but for serious research they use and trust library resources.

3. Online Resources: Is the Information Really There or Not?

User expectations that all resources are online have risen. If the information resources are not online, then users want that clearly indicated. They also want to be able to initially limit their search to items that are only online; if that is not available, then they want the results to clearly indicate whether or not there is direct online access.

This lack of online availability proved to be one of the most common issues raised across all services and was particularly problematic with regards to archival finding aids. To most novice users the concept of a finding aid was extremely difficult to comprehend. There was no immediate understanding of the usefulness of a list of physical objects that provided no direct access to their digital equivalents. In the case of the OAC, it became even more complex, and therefore confusing to users, because some finding aids provide access to digital objects, while others do not. As a result of CDL's usability testing, the OAC now contains a clear indication when online items are available (see Figure 2).

FIGURE 2. Example of the indication in OAC search results regarding availability in finding aids of online digital objects.

4. **Collection Title:** California Cornerstones: Selected Images from The Bancroft Library Pictorial Collection
    Contributing Institution: Bancroft Library
    Collection Dates: None given
    Items Online Yes. Must visit contributing institution to view entire collection.
    Online Items 106 items
    Summary: California Cornerstones is a selection of images from various collections in The Bancroft Library. The images have been organized by provenance; that is, they have been grouped around the individual or corporate body that created or collected the materials. Most come from collections of photographs, such as the William C. Barry Collection or the Frank B. Rudolph Collection. Some come from collections made up primarily of textual records. These, like the Henry J. Kaiser papers or the Sierra Club records, are large collections that include, in addition to photographs, materials such as correspondence, reports, minutes of meetings, diaries, and published pamphlets. A number of the oldest images have been reproduced from illustrations in published books, such as Georg von Langsdorff's Observations on a journey around the world, an account of an exploring expedition that visited the California coast in 1806. One particularly important source has been the Robert Honeyman Collection, an extensive group that includes paintings, drawings, prints, and photographs, most of which relate to the history of California in the 18th and 19th centuries....
    Search terms in context (11):
    ...Ernest Etienne Painting, oil Subjects/Genres: Gold rush 1963.002.1380-FRThe Elopement. Nahl, Charles...
    ...Lithograph, hand colored Subjects/Genres: Gold rush Portraits1963.002.1529-FRS. E. Hollister, the...
    ...colored (watercolor?) Subjects/Genres: Gold rush Mining1963.002.270-CSan Diego, 1850. Conts, C.G....

5. **Collection Title:** Gay (Theresa) Papers
    Contributing Institution: Stanford University. Libraries. Dept. of Special Collections and University Archives.
    Collection Dates: 1946-1960
    Items Online None online. Must visit contributing institution.
    Summary: The bulk of this collection consists mainly of research notes, correspondence and manuscript material pertaining to Theressa Gay's historical research on the California Gold Rush. This collection also includes materials relating to other areas of historical research as well (see contents listings for specific topics); some biographical material and teaching files. The focus of this collection are the original manuscript of Theresa Gay's biography of James W. Marshall, and a group of about two hundred Gold Rush Songs that she collected. The papers in this collection reflect her work over a period of approximately fifteen years, from about 1946 to 1960. It comprises about ten and a half linear feet of material....
    Search terms in context (17):
    ...to the James Marshall, or the California Gold Rush, but photographs having to do with other subject...
    ...AND PRINTED MATERIALS Pamphlets and Fliers: 8 13 Gold Rush 9 1 American Politics—Campaigns, etc....
    ...Maps and Travel Guides: 9 2 Gold Rush Country 9 3-4 Misc. 9 5-8 Book Catalogs 9 9 Misc. items and...

4. Recommendations: Tell Us What You Think

Not surprisingly, students and faculty feel overwhelmed by the amount of information available. Both audiences expressed interest in the library providing recommendations in the form of "top ten" lists of most used resources, "best" resources as defined by librarians, and other similar formats. To be clear, they still want access to all library resources, but they also would like to see a vetted list. In the case of an archival site this might mean highlighting the most viewed or most popular items, or pointing out collection strengths on the home page. Many respondents also expressed a strong interest in something similar to the www.amazon.com feature "Customers who bought this book also bought ..."

5. Navigation and Choices Are Not Where They Should Be

It is easy for users to feel lost or disoriented while navigating through information-rich resources such as those on archives and library sites. It is helpful to make common navigation elements such as links to Home, Search, About, and Contact Us available and prominent on all pages. This issue was glaringly evident during OAC usability testing of the Dynaweb interface. In that interface, all navigation elements were at the bottom of the page–home, help, view collections, etc.–where users least expected them (see Figure 3). In addition, regarding general navigation, respondents expressed a desire to be able to easily undo an action or return to the previous screen.

6. Choosing the Right Search Terms

When using a new interface, users are unsure of what search terms to enter. Some users feel that the system is using specialized vocabulary and since they don't know it, they will not get good results. Likewise, if they do not know the collection's scope, they are unsure how to get started. Users appreciate sites that clearly indicate the scope and extent of the collection on the home page. In addition, clear browse options help them choose the correct terms, and also help them understand what the site has to offer. With regards to archival materials, users want, at minimum, subject, location, and date browsing options.

A related issue is that users are unsure of how to enter search terms such as author names (e.g., last name first or first name last) and dates (e.g., MM/DD/YY or some other format). Users admit that they will not

FIGURE 3. This screen shot of the 2001 version of the OAC Dynaweb interface illustrates that all the navigation elements were originally at the bottom of the page, where users least expected them to be.

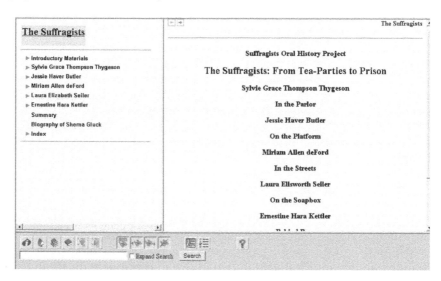

use help pages so would prefer to have examples directly on the search page. The Melvyl Catalog home page (Figure 4) provides an example of date entry help and other tips directly on the search page.

7. Offer Simple and Advanced Search Options

The assumption that users only want the simple Google-like search box was proven wrong many times. Users expressed a preference for a choice of simple and advanced search options. They indicated an appreciation of simple search options (taking into consideration their confusion about how to enter search terms discussed above) when unfamiliar with a site or topic. On the other hand, users familiar with a topic preferred advanced search options. Some of the advanced options they wanted when searching finding aids and other historic materials included date, geographic location, proper names, and repository.

8. Useful Search Results and Sorted by Relevance

There were two main findings with regard to search results. First, users require a clear understanding of why they got the results they did. If they don't understand why they received certain results, they quickly

FIGURE 4. The Melvyl Catalog home page illustrates how CDL chose, in response to usability testing feedback, to include help tips directly on the search box page.

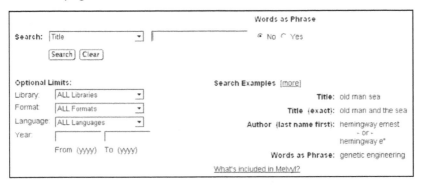

become frustrated and critical of the search engine. Second, users want search results to contain enough information to help them choose the best match, information such as an informative title, date, and a short description. Results on the retired OAC Dynaweb platform contained only the title (see Figure 5), while currently results (see Figure 2) contain more descriptive information. In addition, users prefer Google-like results showing a snippet of text from the site with the user's search term(s) highlighted, a feature now available in the OAC (see the highlighted "search terms in context" illustrated in Figure 2).

Finally, users have a strong expectation that the top search results are the best results. This may seem like an obvious statement, but in the case of finding aid searches on the old OAC Dynaweb platform, results were returned alphabetically. Though alphabetical ordering was indicated on the results page, users did not take notice. They expect the best results at the top. The current OAC interface sorts results by relevance by default, and other sort options are also provided (see Figure 6).

9. Unclear Labels and Icons

Unclear labels and icons are a common barrier to successful interface navigation. Examples of archival terms that users found confusing included the following:

- Finding aids
- Repository

FIGURE 5. The OAC Dynaweb interface as it existed in 2001, illustrating search results that provide minimal information, in this case only the title.

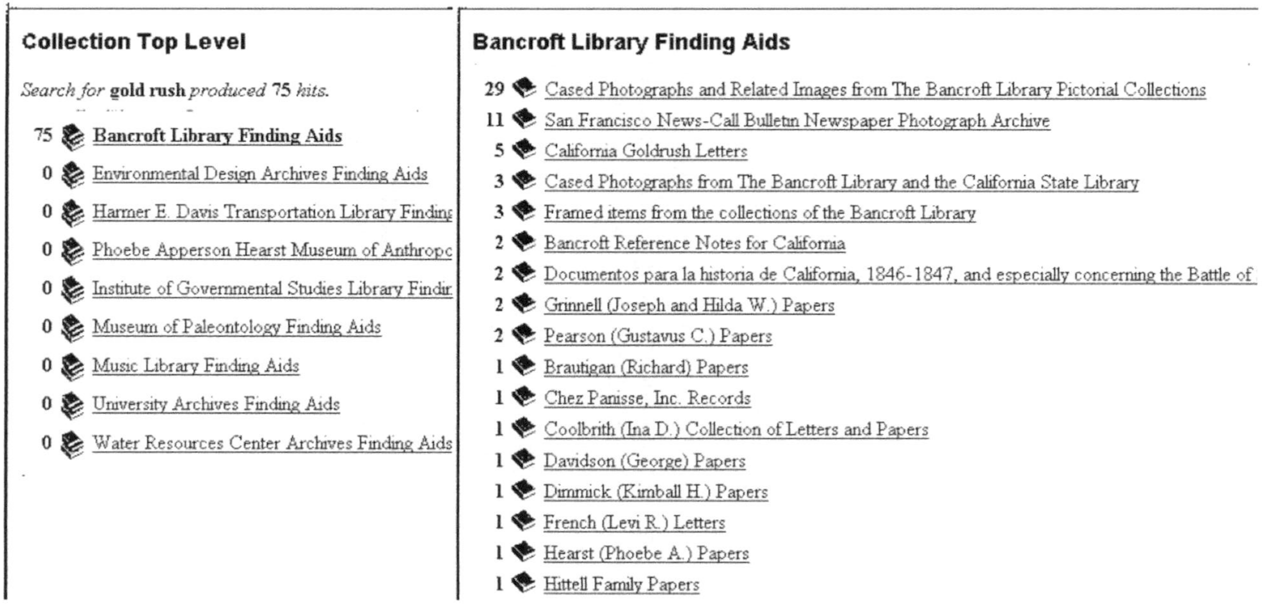

Collection Top Level

Search for gold rush produced 75 hits.

75		**Bancroft Library Finding Aids**
0		Environmental Design Archives Finding Aids
0		Harmer E. Davis Transportation Library Finding
0		Phoebe Apperson Hearst Museum of Anthropo
0		Institute of Governmental Studies Library Findir
0		Museum of Paleontology Finding Aids
0		Music Library Finding Aids
0		University Archives Finding Aids
0		Water Resources Center Archives Finding Aids

Bancroft Library Finding Aids

29		Cased Photographs and Related Images from The Bancroft Library Pictorial Collections
11		San Francisco News-Call Bulletin Newspaper Photograph Archive
5		California Goldrush Letters
3		Cased Photographs from The Bancroft Library and the California State Library
3		Framed items from the collections of the Bancroft Library
2		Bancroft Reference Notes for California
2		Documentos para la historia de California, 1846-1847, and especially concerning the Battle of
2		Grinnell (Joseph and Hilda W.) Papers
2		Pearson (Gustavus C.) Papers
1		Brautigan (Richard) Papers
1		Chez Panisse, Inc. Records
1		Coolbrith (Ina D.) Collection of Letters and Papers
1		Davidson (George) Papers
1		Dimmick (Kimball H.) Papers
1		French (Levi R.) Letters
1		Hearst (Phoebe A.) Papers
1		Hittell Family Papers

FIGURE 6. Currently OAC search results are sorted by relevance and additional sort options (collection title, contributing institution, and collection dates) are provided.

Search Results

Your search for gold rush in Entire Finding Aid found 181 item(s).   New Search

Sort by: [Relevance ▼] [Go!]

   Relevance
   C Collection Title
1. C Contributing Institution
   C Collection Dates

Displaying 1 - 20 of **181** iter

Page: **1** 2 3 4 5 6 7 8 9 1

n (Robert B., Jr.) - Collection of Early Californian and Western American Pictorial Material
: Bancroft Library.
en

Items Online Yes. Must visit contributing institution to view entire collection.

[**Online items**] 🔍 2271 digital objects

Summary: The Robert B. Honeyman Jr. Collection of Early Californian and Western American Pictorial Material is comprised of over 2300 items, with formats and media ranging from original oil paintings, watercolors, drawings, lithographs, engravings, etchings, lettersheets, clipper cards, and ephemera, to plates and spoons featuring western themes, and a fore-edge painting. The collection focuses on pictorial interpretations of the old West, with emphasis on the early California and Gold Rush periods. Views depict the changing landscape of the West under the impact of westward migration, the development of towns and cities, early settlements, California missions, railroads, gold mining scenes, pioneer and frontier life, native populations, social history, and many other topics. "Well-known painters of the West... are represented by oils and watercolors and drawings in the collection. Charles Christian Nahl may be considered the most important resident artist of the early American period in California history. Besides a sketch-book, dated 1853 and 1854, Mr. Honeyman managed to acquire five Nahl oils, including the beautiful and exciting A watercolor by Charles Russell, i small but of prime quality. Alexander Edouart's is a superb documentary of an important mining activity. There is a magnificent oil painting of by A. D. O. Browere; and impressive scenes by the French artist E. E. Narjot de Francheville, a early arrival on the West Coast, attracted by news of gold." ...

Search terms in context (32):

...engraver [Two satirical drawings relating to Gold Rush in California] [185-?] print on paper:...
...music sheet covers, primarily related to Gold Rush, mining, and frontier and pioneer life. Atwill &...
...1756--AXContent/Description: Related to Gold Rush. Notes/Inscriptions: Printed title. Printed (LC):...

83

- EAD
- Descriptive summary
- Folder list

In general, users found most of the icons in the OAC Dynaweb interface confusing (see the icons at the bottom of the Web page in Figure 3). In particular, the book metaphor used in Dynaweb was problematic.

Usability testing is the best way to discover whether a particular label or icon is intuitive or not. There are a variety of good interface-design resources that can assist librarians and archivists in avoiding common pitfalls relating to labeling and icon design.[19]

10. Promote Your Sites and Services

As important as it is to create useful and usable services, getting the word out about them is equally so. Over and over again respondents expressed that they had not heard of or used many already existing services. While some participants were surprised that the library had a Web site at all, others were amazed and impressed at the breadth of library services. It is crucial to explore and expand the ways in which services are promoted to prospective audiences. Related to this point, it is important to note that evaluation activities double as outreach efforts. Getting feedback from potential users is a great way of spreading the word about the variety of other services offered.

CONCLUSION

Sound Web design principles and methods are useful for all types of library services and audiences. Even archives, with their special features and needs, can benefit from the same methods used by other types of sites, commercial as well as educational.

In this article I have provided an overview of the findings and methods used by CDL staff to gather and understand user needs. Across all projects, it is clear that getting input early on, before plans are set in stone, allows for modification and improvements based on feedback from prospective user groups. At times, because of knowledge gained from current users and/or prospective users, the end product was in fact quite different than what was initially envisioned. Though there are many ways to design a Web site, the best sites result from a clear understanding of user needs, behaviors, and goals gained through the use of focus groups, structured interviews, questionnaires, usability testing, and other user-centered information gathering techniques.

NOTES

1. Christine L. Borgman, *From Gutenberg to the Global Information Infrastructure: Access to Information in the Networked World* (Cambridge, MA: MIT Press, 2000), 117.

2. Ibid., 141.

3. Mark Pearrow, *Web Site Usability Handbook* (Rockland: MA: Charles River Media, 2000), 15-16.

4. Additional information about the CDL is available at: http://www.cdlib.org. Accessed 2006-01-03.

5. For additional information on CDL's Assessment and Evaluation Program, see http://www.cdlib.org/inside/assess/. Accessed 2006-01-03.

6. Several of these resources are no longer available. For further information on those that are, see: eScholarship editions (http://content.cdlib.org/escholarship/), Online Archive of California (http://www.oac.cdlib.org/), Counting California (http://countingcalifornia.cdlib.org/), SearchLight (retired in 2005, for information see http://www.cdlib.org/inside/projects/searchlight/), Melvyl catalog (http://melvyl.cdlib.org/), UC Image Service (http://imageservice.cdlib.org/). All URLs accessed 2006-01-03.

7. A summary of a variety of methods along with their strengths and weaknesses can be found in Chapter 7 of Jakob Nielsen, *Usability Engineering* (San Francisco: Morgan Kaufmann, 1994).

8. Richard A. Krueger, *Focus Groups: A Practical Guide for Applied Research* (Beverly Hills: Sage Publication, 1988), 17-48. David Morgan, *Focus Groups as Qualitative Research*, Qualitative Research Methods Series 16 (Beverly Hills: Sage University Press Paper, 1988), p 9-30.

9. For information on CDL's Metasearch project, which will replace the retired SearchLight service, see http://www.cdlib.org/inside/projects/metasearch/. Accessed 2006-01-03.

10. A note about using screen shots rather than conducting a live demo during the session. We deliberately chose to use screen shots over a live demo because of time constraints; each session was one hour and we wanted to stay in control of the conversation. Use of a live demo runs the risk of spending more time than planned exploring the interface.

11. Morgan, *Focus Groups as Qualitative Research, 15-24.*

12. For more detailed information about the assessment activities conducted as part of the UC Image Service Demonstrator Project, see Maureen Burns' article in this volume, 115-143.

13. Nielsen, *Usability Engineering*, 209-214.

14. Two excellent resources for step-by-step guidance in planning, conducting and analyzing results from usability testing are Jeffery Rubin, *Handbook of Usability Testing: How to Plan, Design, and Conduct Effective Tests* (New York: Wiley, 1994), and Nielsen's previously cited *Usability Engineering*.

15. Dynaweb is a Standard Generalized Markup Language (SGML) indexing and Web-publishing application. For a currently functional instance of this software that resembles the now-retired OAC implementation see http://scriptorium.lib.duke.edu/dynaweb. Information about DLXS (Digital Library Extension Service), a suite of open source tools developed and supported by the University of Michigan's Digital Library Production Service, is available at http://www.dlxs.org/. URLs accessed 2006-01-03.

16. Although not fully functional, browsing access to the OAC site as it looked on the Dynaweb platform just prior to the shift to a DLXS platform is available via the Internet Archive (captured on June 3, 2002) at http://web.archive.org/web/20020604025706/www.oac.cdlib.org/dynaweb/ead/. Accessed 2005-01-03.

17. See the Bentley Historical Library's finding aid access site at http://www.umich.edu/~bhl/EAD/index.html. Accessed 2006-01-03.

18. A selection of studies and resources include: Martha A. Brogan, *Survey of Digital Library Aggregation Services* (Washington DC: Digital Library Federation/Council on Library Resources, 2003), (http://www.diglib.org/pubs/brogan/); Nielsen's previously cited *Usability Engineering*; Steve Krug, *Don't Make Me Think: A Common Sense Approach to Web Usability* (Indianapolis, IN: New Riders, 2000); J. Spool, J. T. Scanlon, W. Schroeder, C. Snyder, and T. DeAngelo, *Web Site Usability: A Designer's Guide* (San Diego, CA: Academic Press, 1998); and Jeff Johnson, *GUI Bloopers Don'ts and Do's for Software Developers and Web Designers* (San Francisco: Morgan Kaufmann Publishers, 2000). Cited URL accessed 2006-01-03.

19. Two good resources are the previously cited *GUI Bloopers Don'ts and Do's for Software Developers and Web Designers* by Johnson, and *Don't Make Me Think: A Common Sense Approach to Web Usability* by Krug. In addition, Jakob Nielsen's Web site *Useit.com* (http://www.useit.com) is a useful resource. Accessed 2005-08-30.

doi:10.1300/J201v04n01_05

How and Why of User Studies:
RLG's RedLightGreen as a Case Study

Merrilee Proffitt

SUMMARY. This article documents a lifecycle approach to employing user-centered design, covering both qualitative and quantitative data gathering methods in support of using this approach for product design, usability testing, and market research. The author provides specific case studies of usability studies, focus groups, interviews, ethnographic studies, and web log analysis. The article supplies practical advice and tools for those interested in exploring user-centered design concepts for web-based tools and services in archives, libraries, and museums. doi:10.1300/J201v04n01_06 *[Article copies available for a fee from The Haworth Document Delivery Service: 1-800-HAWORTH. E-mail address: <docdelivery@haworthpress.com> Website: <http://www.HaworthPress.com> © 2006 by The Haworth Press, Inc. All rights reserved.]*

KEYWORDS. User studies, user-centered design, usability testing, focus groups, interviews, market research

Merrilee Proffitt is Program Officer, RLG, 2029 Stierlin Court, Suite 100, Mountain View, CA 94043 (E-mail: merrilee. proffitt@rlg.org).

The author would like to thank Arnold Arcolio for reviewing this article, and for his valuable feedback and advice.

[Haworth co-indexing entry note]: "How and Why of User Studies: RLG's RedLightGreen as a Case Study." Proffitt, Merrilee. Co-published simultaneously in *Journal of Archival Organization* (The Haworth Information Press, an imprint of The Haworth Press, Inc.) Vol. 4, No.1/2, 2006, pp. 87-110; and: *Archives and the Digital Library* (ed: William E. Landis, and Robin L. Chandler) The Haworth Information Press, an imprint of The Haworth Press, Inc., 2006, pp. 87-110. Single or multiple copies of this article are available for a fee from The Haworth Document Delivery Service [1-800-HAWORTH, 9:00 a.m. - 5:00 p.m. (EST). E-mail address: docdelivery@haworthpress.com].

Available online at http://jao.haworthpress.com
© 2006 by The Haworth Press, Inc. All rights reserved.
doi:10.1300/J201v04n01_06

INTRODUCTION

RLG is a not-for-profit organization of over 150 research libraries, archives, museums, and other cultural memory institutions. For more than thirty years, RLG has provided solutions to the challenges presented by information access and management, made more complex in an increasingly digital era. RLG supports researchers and learners worldwide by expanding access to research materials held in libraries, archives, and museums.[1]

RLG works with and for its member organizations, enhancing their ability to provide research resources. RLG designs and delivers innovative information discovery services, organizes collaborative programs, and takes an active role in creating and promoting relevant standards and practices.

RLG's flagship product is the RLG Union Catalog. The catalog has close to 140 million bibliographic records, spanning a range of material types and languages, reflecting holdings from ancient times to the present. There are two interfaces for the Union Catalog. The RLIN21 interface helps to support technical processing functions for librarians, allowing catalogers to search for, evaluate, export, and maintain information in the MARC format, as well as facilitating contributions to LC/NACO Authority File. The Eureka interface is designed for the reference and scholarly use of those interested in locating information resources. Both interfaces are available only via subscription; neither is optimized for novice researchers.

REDLIGHTGREEN BACKGROUND,
AND USER CENTERED DESIGN

In 2001, RLG embarked on a project funded by the Andrew W. Mellon Foundation. The project goal was to create a new service based on the data from the RLG Union Catalog, aimed at reaching new Web audiences. The result was RedLightGreen.[2] A free service aimed at college undergraduates, RedLightGreen helps students locate books of interest for their research.

RLG has long been interested in making useful products and interfaces to aid scholarship and learning. Although we have done user studies with other products, RedLightGreen was the first product to take a user centered design approach[3] from the very beginning. We employed various tools and techniques from user studies in the development of

RedLightGreen. RedLightGreen makes a very nice case study for user studies.

In this article, I am using the term "user studies" in a very broad way, to encompass both qualitative and quantitative data gathering methods. I discuss: usability studies, focus groups, interviews, ethnographic studies, and Web log analysis. Other methods and tools, such as surveys, questionnaires, polls, card sorting exercises, and other techniques are not covered in this article, but also fall under the broad definition of user studies.

Users can teach us so much, and there is a huge range of techniques for gleaning information from a particular audience for a particular purpose. There is not one "best way" to proceed with user studies. Rather than thinking about a single best way to work with users, think of numerous different options; the best way will depend on the questions you want to answer.

Since I want to reinforce the idea of using users to help answer what essentially amount to research questions on our end, this article will give examples of the types of questions we had in the RedLightGreen project, and how we set about answering them.

WHAT ARE THE AUDIENCE NEEDS?

As outlined above, RLG already supports the RLIN21 and Eureka interfaces to the RLG Union Catalog. These interfaces are not designed for novices, but for scholars and librarians. We didn't want to simply replicate or "dumb down" those interfaces, but instead approached this project as new product development, since we were designing for a new and entirely different audience. It is important to think about your audience whether you are designing a Web page, an exhibit space, a data entry manual, or signage. Design for the audience, and not for yourself.

Our first research question in this project was to determine audience needs. The RLG Union Catalog represents a huge body of bibliographic data; what services could we develop, based on bibliographic records, that undergraduates want and need. What do students want in a research environment, and what do they not care about. We had an idea of who our users might be, and some ideas of what they would want, but needed to confirm before we started extracting data from the union catalog, and certainly before we started coding for an interface.

We determined that the best way to answer this question was by employing guided discussion groups, using eighteen "friendly dyad pairs"[4] to explore our service ideas. We recruited college students[5] who we thought would use the service and who had some research experience under their belts: juniors and seniors who had a social sciences or humanities major, and who had written at least two ten-page papers that required them to identify and use their own sources.

We had two rounds of studies with the dyad pairs. We used a single skilled facilitator[6] to lead the ninety-minute discussions. The facilitator employed a discussion guide that had been developed with the project team ahead of time. The discussion guide was paired with wireframes,[7] which were paper prototypes in one round and, HTML screen mockups in a second round. The students and the facilitator sat in one room, with members of the project team watching from a second room, and the interaction between the students and the facilitator was videotaped. We felt it was important to capture the interaction on videotape for a number of reasons. Not all members of the project team were able to attend all the "live simulcasts" of the discussions, we wanted to preserve the discussions so we could watch them a second time as a group, and we wanted a visual documentation of the interchange in order to let the students themselves sway any skeptics.

These discussion groups helped us to learn what students wanted in our service and, even more importantly, what they didn't want. The dyad discussion groups were done in two rounds, about four weeks apart. When we felt we had an answer to a question–for example, if three pairs in a row responded exactly the same way to a question on the discussion guide–we would swap in a new question in order to solicit student responses to more questions. There seemed to be no reason to repeat a question once we knew how the students would respond. Below is a short summary of what students liked and disliked.

We presented students with a potential front page for the service (see Figure 1), which featured a simple search box, with browse by date and browse by subject options.

Students indicated that they were unlikely to use the browse by date or browse by subject options. They were unsure from the presentation if date was date of publication or date of coverage, and in many cases these labels were not meaningful to students. Students were disinclined to use the browse by subject option because they were afraid of going down the wrong "branch" of the subject "tree" and getting lost. Students

FIGURE 1. Students were presented with this wireframe, a sample search page that included a browse by date and browse by subject option. Clicking on a subject would open a subject sub-tree, shown in Figure 2.

Search

To begin your search enter your search terms into the text box and click on "Search."

	SEARCH

Browse by Date

Use the timeline below to locate materials by date.

<<
1100s   1200s   1300s   1400s   1500s   1600s   1700s   1800s   1900s   2000s

Browse by Subject

Use the links below to browse by Subject.

Architecture and Engineering
Architecture | Structural Engineering |
Electrical Engineering...

Business & Economics
Economics | Management | Marketing...

Communications
Advertising | Radio, Television, & Film | Journalism...

Education
Curriculum & Instruction | Educational Administration |
Educational Psychology...

Fine Arts
Music | Art and Art History | Theatre and Dance...

Humanities
Literature | Philosophy | Language Studies...

Library & Information Science
Library Administration | School Libraries |
Academic Libraries...

Mathematics
Algebra | Number Theory | Statistics...

Public Affairs
Foreign Affairs | Policy Research | Public Policy...

Life Sciences
Biology | Chemistry | Physics...

Social Sciences
Psychology | Sociology | Anthropology...

Social Work
Corporate | Adolescent | Dependency...

also indicated that they were unlikely to use the browse by subject option unless they had some understanding of where the categories came from and how they were populated.

Students did appreciate the simple search box, however, and almost universally expressed a desire to use their own keywords, then evaluate the result set (see Figure 3).

We proposed a potential interlibrary loan (ILL) feature, which also failed to strike a chord with students. Some students were unaware of ILL as a service on their campus, and those that were aware of it felt that the materials would reach them too late to be of any use for their research projects. Many students had a maximum of a two-week

FIGURE 2. Wireframe for a subject sub-tree

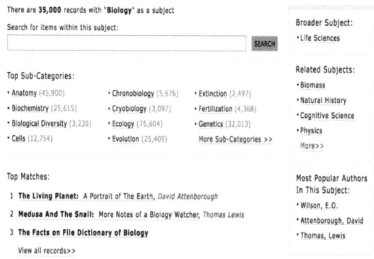

deadline, and it was not uncommon for project deadlines to be even shorter.

A few other ideas also failed to gain traction. Undergraduates were uninterested in reviews or rating features for titles. Many students do not trust their peers to give reviews or to rate books, fearing that they would be misled or waste their time. Students would be interested in professors rating or ranking books, but only their professors, and only when they were taking courses from them. Students did not react positively to the idea of a research-based social destination. They want to do their research and get out; they did not see a service like RedLightGreen as a place to linger or spend time beyond what was necessary to do their work. Although social tagging features are very popular on some Web sites, our discussion groups showed that students would put very little faith in the opinions of others for a service like RedLightGreen. This could be because the opinions of anonymous others mean very little in a research context; whether or not someone values a resource may vary greatly depending on the nature of a given research project. There also may be significant differences between trusting advice on resources used for assigned research rather than resources used for more personal reasons.

FIGURE 3. Students appreciated the simple search box shown in Figure 1; this design element remained when other elements were removed. The simple search box continued to receive favorable reviews in later testing.

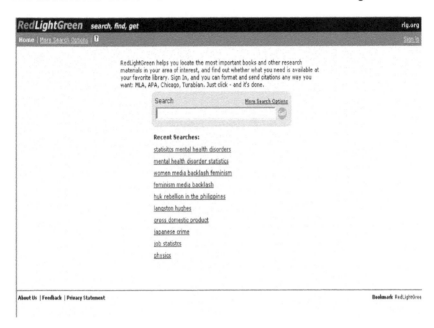

Students were also presented with a feature that would create a bibliography by formatting results to common citation formats on the fly. This was a hit. We thought this would be well-liked, but we were a little surprised by how popular this actually was. When we discussed or showed the feature to students their responses were categorized by the following statements: "totally cool," "really helpful," "awesome," "sweet," "very appealing," "that would excite me so much," "that's so huge," and "that is the best idea I've heard today." Some students suggested the feature independently, before being prompted. Students lamented the effort that it often takes to compile bibliographies, even for simple papers. Students characterized the effort of compiling a bibliography as "[taking] half the time [as writing the paper itself]," "so painful," and "quite annoying."

It's important to keep in mind that we were only presenting students with ideas expressed as mockups of the system, either represented on a computer screen or on paper (see Figure 4). At this point, we focused

FIGURE 4. Wireframes don't have to be complicated. This hand drawn wireframe was used in a guided discussion group about RLG Archival Resources.

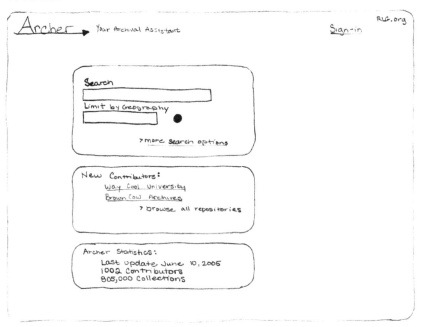

our attention on discussions with students, so the dyad pair discussion groups required no in-depth programming. Having our findings before we did any programming saved us a huge amount of time, and enabled us to spend our programming and development time more wisely.

The discussion groups were a great way to get to know more about our audience and their sensibilities. Apart from the idea of a bibliographic formatting service, students were generally lukewarm about going to the library. Some students even went so far as to say, "I'm lazy, I don't like going down to the library.... If I can do it all from the comfort of my home, in my PJs, then I'm happy"; and "I tend to avoid the library if possible." Although these sentiments were somewhat discouraging, uncovering services that the students found exciting, like citation formatting, gave us confidence that we could provide valuable services that would be meaningful to our audience.

These discussion groups were important because they helped us to gain insight into what the students considered valuable and what they didn't care for; additionally, we also gained some important insight into language and labeling. There was a huge disconnect between what we, as library professionals, meant and what students thought we meant. In an interface review, the term "maps" was perceived as a possible link to online roadmaps, the term "scores" brought to mind sports instead of music, and a term like "edition" was not easily understood. This finding–that what is well understood in the library community may not be comprehensible to students–was perhaps one of the most valuable findings of the study, and something we continued to pay close attention to in other studies. The focus group also revealed that at least some students would avoid an "expert search" page, saying "I'm not an expert." The "expert search" label was replaced with a more inviting "more search options" label.

WHO IS THE AUDIENCE?
(OR GETTING TO KNOW YOUR AUDIENCE)

The more time we spent with our undergraduate subjects, the more we realized that we were most definitely "not our own audience." In the words of RLG Information Architect Arnold Arcolio, "Undergraduates live in different universe than we do." As a group of librarians with average age of forty, and little day-to-day contact with undergraduate students except in some cases at home, the RedLightGreen project team[8] realized that we had many questions about the general research habits and sensibilities of college students. Rather than calling the students back to RLG for another round of focus groups, we followed them into their native habitat. We did a brief ethnographic study,[9] which involved observing students, with their prior consent, in the environment where they conduct bibliographic searches (see Figure 5).[10] Using a notepad, digital camera, and worksheet (which served as our discussion guide), we attempted to learn how students approach research and gain a clearer understanding of the lifecycle of a student research project (see Figure 6). It was very important to see and realize that research happens in dorm rooms, sorority houses, apartments, coffee shops, and also in the library. It also was important, and humbling, for us to see that students and researchers in general have a multitude of tools. Getting to know your audience as much as possible is vital. It is important to know what they bring to the table in

FIGURE 5. From the ethnographic study, a photo of a student in her sorority room, a place she identified as the location where she usually located sources for papers. Many students located sources away from the library.

Used with permission.

terms of knowledge and expectations and, further, what you bring to their table.

Our ethnographic study revealed that the students we spoke with are excellent time managers, and are very concerned about wasting a lot of time; fifteen minutes is a block of time that they want to invest wisely in their research efforts. Only two students out of the six who participated in the study left their paper writing to the last minute. Most students gather their sources in one sitting, then spend quite a bit of time winnowing down, and may not wind up using all the sources they have identified. All students reported that they had two or three papers or projects going on at the same time.

FIGURE 6. In the ethnographic study, students were asked to draw a flow diagram of their research and paper writing process. As you can see, students took very different approaches.

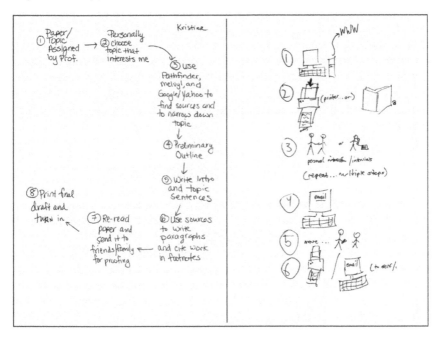

HOW BEST TO DESCRIBE OR PROMOTE A RESOURCE?

Once we had a handle on what the service should do, we again turned to our audience to help us design a promotion plan. For this we again convened focus groups, populated with students who fit the profile of a likely RedLightGreen user. We conducted two focus groups, each with between eight and ten students.[11] Again, a facilitator led the discussion following a discussion guide. (See Appendix 1 for a sample from the discussion guide.) We had a similar setup to the study with the dyad pairs: RLG staffs observed from a second room and we documented the discussions by videotaping them.

The discussion guide was designed to help us learn how students would find out about this resource, which in turn helped us design a communication map for the project. We learned that students would be likely to hear about a resource like RedLightGreen from a number of sources: faculty, teaching assistants, librarians, and their peers. Not surprisingly, students tend to value what faculty members tell them, and if an instructor tells them to check out a new online resource they will do so. Librarians are the next most important resource, and their peers are last. The students didn't feel that print or online advertising would catch their attention for a resource like RedLightGreen. In developing our communications texts for RedLightGreen, we focused on trying to appeal not only to librarians, but also to instructors. We also listened very carefully to the language that students used in expressing their perceived value for RedLightGreen, and used this language in our promotional materials.

DOES THE INTERFACE WORK?

Perhaps the most well-known aspect of user studies is a usability test, which will help evaluate a user interface. Once we built RedLight-Green, based on student needs articulated in our dyad pair study, we undertook usability testing on the live system. Each test involved a single student who was given a set of tasks, and asked to use a "think aloud" protocol.[12] Again, students[13] who participated in the testing matched our audience profile. The facilitator followed a discussion guide. We not only videotaped the session, but also used screen capture software[14] in order to see more clearly where the student was succeeding or foundering as he or she went through the tasks.

Usability testing helped us to learn where the system was confusing and where it was working well. The testing was staged into two rounds, which is about the minimum number of rounds you would want to do. Before the second round we fine-tuned the interface in response to findings from the first round. Once you've changed the interface, it is critical to retest so you can be sure that the "fix" you have made really does work.

In our first usability test, we found that students did not understand our ranking system, indicated with two sets of stars (one set of stars to indicate how many libraries widely held a work, and another set of stars to indicate how relevant the work was to the search term or terms). We abolished the two sets of stars and found in a second round of testing that even one set of stars confused students as well; they thought the stars meant that someone had rated the work. Eventually we converted the stars to a more neutral set of bars.

IS THE RESOURCE VALUABLE?

After all that work, have we made a difference? Were we filling the needs we had identified early on? These constituted a final set of RedLightGreen research questions.We also wanted to know which communication methods had worked best. How had students found out about RedLightGreen? In order to answer this question we once again convened focus groups of between eight and ten students. We held eight meetings in four different locations (Columbia University, New York University, Swarthmore College, and University of Minnesota). Each student who participated had used the system for a semester or more. Using a discussion guide a facilitator conducted each session, and we documented the discussions with audiotape.

This assessment round was useful because we learned how students found out about the resource, what was highly valued, and what was missing. Students who had started using RedLightGreen early on missed features that were added later. Students also indicated that even though they had used RedLightGreen, they may have forgotten about it. These findings prompted us to e-mail reminders and updates to registered users (allowing them to opt out of such mailings, of course). We noticed, in looking at registration data, that we had more graduate students than we would have expected, so we included them in our interviews. They told us that even though it had been designed for undergraduates, it worked well for them for general research. We also learned how difficult it can be to promote a new resource, and that a combination of approaches (e.g., demonstrations, Web site notices, e-mails, fliers) was more likely to be effective than relying on any one approach.

IS THE RESOURCE USED? (AND IF SO, BY WHOM?)

This section could be called, "If you build it, do they come?" and is a reminder that not all user studies involve interacting with users directly. Once you've established your service or site, you can step back and observe or count who is using it and how. In the case of a Web-based resource, this can be done by analyzing transaction log data. But you can also look at gate counts, registration information, and other traces of usage. The important thing here is to try to tease out who is deriving value from your service, the impact of your promotional efforts, and whether or not you're reaching the audiences you hoped to.

Sorting through Web transaction logs is time a consuming task and something that takes some orientation. Fortunately, there are a number of software packages that will help make this task easier.[15] Even with a Web analysis tool, Web log data is famously misleading, and you need to be sure you know exactly what is meant by terms like "hits," "visitors," and "sessions" so that you don't misinterpret the numbers.

When analyzing any sort of numerical data, it is useful to pose clear questions, just as you would when setting up a usability test. With a usability test, your question might be "can a visitor find what hours we're open?" Your usability test should be designed to help to answer that question. When analyzing numeric data your question might be, "How much has reading room attendance changed over the last year?" or "Did the promotion we did in the online campus newspaper bring more traffic to our Web site?" Make sure that you have the data to answer the question you are asking, and if not, work with others to see if you can answer your important questions about use and usage. It might mean buying new software, tweaking existing software, or adding a few more checkboxes to an existing registration form.

For RedLightGreen, we use WebTrends to help answer specific questions, like "How many of my users are coming from the .edu domain?" or "What terms do my users search on most often?" and "Which parts of the system are they using most?" In terms of how users find the system, you may be asking, "What external links are they following in order to get to it?" This process can in turn drive more questions: for example, if no one is using the help screens, is that because the system is already easy-to-use, because they can't find the help screens, or because they are reluctant to do so for other reasons?

OTHER TAKE AWAYS

Developing a Discussion Guide

A discussion guide is a critical component in your user study, especially if you are conducting a usability study or a guided discussion. The guide will give structure to participant interaction, through discussion questions or prompted tasks. Developing your discussion guide in concert with others can provide a useful check that the people on the project team have a shared sense of what research questions are to be investigated and why. After you have drafted your discussion guide, you might run through it and make sure that the project team is prepared to act on discoveries based on what the guide will elicit from users.

The Importance of Facilitator Skills

This article frequently references the "skilled facilitator" or the "facilitator." For the RedLightGreen studies, we employed professionals who consulted with us throughout the user study and also facilitated the discussions. If you can afford to work with a professional, that may be a good way for you to go. However, a small user studies budget should not deter you from trying this on your own. Facilitating discussions or usability studies is a skill, but one that you can learn. There are many good books and articles about this topic,[16] but probably the best advice is that facilitating a user test is a great time to pass up the proverbial "teachable moment." If you are usability testing your Web site and a student can't figure out to search across your finding aids, for example, pass up the opportunity to show them how. Instead, listen and observe. This is your opportunity to learn from the student.

Practice

This article has mentioned the importance of testing your discussion guide. If you will be facilitating a discussion, run through it yourself and be familiar with the material and the order of tasks. During the session, don't be afraid to use the discussion guide you and your team have developed. This is not a performance. Finally, remember that this will get easier the more you do it.

Human Subject Considerations

If you are affiliated with an academic institution, you will probably have to get clearance to conduct your study with the your Institutional Review Board (IRB). The IRB is a campus organization that looks after the welfare of human subjects in campus research. In order to receive clearance to go forward with your usability study, focus group, or survey, you may have to go through this organization. They will ask about your protocols, and you can show them your discussion guide (you *do* have a discussion guide, don't you?) and a waiver that participants will sign. Whether or not you have an IRB to guide your actions, you should have participants read and sign a waiver. Waivers will typically outline what you hope to get out of their participation, how they will be compensated (or not), and what will happen with the data you collect (including audio or videotapes). Waivers will also state that the participant can ask for the study to stop at any time.

Recruiting and Creating a Screener (Defining Your Audience)

It's important to define up front who your audience is and then create a screener, which is simply a questionnaire that will help you find participants who match your profile. These questions are designed to ensure that participants accepted into the study are representative of your target audience(s). For the RedLightGreen user studies, we targeted a very specific demographic; our screener was quite lengthy in order to help us determine if would-be participants were college students, undergraduates, upper division humanities or social science majors; if they had written enough lengthy papers; done enough independent location of sources; and cited sources using footnotes. After an initial round of focus groups, we found that journalism students were not suitable for our study, so the screener was adjusted to screen them out in future rounds. (See Appendix 2 for a sample screening document used in RLG's Archival Resources user studies.)

Compensation

Participants in user studies are giving invaluable insights that contribute greatly to increasing your knowledge base. In order to attract participants, you should consider compensation. After all, you are asking that they give up anywhere from fifteen minutes to two hours of their time. Compensation need not involve a lot of money. Consider enticing participants with a gift certificate, a small trinket, or pizza. If you are having problems attracting participants, or participants that meet your screener requirements, you may have to consider upping the ante.

Record Then Watch/Listen (Again, and Again, and Again...)

But do it soon! User studies have a limited shelf life; you will find that if you do not process, prioritize, and act on your findings quickly, they will cease to be meaningful and recede into background noise. It is important to garner what information you can, decide which things you can and will act on, then implement the changes. The process of analyzing your findings can be quite time consuming, so plan to revisit the recordings, discuss them with colleagues, and document what your findings are. Then make a plan. Follow up your findings with more user studies. Your results are valuable, though not all will be implementable, or perhaps not all in the short term. Nonetheless, you will have gained an appreciation of your audience, their needs, and the pluses and minuses of your service.

As illustrated by the RedLightGreen experiences with user studies, no one size fits all. User studies are hard work, but also very worthwhile and rewarding, even addicting. Users can tell us so much, if only we'll ask, listen, and act.

NOTES

1. Additional information about RLG can be found at http://www.rlg.org/. Accessed 2005-11-30.

2. RedLightGreen is available at http://www.redlightgreen.com. Accessed 2005-12-01.

3. Rosalie Lack's article, "The Importance of User-Centered Design: Exploring Findings and Methods," included in this volume, 71-88, does an excellent job of defining User Centered Design. The approach followed by RLG mirrors that of CDL, as outlined in Lack's article.

4. A "friendly dyad pair" comprises two friends, the first of whom was a student meeting the requirements for the study. This first student was asked to bring along a friend who was like them in terms of class status and major.

5. Students for "friendly dyad pairs" came from San Jose State University, Santa Clara University, and Stanford University.

6. Throughout the RedLightGreen user studies, RLG employed consultants to assist us along the way. We are grateful to Azimuth Consultants LLC, idbias (http://www.idbias.com/), and UsabilityWorks (http://www.usabilityworks.net/) for their help. All URLs accessed 2005-11-30.

7. A wireframe is a representation of a single screen or Web page, and is useful both in user studies and in system architecture discussions.

8. Members of the RedLightGreen project team involved with user studies included: Arnold Arcolio, Judith Bush, Pam Carls, Pamela Dewey, Hava Kagle, Brenda Lee, Merrilee Proffitt, Lennie Stovel, Bruce Washburn, and Joe Zeeman.

9. Ethnography in user studies is outlined in Hugh Beyer and Karen Holtzblatt, *Contextual Design: Defining Customer Centered Systems* (San Francisco: Morgan Kaufmann Publishers, 1997).

10. Students for the ethnographic studies were drawn from Santa Clara University and University of California, Berkeley.

11. Students for the marketing focus groups were drawn from Santa Clara University, College of Notre Dame, and University of California, Santa Cruz.

12. The think-aloud protocol is outlined in Clayton Lewis and John Rieman, "Task-Centered User Interface Design: A Practical Introduction," available at:

http://hcibib.org/tcuid/. Accessed 2005-09-13. Typically, study participants are asked to say aloud what they are looking at, thinking, doing, and feeling as they go through tasks.

13. Students for the usability tests were drawn from Notre Dame de Namur University, Santa Clara University, Stanford University, and University of California, Berkeley.

14. We used a video camera both to tape the sessions for later and to send a feed to observers in another room during the tests. In addition, we used HyperCam from Hyperionics (http://www.hyperionics.com/) to log the user's screen activity, and VNC (http://www.realvnc.com/) to send a feed of this activity to observers in another room during the tests. The feed from Hypercam was shown to observers in a second room, along with the live feed from the video camera. Both the Hypercam file and the videotape were saved, and could be watched again. In more recent usability tests, RLG has used Morae from Techsmith (http://www.techsmith.com/morae.asp) instead of Hypercam. Although Hypercam is perfectly good at capturing screen activities, Morae makes it easier to mark segments of interest for reuse, and synchronizes video (captured through a Webcam) with the screen capture. All URLs accessed 2006-03-27.

15. There are many Web transaction log analysis software packages available commercially. Examples of these, implying no endorsement by the author, are WebTrends (http://www.webtrends.com/) and Urchin, recently taken over by Google and now renamed Google Analytics (http://www.google.com/analytics/). All URLs accessed 2006-03-27.

16. Steve Krug, *Don't Make Me Think: A Common Sense Approach to Web Usability* (Indianapolis: New Riders Press, 2000); and Jeffrey Rubin *Handbook of Usability Testing: How to Plan, Design, and Conduct Effective Tests* (New York: John Wiley & Sons, 1994).

doi:10.1300/J201v04n01_06

APPENDIX 1

DISCUSSION GUIDE SAMPLE FROM RLG'S ARCHIVAL
RESOURCES USER STUDIES[1]

Session script

Introduction to the session (5 minutes)

Help participants get a snack and get seated.

Thanks for coming today. My name is <*your name here*>. I'm a <*research specialist/archivist/fellow researcher, whatever* > and I'll be moderating our session today. I'm here to learn from all of you.

Today we're going to present some ideas that RLG has for redesigning its service called Archival Resources. For the purposes of this exercise, we're calling the prototype "Minerva." The redesigned service will have a different name.

RLG is an international, not-for-profit membership organization of libraries, archives, and museums, working together to create solutions to the challenges of information access and management.

RLG's Minerva will provide access on the Web to detailed descriptions of archival collections–the actual collection guides or inventories that reveal where a collection came from, how it is organized, and what it contains.

We have invited you here today to get a reality check on what RLG has in mind for this service. Your participation today will help the design team at RLG make important decisions about their design for Minerva.

You've probably already seen the current version of RLG's Archival Resources service before this session. The prototypes we're looking at today will be a replacement for that version. So we're not going to spend time talking about the design of the old version, but we did want to give you some idea of how vast the content of the service is.

My role is to ask you questions that the team most want answered. But I'm also interested in knowing what questions you have about the prototype.

We're going to be here for about an hour and a half from this point. The session will work like this: First, I want to get some impressions from you about how you find primary sources. Then we'll present a prototyped redesign of how the new system would work–and get your feedback on those ideas. This will take up most of our session. In the end, I'll have some follow-up questions.

[*If observers are present in a nearby room*] "When our time is up with the main questions, I'll invite some of the people who are observing the session from another room to introduce themselves and ask anything that I haven't thought of. You may be able to ask questions of them, also.

Before we go on, would you please silence phones and other devices? Thanks!

APPENDIX 1 (continued)

Your comments are important, so we'll be taking notes and recording the session on audio (and video).

Do you have any questions before we begin?"

Instructions (5 minutes)

Please introduce yourselves. Tell us your name; tell us what your research specialty is.

<Participants introduce themselves around the table.>

Thank you. Now just a few guidelines for the session:

It is my job to keep the discussion on track. I have a list of questions for you, and I would appreciate your attention on those specific questions.

Please speak clearly, and one at a time–this is so we can accurately capture all of your comments and ideas.

I need input from all of you–it's very important that everyone get a chance to take part.

"There are no right or wrong answers here. We are not trying to reach an agreement. The goal of this session is for you to express your own ideas and to talk about your own experience, so we can all learn."

Warm up: Researcher Priorities (up to 15 minutes)

Follow up questions are bulleted. These questions may be answered in the course of the discussion.

Question	Timing
How do you find primary sources? What did you do the last time you needed to find primary sources?	14 min
• What about electronic services for finding sources?	
What do you do to keep track of these online services and sources?	
Have you shared information about services and sources? How did you do that?	
• When you wanted to tell someone about a resource, what did you do?	
What makes a good resource?	7 min
Time for topic	21

Prototype Demonstration (up to 45 minutes)

Okay, now we're ready to show you some of the thoughts and ideas RLG has had about redesigning its electronic archival resources service, Minerva.

Imagine as we go through this that you're looking for resources having to do with Irish immigration.

We also have printed copies of the pages that I'm handing out. You can follow along that way, if you like. As we go through this part of the discussion, feel free to mark up the printed copies you have. Make notes, make changes–but please leave them here when we're done. We can use them as artifacts of the session.

This is a discussion, so we welcome your comments and questions as the presentation progresses. [As participants ask questions, turn the questions back on them. For example, if someone asks, "What do the numbers mean next to the repository items?" You then ask, "What do they suggest to you? How useful is that?"]

Show this...	Say this...	Timing
home page with blurb	What does this show you?	5 minutes
	What does this tell you about RLG?	
	Have you ever bookmarked anything like this?	
	If you wanted to search for primary sources that might contain materials relating to the immigration of Irish people to Michigan, what do you do here? [Probe on formats: dates, places, what else do participants want to include in the search?]	
	Is this search box enough? Why or why not?	
	What might be in Advanced Search?	
home page with blurb, search box filled in with "irish immigration"	As you start a search for primary materials, what is your focus:	5 minutes
	☐ Finding every relevant collection?	
	☐ Finding collections at particular institutions?	
	☐ Something else? Such as?	
result list	Having filled in the blank and clicked Go, you'd get a page like this one.	10 minutes
	What do the lists represent?	
	Based on what you see here, how well can you tell what is on the shelf in the archive?	
	How are the lists organized?	
	How might you determine which results are relevant?	
	Is organizing the list by relevance the right thing to do? Or are there other orders that might make more sense for you?	
	How useful is seeing a summary of institutions here?	
	How useful is having a summary of institutions in Minerva–anywhere but here? Where might be a good place?	

APPENDIX 1 (continued)

Show this...	Say this...	Timing
	How many results did the search turn up? <817>	
	How does this quantity feel to you? Is this small? Okay? Large? Too large?	
	For very large sets of results, what do you expect to be able to do here to narrow the results?	
	Let's say you want to you want to see what is in one of items on the results page	
	Let's say you want to see what is in one of the items on the results page. What do you do?	

[1] Both appendices were created for the RedLightGreen user studies by UsabilityWorks (San Francisco, California) and are used here with permission.

APPENDIX 2

SCREENER SAMPLE FROM RLG'S ARCHIVAL RESOURCES USER STUDIES

Participant Screening Script: Archival Resources Task-Based Focus Groups–Genealogists

The participant mix for the session with genealogists should look like this:

Characteristic	Desired Number
Total regular participants	7
Experience: Minimum of 1 year doing personal research	7
Use electronic resources for research	7
Have used physical archives–recommended by an archivist	7

Screening Script

"Hello, this is <name> at <place>. Our client is conducting a discussion about how genealogists use archival resources on [October 28 or 29] in Mountain View. Does this sound like something you might be interested in? This project involves absolutely no sales. If you're selected and complete the session, to thank you my client will pay you <amount>.

First, let's find out if you qualify for taking part in the study.

[If the person is receptive, continue. If the person is not receptive, thank him or her, and hang up.]

1. First, are you or any of your family currently employed in any of the following types of industries?
Advertising, sales promotion, public relations or marketing research:
_____ Yes   [Reject]
_____ No   [Continue]

Website design/development:
_____ Yes   [Reject]
_____ No   [Continue]

2. During the session you'll be observed by people you won't be able to see and the session will be recorded for internal use. Do you have any objection to this?
_____ Yes   [Reject]
_____ No   [Continue]

3. How long have you been a genealogist or family researcher?
_____ Haven't started yet   [Reject]
_____ 1-4 years, or it is a hobby   [Accept up to 7, continue]
_____ 5 or more years   [Accept as many as as possible, continue]

4. Are you a certified genealogist or family researcher?
_____ No   [Continue]
_____ Yes, by whom: [Continue]
_____ Board for Certification of Genealogists (BCG)
_____ International Commission for Accreditation of Professional Genealogists (ICAPGEN)
_____ Member of Society of Genealogists or Association of Professional Genealogists, but not certified

5. In your most recent work, which of these types of sources did you use?
_____ Interviews   [Continue]
_____ E-mail, electronic conversations   [Continue]
_____ Public Web sites   [Continue]
_____ Electronic databases [such as Proquest, Ancestry.com, WorldCat   **[Required**; continue]
_____ Books   [Continue]
_____ Rare books or manuscripts   [Continue]

APPENDIX 2 (continued)

_____ Articles from printed periodicals	
or journals	[Continue]
_____ Archival materials	[**Required**; continue]
_____ Other; what?_____	[Continue]

*[**Recruiter:** the participant <u>must</u> have used databases and archival materials; <u>only</u> select people who have, regardless of the other sources used.]*

Thank you for answering these questions.

In this group discussion, you'll spend an hour and a half talking with other professional genealogists and telling us what you think about a prototyped electronic tool. Based on your comments and experiences, my client may make changes to the design of their tool. And, to thank you for your valuable input, we're offering participants <amount>. [*DO NOT say who the study is for. If participant asks, say you don't know.*]

We'll be conducting the discussion session in Mountain View on [October 28 or 29] from […] to […] p.m.

By the way, please plan to arrive 10 minutes before your scheduled appointment.

We'll tentatively schedule you now, and we'll confirm your appointment after we finish interviewing all our candidates. At that time, we'll give you directions and other important information for the session.

[Confirm contact information – ask if they prefer to be contacted by e-mail or phone. If e-mail, get e-mail address]

From Horse-Drawn Wagon to Hot Rod:
The University of California's Digital
Image Service Experience

Maureen A. Burns

SUMMARY. This article proposes that a viable approach archivists might consider to meet increasing demands for access to digital images with functional presentation tools is to develop a reciprocal partnership with a digital library. The University of California's experience with the federation of licensed and UC-owned digital image collections is summarized to illuminate core issues related to collection development, system functionality, and patron usability. The resulting UC Image Service is then examined against a backdrop of comparable digital imaging projects with reflections on strategies and intersections. The range of business models and approaches to digital image collection access and developing image management and presentation tools highlight the unprecedented opportunities digital technology provides for moving archives towards an integrated environment through collaborative action. doi:10.1300/J201v04n01_07 *[Article copies available for a fee from The Haworth Document Delivery Service: 1-800-HAWORTH. E-mail address: <docdelivery@haworthpress.com> Website: <http://www.HaworthPress.com> © 2006 by The Haworth Press, Inc. All rights reserved.]*

Maureen A. Burns, EdD, is Humanities Curator, University of California, Irvine's Visual Resources Collection-Slide Library, 61 Humanities Instructional Building, Irvine, CA 92697-3375 (E-mail: maburns@uci.edu).

[Haworth co-indexing entry note]: "From Horse-Drawn Wagon to Hot Rod: The University of California's Digital Image Service Experience." Burns, Maureen A. Co-published simultaneously in *Journal of Archival Organization* (The Haworth Information Press, an imprint of The Haworth Press, Inc.) Vol. 4, No.1/2, 2006, pp. 111-139; and: *Archives and the Digital Library* (ed: William E. Landis, and Robin L. Chandler) The Haworth Information Press, an imprint of The Haworth Press, Inc., 2006, pp. 111-139. Single or multiple copies of this article are available for a fee from The Haworth Document Delivery Service [1-800-HAWORTH, 9:00 a.m. - 5:00 p.m. (EST). E-mail address: docdelivery@haworthpress.com].

Available online at http://jao.haworthpress.com
© 2006 by The Haworth Press, Inc. All rights reserved.
doi:10.1300/J201v04n01_07

KEYWORDS. Digital image service, image management, presentation tools, Luna Imaging's Insight software, qualitative assessment, institutional and personal collections, outreach, integrated environments, access, usability, sustainability, strategic planning, collaboration, digital libraries, University of California, California Digital Library

INTRODUCTION

From photographs, to lantern slides, to 35-millimeter slides, analog images have a history of being made available in portable formats for a variety of educational purposes.[1] We have come a long way from the first horse-drawn wagons that delivered lantern slides to public schools as a result of the 1905 nationwide visual instruction movement.[2] In 100 years, such images have become easier to create, duplicate, collect, share, present, and preserve. Digital technology has dramatically accelerated this progression by making image accessions as simple as an Internet search and a few computer keystrokes. Such simple image acquisition has huge implications for those who have traditionally collected images, whether in archives, libraries, museums, or visual resources collections. The analog challenges of organizing, making accessible, and conserving tangible image collections are now compounded by the formation of relatively ephemeral digital image compilations with some of the same and new sets of complex issues to address. Over the last decade, image archivists have learned a great deal about what it takes to make digital image collections accessible and who might be interested in using such compilations.[3] In a world increasingly dominated by visual media, both long-established and new patrons are requesting images and/or assistance with digital media.[4] How might archivists meet these demands and insure that digital image services provide the content and tools their patrons need?

Reciprocal partnerships with digital libraries provide a viable alternative in the quest to make image collections more readily available.[5] The University of California (UC) has spent the last two years experimenting with the federation of digital image collections, thereby exploring technical and usability issues for the ten-campus state system.[6] Through the leadership of the California Digital Library[7]–with a project team including staff from UC libraries, museums, and visual resources collections[8]–a UC Image Service demonstrator project was developed to obtain practical experience (subsequently referred to as the UC Image Service for brevity).[9] The project explored many core issues and addressed a number of important questions about collection development, work flow, image management, and patron usage: What roles might the various partners play? How might such a digital image service be used and promoted? What are the benefits of such collaboration?[10]

This article provides background information about the UC Image Service, followed by a report on the early usability testing and results. The UC Image Service is examined against a backdrop of larger digital imaging trends and projects bringing to the surface issues related to development and collaboration, exploring what UC has learned to date as well as plans for future development. Discussion concludes with consideration of the implications of cross-disciplinary access to image-based collections, including some reflections on strengths and weaknesses in a variety of high-profile digital image services.

THE UC IMAGE SERVICE

Found in a variety of contexts on the ten University of California campuses, image repositories might be in archives, libraries, museums, or visual resources collections.[11] Some collections provide centralized archival services in the libraries, others are distributed locally in departments, schools, colleges, or off-campus to more immediately support the research and instructional needs of faculty, students, and the community. Recent surveys (formal and informal) indicate that the UC libraries have over eleven million images in their collections with approximately 250,000 digitized. The UC Visual Resources Collections have at least three million images with about 150,000 digitized.[12] The present estimate indicates only two to five percent of UC image collections are digitized; of these, not all are readily accessible. This approximation does not include all of the museum and independent archival materials.[13] All of these archival image collections support faculty and students' educational activities, with the types of image holdings ranging from unique or rare materials used primarily for research, to canonical surrogates intended for classroom instruction.

Prototypes

Starting in the 1980s, many UC archivists began exploring the potential of their images in digital systems, either working in isolation or in small, collaborative groups. Some slowly, others more systematically, were working their way out of analog isolation, but most were struggling to find the time and resources to transition to the new digital technology. Experimentation with various collaborative models and full-scale operations resulted in a deeper understanding of what it takes to get digital image projects started and a growing familiarity with the challenges of scalability and sustainability.

Slide and Photograph Image Retrieval Online (SPIRO)–one of the earliest UC imaging projects, started in 1985–is a visual public access catalog for Berkeley's architecture slide library.[14] With technical support provided by the Museum Informatics Project, about 25 percent of the analog image collection at this Berkeley campus repository has been transitioned into digital form retrievable from a Sybase database containing approximately 65,000 records.[15] Through the Web, thumbnail images are provided worldwide and high-resolution images are available to the Berkeley campus for a variety of educational applications. With SPIRO and other grass roots/fair use Web sites for inspiration, the UC visual resources curators decided to experiment with a digital image databank prototype project in 1996.[16]

Like SPIRO, the Library of University of California Images (LUCI)[17] was conceived as a searchable data bank of UC digital images in a universal format shared on the Internet. The first phase of the pilot project brought together 1,200 digital images of classical art and architecture, whereas the second phase included over 3,000 images of current California art and architecture. Content decisions were made by consensus based upon the availability of material, copyright considerations, thematic grants, and faculty interest.[18]

A little earlier than LUCI a more ambitious prototype union database, the Online Archive of California (OAC),[19] emerged from the UC libraries. This searchable database of information about primary sources and selected digital facsimiles from more than sixty contributing repositories (UC and statewide) currently includes more than 8,000 finding aids and 150,000 digital images.[20] An associated entity, the Museums of the Online Archive of California (MOAC) focused on developing the museum and other image content covering California history, ranging from early cultural heritage materials, like pre-Columbian artifacts, to those documenting more recent events, such as the free speech movement.[21] The practical experience of large-scale development has enabled the OAC to lead UC digital resource planning, making significant contributions to the archival and digital library communities with progressive standards for system architecture, metadata and encoding, interface design, user tools, and preservation.

OAC is now a core component of the California Digital Library (CDL), founded in 1997 by University of California President Emeritus Richard Atkinson to focus on virtual collections and digital library development. In addition to building digital collections, the CDL invests in applications to promote technological innovation and provides leadership with new forms of scholarly communication, achieving its mission through strategic partnerships with UC campuses and the communities they serve.[22] The arrival of this new entity has allowed UC to federate these prototypes with other image content in a robust digital image service.[23]

Building a Digital Image Service

Although still establishing itself, the CDL took an interest in these early digital imaging efforts and image archives as important components of UC's diverse and distributed information resources. The challenge was how to connect with all the image stakeholders and create a networked online information space that users can locate, access, and use for educational purposes. The UC prototype projects, mentioned above, were primarily arts and humanities based, and there also happened to be a number of commercial image sources supporting instruction in these academic areas. Because most intensive academic image users are in the arts and humanities and frequent requests for access to such image content derive from these disciplines, this was the logical area to start assembling a UC-wide digital image collection. A great deal was learned from the early digital imaging experiences of SPIRO, LUCI, and OAC; primarily that building cooperatives, sharing collections, drawing upon a variety of staff expertise, and distributing the workload were effective approaches to digital image collection development. However, concerns about sustaining and integrating imaging projects emerged, including such issues as: resource allocation, usability, scalability, maintenance, technological change, and preservation. The prototype partners were ready to take the next step, but needed guidance and leadership to insure it was in the right direction.

Since the California Digital Library is part of the UC library system, it is heavily reliant on campus librarians to inform and assist with building a robust digital service environment. Two systemwide library committees played integral roles in assembling the UC Image Service. First, the Joint Steering Committee for Shared Collections (JSCSC), which focuses on UC collection development, began assisting CDL in filtering information on digital image resources.[24] This group recommended several external image databases for licensing consideration and UC access, provided by the Art Museum Image Consortium, Saskia Ltd., and Hartill Art Associates, with good coverage of the history of world art.[25] The established UC cost-sharing model spread the financial burden across the libraries on the ten campuses.

Next, the Systemwide Operations Planning Advisory Group (SOPAG), which researches current issues impacting UC libraries and devises action plans for consideration, formed a Digital Visual Resources Planning Task Force (VR Task Force).[26] This group was charged with the following tasks: (1) to identify all the visual material UC libraries own, (2) to determine the degree of digital "readiness," and, (3) to identify the pertinent issues that needed to be addressed for digital image library development.[27] The VR Task Force accomplished their goals by surveying all the UC library image collections and providing a detailed, thought-provoking report with an architectural model for digital library development. Identifying a number of complex concerns and potential barriers, such as copyright considerations, the bottom line indicated that UC library image collections were not as "ready" as anticipated, with only approximately two percent of these holdings digitized.

Building upon the research of the VR Task Force, the advice of the JSCSC, and the work of UC prototype projects, the UC Image Service was developed by CDL to obtain experiential learning about the federation of image collections through a demonstration project. The goal was to form a digital image collection policy and evaluate technical issues as well as assess workflow, content management capabilities, presentation tools, and faculty/student needs. The CDL implemented a layered service model, in which services are layered on top of a central image base and data can be harvested, ingested, or accessed from institutional, licensed, and freely available image collections, thereby providing users with content and functional tools for image management and presentation.[28] Thanks to the important foundational work of grass roots digital image projects and the creative development of powerful software tools, the UC Image Service was ready for testing in a mere six months.

Content

Starting with eight discrete image collections, the UC Image Service has expanded since its inception to contain thirteen discrete collections, totaling over 335,000 digital images. The images are an eclectic mixture (dependent upon digital readiness) generally surveying the history of world art and architecture with particular strengths in California material,

American museum collections, and cartography. Table 1 summarizes the collections included to date (October 2005).

Functionality

After research into a variety of presentation tools and delivery system options, Luna Imaging's Insight software was decided upon by the CDL as the platform of choice.[29] It was ideal for a demonstrator project since Luna Imaging could host the server and provide additional services to facilitate prompt uploading and ready access to the image collections.[30] Luna processed the metadata, created the necessary file formats, developed a new data structure for MOAC, and provided user training.[31] CDL focused on developing the infrastructure, guidelines, and providing other services, from metadata mapping to user support.

Insight was the only product with such an advanced suite of image management and presentation tools. The software's cross-collection search capability was enticing since it allows the user to access images from one or multiple collections, singly or in a variety of combinations, with each retaining its unique identity. Insight's tools support the following functions:

- multiple juxtaposition options
- zooming
- panning

TABLE 1. UC Image Service 2005 Content Summary (Numbers of Images in Parentheses)

- Art Museum Images from Cartography Associates (115,288)
- Estate Project Virtual Collection (3,065)
- Farber Gravestone Collection, American Antiquarian Society (13,527)
- Hartill Art and Architecture Collection (16,660)
- Hoover Institute Archives Poster Collection, Stanford University (53)
- Japanese Historical Maps, UC Berkeley East Asian Library (896)
- Library of University of California Images, (3,690)
- Medical Imagery, UC San Francisco Demonstration Project (99)
- Museums of the Online Archive of California (77,193)
- Rumsey Map Collection (12,645)
- Saskia Ltd. Cultural Documentation (27,385)
- Slide and Photograph Image Retrieval Online, UC Berkeley Architecture (65,966)
- Tebtunis Papyri Collection, UC Berkeley Bancroft Library (55)

- searching (simple or advanced)
- showing or hiding descriptive metadata,
- creating groups
- building presentations from groups
- printing
- exporting
- annotating
- Web linking
- adding audio
- adding video
- scaling/measuring
- multiple views of three dimensional objects
- paging through multi-page documents

The most recent version includes personal collection-building tools that allow users to spontaneously upload local image collections and use them in conjunction with the centralized collections in the UC Image Service. This extensive suite of tools, the fine aesthetics of the system, the added value of non-UC collections available in the software, and Insight's ability to "play well with others" were persuasive factors for adoption.[32] The image Web-linking and export options provide the user with the flexibility to use this powerful software live in the classroom, to export images to a familiar presentation tool such as Microsoft PowerPoint, or to incorporate the images into existing course Web sites or learning management systems. Luna also offered an attractive consortial licensing discount allowing all ten UC campuses to participate in the demonstrator project.

LEARNING FROM UC IMAGE SERVICE USERS

Reaching targeted users and finding enthusiastic early adopters of new technologies is one of the big challenges in providing digital services.[33] After using analog images for more than a hundred years, traditional academic image users cannot be expected to embrace digital images without encouragement, motivating factors, and support. UC information professionals strive to continually improve systems and stay current with technological change in order to anticipate academic users' needs. This somewhat speculative work is necessary at research institutions where faculty do not usually have the time or the inclination to develop teaching resources. The local facilitator's role becomes crucial to the success of projects where such mediation is needed. Librarians traditionally provide campuswide training for users of new information systems, but Insight's extensive suite of presentation tools for classroom usage goes beyond the type of training services usually provided. In UC's visual resources collections, curatorial staff have traditionally worked at the departmental level to provide image content (35-millimeter slides still prevail) and facilitate the use of audiovisual equipment for classroom projection, but the latter piece might also be provided by centralized instructional technology staff who equip classrooms and provide training for new tools and equipment. To allow for potential image service adoption, extended partnerships between these three groups are imperative and some adjustment to traditional roles may be necessary.

A soft rollout of the UC Image Service occurred in spring 2003, involving training of relevant staff, modest announcements, and assessment activities. Providing hands-on training to UC campus librarians and visual resources curators was a way to obtain early user feedback, communicate news about the image service, and provide support for potential adopters. These groups were consulted about faculty who might be willing to experiment with the UC Image Service. Several faculty and graduate students were identified on three UC campuses as subjects for a round of formal assessment activities.

Assessment

While the CDL focused on the technological capabilities and limitations of the UC Image Service, usability testing needed to take place with teaching faculty and students at the UC campus level. Rosalie Lack from the CDL outlined an assessment plan, designed the data collection instruments, and worked closely with UC librarians and visual resources curators to obtain a better understanding of the usefulness of the image service and identify the associated support issues.[34] An interview format was employed since a qualitative model could be implemented quickly with a small sample of informants and the data would be rich in detail.

Assessment activities were conducted with twelve faculty and four graduate students, all of whom had worked as teaching assistants at some point in their studies, representing the intensive image-using disciplines of art history (10), architecture (1), visual studies (2), history (1), and education (2). The informants[35] came from three UC campuses (Berkeley, Santa Barbara, and Irvine).

Loosely structured interviews with faculty and graduate students took place over the 2003/2004 academic year. Informants were asked to provide one hour of their time to focus on the look, feel, and functionality of the UC Image Service. Each interview included the following activities:

1. General discussion about digital images (present use, barriers to use, tools used or needed, etc.).
2. Hands-on experimentation with the new UC Image Service, using the Insight Java Client without prior training.
3. A demonstration of additional functionality.
4. More discussion about perceptions of digital image services.
5. The completion of a short questionnaire with ten multiple choice and short answer questions.

From the general discussion at the beginning of each interview a better understanding of the participants' use of digital images, or lack thereof, was obtained. At first, most respondents said they did not tend to use digital images, but when the definition was expanded to include Web image resources, it became clear that most had favorite sites they frequently visited related to their specific areas of expertise. However, most participants had never taught with digital images in the classroom. Of the two respondents who regularly did, one used Microsoft's PowerPoint software to manage and deliver the images and the other taught directly from a highly-developed course Web site. The digital images used by informants were found online, copied from CD-ROMs, or scanned locally. Figure 1 illustrates the informants' responses, with research being the most frequently mentioned use of digital images followed by course assignments; little use of digital images in the classroom for teaching was confirmed.

FIGURE 1. Informants' Digital Image Usage

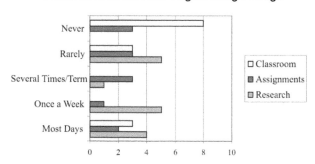

The interview data documents some obstacles and a natural resistance to change. As expected, a group dominated by art historians had very high image quality standards, exacting image content needs, and an attachment to existing institutional analog collections built upon their specific teaching needs. As intensive image users, the initial transition from analog to digital image usage is a substantial commitment, even with the promise of long-term efficiencies. At the University of California, members of the faculty are promoted primarily for research activities, with the concomitant pressure to publish, leaving little time or motivation to focus on instructional technology. Classroom readiness and adequate staff support emerged as central issues for these respondents. There was some uncertainty about the legal use of digital images and what faculty should allow students to download, evidence of the effects of recent copyright controversies, but also an indication of an underlying concern for how technology is changing pedagogical practice. Mention of a hybrid world, with analog images for classroom use and digital images for student assignments and study images, indicated that traditional approaches to the use of images in research and teaching will not be easily changed. Nonetheless, when asked about the future, all responded that they anticipated using digital images within the next three years and one remarked, "It is inevitable."

Hands-on Activity

Without a prior demonstration or any formal training, faculty and student informants were seated at a computer with the opening page of the UC Image Service listing the collections available for perusal. They were more than willing to "jump right in" without hesitation and were encouraged to experiment with the various features of the interface; as a result they did not all complete exactly the same tasks. After choosing one or more collections, informants found themselves in the group workspace as seen in Figure 2.

Here they were asked to search for an image or multiple images of interest for their research and teaching. The group workspace is where image searches take place and images are selected for presentation, printing, or export. Comfort levels were high with the menu choices in the group workspace, visually and functionally similar to online resources and other software programs.

When one or more images were found and selected, informants found themselves in the image workspace as seen in Figure 3. Here, a suite of advanced tools allows users to manipulate images.

FIGURE 2. Group Workspace in UC Image Service

They were then asked to experiment with the toolbar to see what functionality was available. Informants became adept at the basic functions: moving, juxtaposing, maximizing, zooming, and closing images as well as finding descriptive metadata. Although all the participants were able to use it, the toolbar in the image workspace posed more challenges. Since most of the icons were unfamiliar to users and the user must click on the icon and then on the image, some referred to the toolbar as "unintuitive." Repetition of use, with some encouragement to try the various buttons, improved participants' ability to accomplish basic functions.

Once participants accomplished the basic tasks and seemed interested in moving on, staff proceeded to demonstrate additional system attributes and functionality. A number of advanced features were shown, some through a presentation prepared in advance, such as juxtaposing images, panning/scrolling, scaling, annotating, linking to media or Web sites, multi-views, and multipage documents.

FIGURE 3. Image Workspace in UC Image Service

Analysis and Lessons Learned

Overall, participants were impressed with the aesthetics and functionality of the UC Image Service. During the session, they were able to perform the basic functions requested with little difficulty. For the most part, the problems encountered were not significant enough to impede use, but frustrated participants at times. A number of constructive usability recommendations were shared with Luna Imaging staff to assist with software development, some of which have already been implemented. When participants were asked for their opinion of the interface, half replied that it was easy enough to use, while others thought with time they could "figure it out." No missing features were suggested or additional functionality identified, although informants felt that more time to explore and use the tools might enable them to do so. Interestingly, system performance was not an issue raised by any of the participants, even though it was slow at times and froze on a few occasions. The majority of the informants mentioned that they would like 24/7 access to the system from home, where they tend to accomplish much of their work. Proxy access was not yet available at the time of the assessment, but has since been provided through virtual private network capability on the UC campuses.

One of the initial challenges for anyone using Insight is getting into the mental mode of navigating back and forth between the two workspaces–group and image–and determining the functions that can be accomplished in each place. Participants were unsure about how to go back and forth between workspaces and needed guidance. Subsequent to the testing, Luna changed the image workspace toolbar so it now states "return" rather than just indicating this with an arrow. Although informants were not asked to engage in the more advanced functions of the software–such as adding annotations, scaling, creating groups, and exporting data–some spontaneously experimented with such features from the group workspace menu or using the image workspace tool bar.

The image search capabilities of Insight enabled informants to find images with a simple keyword search, but doing more complex searches proved more challenging. They were unprepared for the wide array of search options in the pull-down menu, many of which were difficult to equate with familiar library tools and caused uncertainty in terms of selection. They expressed appreciation for substantial number of thumbnail images returned (fifty can be viewed before having to move to the next page). Some dissatisfaction was voiced about the minimal descriptive metadata attached to the thumbnail images. Insight allows some user rearrangement of the textual information in the thumbnails, but this was a function that was not demonstrated to the informants.

In terms of the more detailed descriptive metadata associated with images, there was a split between those who thought it was comprehensive enough and those who felt there was too much textual information. Many liked the detailed descriptions in some of the museum records, but found that the information they wanted quickly was buried too deeply. Informants suggested re-ordering the information, placing the basics traditionally found on a 35-millimeter slide or museum object label–artist or site, title, date–at the top. All of this tester feedback about metadata and the variations between collections resulted in the CDL developing principles for the search, sort, display, and naming of fields.[36] These principles were implemented and have greatly improved image discovery as well as simplifying the end-users' experience when searching across collections.

One of the biggest revelations of the early assessment was that participants did not have a deep understanding of the concept of presentation software. Many did not realize that the Insight software was designed to provide advanced tools for classroom use and were seeing this kind of software functionality for the first time. Rather, they tended to first consider it as a resource to mine for images, similar to their present experiences using the Web. Informants confirmed the predominance of Microsoft PowerPoint as something they were already using, or knew colleagues who were using, for classroom presentations. Those who had already made the effort to learn PowerPoint wanted to ensure they could continue to use it with images from the UC Image Service (an export to PowerPoint function in Insight supports this) and gave little indication they would want to switch to Insight's more sophisticated tools.

Informants indicated a disinclination to teach live from the Internet, expressing a general perception that things can go wrong quickly and easily with computer technology, that classroom connectivity is either nonexistent or unreliable, and that there is not enough staff support, all of which are certainly valid concerns. When using slides in classroom settings, many presently rely on student projectionists who are prepared to deal with technical problems for support. Faculty will need similar technical support reassurances, access to technologically upgraded classrooms with reliable network connectivity and high quality digital projection, and more information about image service interoperability and back-up capabilities to gain confidence in using something like the Insight software live in a classroom setting.

Although these interviews elicited much useful interactive discussion, thoughts about digital image usage, and specific feedback about the UC Image Service, a short questionnaire at the end also provided valuable data. Eighty-seven percent of the participants indicated a positive overall impression of the UC Image Service.

Although look, feel, and functionality were the primary foci of this usability testing, some discussion of content was inevitable as well as valuable. Overall, participants were surprised by the breadth of the collections in the UC Image Service, but provided suggestions for potential additions, mostly based on their specific areas of expertise. One informant mentioned the need for more images of material culture, crucial for the teaching of history. Broadening the image content to include non-art-related image resources will be necessary to obtain extensive cross-disciplinary usage of the UC Image Service.

In regard to what sort of visual materials respondents had used previously, most indicated use of 35-millimeter slides from UC campus image archives, particularly visual resources collections. Analog media in other collections (e.g., books, prints, photographs) were also mentioned, as well as online resources. All participants expressed a desire for online access to a broad range of campus visual resource collections.

With visual analysis and building visual literacy at the core of this group's pedagogy, image standards were very high. Informants confirmed that usefulness of digital image quality is measured in comparison to the quality of a 35-millimeter slide. Most art historians are concerned about digital projection systems adversely affecting color and reducing the amount of screen real estate available for image juxtapositions. Informants expressed more concern about having access through digital collections to specific images they need for classroom teaching than they did about federation in these collections of huge numbers of images. Seventy-five percent of the respondents agreed that it is important to have access to personal faculty collections of images in the same digital-tool environment as content owned or licensed by the university. This kind of material includes photographs taken or images purchased when doing research or traveling, or images found on the Web, though informants noted concern about image quality and copyright concerns regarding the latter.

The following responses indicate the pedagogical ways in which respondents envisioned using digital images.

- Student assignments
- Student image review
- Searching for images for research
- Classroom presentations
- Definitely not for classroom presentations
- Teaching from images on Web sites or CD-ROM
- Export to PowerPoint for teaching
- Student presentations

Interestingly, many participants seemed to want their students to use digital images more than they wanted to use them themselves. The responses were equal in number as to those who said they would use the UC Image Service in the classroom and those who said they definitely would not. Informants seemed to be more comfortable with the technologies in which they had invested time, such as PowerPoint, CD-ROMs, and obtaining images directly from Web sites. Nonetheless, most thought the UC Image Service interface looked useful enough to spend time learning how to use, but they also seemed eager to have a staff member who could facilitate the learning process. Other things that would entice them to use the UC Image Service included detailed collection descriptions, expanded content, technical support, online tutorials, helpful guides (online and hard copy), 24/7 access from home, and time to transition.

Although this was a small sample of testers and the results of the assessment are not generalizable to all situations, enough data was provided to get a feel for faculty and graduate student perceptions of digital image services in a research institution context during the 2003/2004 academic year. When compared with other similar assessment information, useful patterns emerge to strengthen the findings and inform future planning. At the opening of the 2005/2006 academic year image archive staff were already reporting an increased demand for digital images from patrons, indicating that the user population has changed rapidly while the UC Image Service has operated in an environment not fully formed.

ONGOING PLANS FOR THE UC IMAGE SERVICE

Data collected by the UC Image Service demonstrator project indicate that the technological constraints to federating and delivering images to all ten UC campuses are minimal, and that the potential for sharing collections, decreasing redundancy, energizing teaching, and stimulating learning are great. A final recommendation to the UC Libraries was that the UC Image Service warrants further strategic planning and experimentation as a potential shared production-level service.

Since the completion of the demonstration project, CDL has moved the Insight server from Luna Imaging to the UC Office of the President (UCOP) offices in Oakland and has added additional collections. A number of other ongoing CDL projects will benefit and merge with the work of the UC Image Service. The Metasearch Infrastructure Project to tailor search portals for cross-database searching, and the Digital Preservation Repository to support the long-term retention of digital objects, are two such examples.[37]

The soft rollout of the UC Image Service to the campuses did not result in extensive usage by faculty or students beyond a handful experimenting with it for specific courses and larger numbers browsing for images. As with most new services, it takes time to build a base of adopters who will incorporate the images and tools into work routines and pedagogy. Online surveys were developed to obtain a continuous flow of feedback.[38] At UC Irvine, one partnership between the art librarian and visual resources curator has resulted in well-attended workshops being taught quarterly involving hands-on training in using the UC Image Service.[39] As a result, a variety of user guides and support materials were developed and added to extended information about digital image resources on the UC Irvine Libraries' Web site.[40] In the summer of 2004, these UC Irvine staff members were asked to partner on a research project in which they could share their workshop experiences and consider how best to promote available digital image services at the UC campus level.[41]

The integration of technology into research, teaching, and learning is a dynamic process involving a balance between strategic planning and experiential learning. The UC Image Service demonstrator project highlighted some important differences between it and the UC prototype projects of the past, among them: (1) the federation of various types of image collections; (2) a layered service model; (3) powerful presentation software as the cohesive interface allowing for flexibility of use and the manipulation of image collections in ways more supportive of the pedagogical needs of patrons; (4) ongoing assessment activities to determine the usefulness of the service as well as its technological capabilities and limitations; and (5) meaningful collaboration between libraries, museums, and visual resources collections. Extending the collaboration to include more stakeholders, such as instructional technologists who plan classroom readiness and provide local technological support, and expanding the UC Image Service to include more UC-owned content, both within the UC Libraries and in archives outside, are among the next logical steps.

COMPARABLE EXPERIENCES WITH
DIGITAL IMAGE DEVELOPMENT

Digital technologies have created unprecedented opportunities to reduce redundancy and promote collaborative action on many different levels–from local archives to worldwide access. Compared to image delivery by horse and wagon, the paradigm one hundred years ago, recent digital imaging services are hot rods. A variety of stakeholders are developing digital image services and experimenting with different content compilations, management systems, delivery mechanisms, and business models. The general historical progression has been that image databases were first developed, the need for presentation tools emerged, and the central importance of user studies to guide the work was realized along the way.[42] Although the digital image service landscape is rapidly developing and all systems cannot be discussed here, the following is a summary of notable projects and developments to date with an emphasis on those associated with or comparable to the UC Image

Service. All of the projects mentioned have great merit and face a variety of interesting challenges. The following discussion highlights several important projects.

Madison Digital Image Database

The Madison Digital Image Database (MDID) is an Internet-based image database system connected to a teaching and learning tool for classroom presentation developed at James Madison University in Virginia.[43] The emphasis has been on educational capabilities–managing faculty personal collections, university-owned images, and commercially licensed images–as well as developing classroom presentation tools.[44] The MDID project provides a model of exemplary campuswide collaboration inclusive of all stakeholders: instructors, information professionals, computer programmers/designers, and instructional technologists.

The MDID experience has been extensively evaluated and widely published providing an exemplary university-based model.[45]

Visual Image User Study

The most ambitious analysis of usability issues has been the Pennsylvania State University's Visual Image User Study (VIUS), a thirty-month project funded by the Andrew W. Mellon Foundation.[46] A university team conducted rigorous assessment activities to determine the need for interdisciplinary image delivery at this large and complex institution producing detailed data on the needs and preferences of academic image users.[47] They also prototyped and evaluated two services: a conventional image database and a more experimental peer-to-peer file sharing system for digital media files.[48] The lessons learned and strategies being employed for successful image delivery have been published, in addition to the extensive online report.[49] The UC Image Service demonstrator assessment team connected with Penn State staff to guide and hone the UC assessment discussed above.[50]

Ohio Library and Information Network

The Ohio Library and Information Network's (OhioLINK) Digital Media Center (DMC) was opened in 1998 as a programmatic effort to archive and access multimedia materials.[51] The consortium has licensed digital images as well as included a full complement of local image collection materials–ranging from faculty personal collections to images from libraries, museums, visual resources collections, and various types of archives–available statewide, with worldwide access to a smaller subset of materials. One of the earliest projects to promote resource sharing through large-scale contributor participation, OhioLINK has managed to leverage expertise and funding. OhioLINK is an impressive model of statewide collaboration with the Ohio State Library working in conjunction with eighty-four academic libraries.

Art Museum Image Consortium

The Art Museum Image Consortium (AMICO), a not-for-profit organization of institutions with collections of world art, collaborated on and provided one of the earliest licensed image services, the AMICO Library, to enable educational use of museum collections in digital form.[52] Members created digital content, AMICO compiled and edited it, and multiple distributors delivered it to educational institutions, who subscribed on behalf of end users. A collaborative endeavor from 1997 to 2005, AMICO member institutions recently voted to dissolve the consortium. However, new and past distributors have negotiated non-exclusive agreements with museum members and continue to license most of the image collections.[53] Although unsure of the details since they have (at the time this article was written) yet to be published, it appears that the Art Museum Image Consortium also struggled with sustainability issues as well as keeping a complex collaborative together.[54]

Cultural Materials

RLG's Cultural Materials (CM) is another strong example of a model multimedia database on the Web. Since 2001, RLG has been building a digital collection of primary sources delivered through a subscription service, similar to AMICO, but focused on cultural heritage artifacts from special collections, archives, historical societies, museums, and other repositories, more than art museums.[55] The Cultural Materials Alliance (CMA) of over fifty institutions works together to establish best practices, to build tools for creating, describing, and contributing electronic surrogates of cultural materials, and to develop a viable business model.[56] For example, the descriptive metadata guidelines developed for CM benefit other archives, libraries, and museums interested in making analog collections accessible online.[57] RLG is presently considering a variety of interface transfer mechanisms for large-scale export and use with instructional technology tools.[58] RLG has also conducted informative interviews with faculty to better understand academic digital image usage.[59]

ARTstor

ARTstor is a digital imaging initiative, supported by the Andrew W. Mellon Foundation, the goal of which is to create a sustainable, scalable, and increasingly authoritative resource for the history of art and the humanities.[60] Since July 2004, the charter collection of 300,000 digital images (soon to expand to 500,000), complete with functional software tools for delivery and presentation, has been made available.[61] More than 300 educational institutions have subscribed to ARTstor and are participating in the research and associated intellectual exchange to further develop this model. Similar economic and interoperability issues arise with ARTstor, but this project is well on its way to becoming the definitive digital image service for the history of art. This disciplinary focus can be seen as a strength, as well as a weakness, in terms of cross-disciplinary usage, but comprehensive, high quality, and authoritative content has been provided from the start and continues to grow at a steady pace.

CONCLUSION

For digital image services, scalability, functionality, usability, sustainability, and preservation are the issues of the day in an environment clearly in a state of rapid change and expansion. Why are so many different stakeholders directing substantial resources toward the development digital image services? Part of it is timing. Although AMICO and OhioLINK started in the 1990s, the rest of the projects and systems discussed above were post-2000 innovations with somewhat parallel developments and slightly staggered release dates.

Another factor is demand for digital image access and delivery. Image archives are finding increased numbers of traditional and new patrons asking for digital images of archival materials for assorted uses to meet various needs. For the UC, the early assessment indicated users may be slow to adopt the UC Image Service, but the need is clearly there and perceptions are changing rapidly. With image holdings numbering in the millions, many of which were specifically built for research and teaching, a way to move from analog isolation into shared digital resources for both the university and the California community is a goal in line with the educational mission of the institution. Whether in archives, libraries, museums, or visual resources collections a way needs to be found to move pertinent content online for shared access across the ten campuses. Image archives need to consider options for making images accessible to meet this demand, whether starting small by digitizing local collections or partnering with digital libraries in large-scale image service development or participating in both.

The content variations in image services also reflect different potential adopters or users' needs. For example, art historians might be better served by ARTstor, historians by Cultural Materials, and museums by AMICO. It has been demonstrated that without these pioneering efforts and prototype projects, the content would not have been there, creating substantial obstacles for the federation of image collections. At the same time, large image compilations do not seem to be meeting all of the needs of users. Image services must continue to develop spontaneous ways for institutional and personal collections to be added or used together with larger compilations. Whether rare materials or canonical surrogates, more content needs to be made accessible to traditional and new patrons. Expanding intra- and cross-institutional sharing could decrease redundancy while easing restrictions on public domain materials could perhaps lead to some resolution of copyright complexities.[62]

The differences in functional tools are also being driven by users' needs. In terms of presentation software, Luna Imaging took the lead in determining that it is not enough to provide access to digital images on CD-ROM or the Web, but that functional tools, such as those in Insight, needed to be developed to facilitate thinking about and using those images, whether for research, teaching, learning, or other purposes. The Madison Digital Image Database's focus on classroom delivery clearly emerged from pedagogical need and showed great foresight in thinking big and including the entire campus community. From UC's experience, digital image users seem to want to make their own choices about which presentation tools will work best for specific educational uses. Of the eight image services discussed, eight different interfaces have been developed or used to distribute the images.[63] Most of these have had to find ways to interoperate with the ubiquitous PowerPoint, the tool of choice for many early adopters.[64] At UC, some users have indicated a desire to use PowerPoint, but four UC campuses now have access to multiple image services–the UC Image

Service, Cartography Associates' Visual Collections (VC), Cultural Materials, and ARTstor–and it will be interesting to see which tools become dominant, if any.[65] In addition to presentation tools, digital image services must interact with collection management systems, images found on the Web, digital image databases, and campus learning management systems. All of these systems need to interoperate and/or the ability to search across them needs to be developed since there is a clear preference for one-stop shopping, i.e., a desire for a single image portal.

Whether commercial, not-for-profit, or locally built, the motivating factors for image service development and distribution vary in detail, but overall seem to have commonalities in trying to reduce redundancy, meet demand, and find economies of scale. Experimentation with different business models needs to take place in order to determine what is sustainable over time. Competition is good for the consumer, for it increases choices, encourages development, and drives prices down. It is significant that the Andrew W. Mellon Foundation has provided substantial funding for various imaging efforts–from assessment to implementation. Cartography Associates' free, internationally accessible content and presentation tools are also noteworthy. Perhaps one model will become the dominant form of digital image distribution or each will flourish in its niche. There is another contender that should not be overlooked–the Internet. As Henry Pisciotta indicated, there are more than ten billion pictures available in the decentralized space on the World Wide Web and more than 500 million Internet users around the world: "These types of cultural institutions have lost the race if we consider 'critical mass' to be quantity of images and users."[66]

Experience at the University of California indicates its users want it all: all types of collections, choices in functional tools, and an integrated environment to access them. The challenge is to determine how best to promote image sharing across collections, services, institutions, and communities. Each image archive needs to make contextual decisions about image access and delivery, but there are roles for everyone to play in reciprocal partnerships and distributed networks. Digital libraries rely on archivists and others at the local level for content, metadata, and direct connections to users, while providing valuable leadership, robust infrastructures, advancing standards, ongoing technological development, and, last but not least, future visions. After 100 years of using photographs in various analog formats, the leap of faith to digital requires elaborate user support networks and the promise of sustainability as well as preservation. It is gratifying to know there are a number of intriguing options and a vibrant developmental community offering the finest of hot rods to test drive.

NOTES

1. Discussion will be focused mostly on still images, but it should be noted that many of the images services discussed below do support multimedia and the demand for such materials is increasing. For more historical information on image usage in educational contexts see Jackie Spafford, "Property and Capital in 19th and Early 20th Century Visual Collections: Tales in Search of the History of the Visual Copy as a Gateway to the Future," *Visual Resources Association Bulletin* 29, no. 2 (Summer 2002): 34-36.

2. To view a 1911 image of St. Louis' first such wagon, see the following: Maryly Snow, "'Visual Copy' Collections in American Institutions," *Art Documentation* 21, no. 2 (2002): 4-7, Figure 1. Many of the papers that were presented in the "Property and Capital" ARLIS/VRA conference session, mentioned above, were published in *Art Documentation* 21 and the panel's combined references are online at http://www.arts. uci.edu/vrc/page15a.htm. Accessed 2005-12-19.

3. The term image "archivist" is being used loosely to refer to image collectors or curators of collections and is intended to be inclusive of various contexts, within and outside of academia–archives, libraries, museums, and visual resources collections.

4. For more on visual literacy, see Jeanne M. Brown, "The Visual Learner and Information Literacy: Generating Instruction Strategies for Design Students," *Visual Resources Association Bulletin* 29, no. 3 (Fall 2002): 28-32.

5. For more on digital libraries, see Daniel Greenstein and Suzanne E. Thorin, "The Digital Library: A Biography," at http://www.clir.org/pubs/reports/pub109/ contents.html. Accessed 2005-12-19.

6. More information about the University of California system is available at http://www.universityofcalifornia.edu/. Accessed 2006-03-21.

7. In 1997, University of California President Richard Atkinson created a new UC entity–the California Digital Library. Described as a "co-library," the CDL was set-up as a collaborative venture with the ten UC campuses. Their focus is on digital materials and services with a mission that includes but is not limited to the following: (a) building, sharing, and preserving digital collections, (b) creating tools and services, (c) influencing and supporting innovation in scholarly communication, and (d) developing strategic partnerships for digital library development.

8. UC Image Service project team: Laine Farley, Project Manager (CDL); Christine Bunting, Content Manager (UCSC); Maureen Burns, Visual Resources Curators Liaison (UCI); Robin Chandler, Digital Content Coordinator (CDL); Rosalie Lack, Usability Assessment (CDL); Rick Rinehart, Museums Liaison (UCB); Brian Tingle, Technical Assessment (CDL), Lena Zentall, Metadata Manager (CDL). The team was assisted by staff from Luna Imaging (Michael Ester, Elicia Richardson-Ellis, Gina Mauss, Michelle deFarra, and Adam Brin), and the following individuals from UC campuses: Jan Eklund (UCB), Mary Elings (UCB), Kathleen Hardin (UCSC), Bill Landis (UCI), Madelyn Millen (UCR), Maryly Snow (UCB), Jackie Spafford (UCSB),

Susan Stone (UCB), Rina Vecchiola (UCI), and Loy Zimmerman (UCI). Farley's reports, articles, and presentations have greatly influenced my thinking about the UC Image Service and provided valuable information for this article, most recently "Digital Images Come of Age" in Campus Technology (May 2004) at http://www. campustechnology.com/article.asp?id=9363. Accessed 2005-12-19. I am very grateful for the invitation to participate on the project team, the encouragement to present and publish about the experience, and for her leadership in providing such a rich learning experience.

9. For more information on the UC Image Service demonstrator project, see http://www.cdlib.org/inside/projects/image/. Accessed 2005-12-19.

10. For more specifics about the project's goals, see http://www.cdlib.org/inside/projects/image/#goal. Accessed 2005-12-19.

11. For sampling of various types of archives primarily outside UC libraries, see http://www.universityofcalifornia.edu/cultural/welcome.html. For more information about UC museums and visual resources collections, see http://www.bampfa.berkeley.edu/moac/ and http://vrc.ucr.edu/luci/uc.htm respectively. All URLs accessed 2005-12-19.

12. This was an informal survey of UC visual resources collections that has not been published.

13. Other types of UC archives, such as the Environmental Design Archives at UC Berkeley (http://www.ced.berkeley.edu/cedarchives/), outside of the library system have yet to be surveyed. Accessed 2005-12-19.

14. Maryly Snow, "SPIRO: FAQ–Frequently Asked Questions about SPIRO," *Visual Resources Association Bulletin* 21, no. 2 (1994): 13-18 and Maryly Snow, "Spiro, a Visual On-line Public Access Catalog," *Computers and the History of Art* 7, no. 2 (1997): 19-34. It should be noted that Berkeley has two large visual resources collections, one located in the Architecture Department and the other in the Department of the History of Art.

15. The Museum Informatics Project at Berkeley supports the electronic resources of a number of archival collections outside the UC libraries; for more information and to peruse these collections, see http://www.mip.berkeley.edu/. For current information on SPIRO and to search the database, see http://www.mip.berkeley.edu/spiro/about.html#Introduction. All URLs accessed 2005-12-19.

16. Maureen A. Burns and Loy Zimmerman, "'If You Build It, Will They Come?' The Library of University of California Images in Transition," *Visual Resources Association Bulletin* 29, no. 4 (2002): 60. For more about the concept of a fair use Web site, see Maryly Snow, "Digital Images and Fair Use Web Sites" at http://www.utsystem.edu/ogc/intellectualproperty/portland.htm. Accessed 2005-12-19.

17. Burns and Zimmerman, "If You Build It," 60-68, and Maureen Burns and Madelyn Millen, "LUCIVISION," *Visual Resources Association Bulletin* 25, no. 4 (1998): 80-84. To access the LUCI image database, see http://vrc.ucr.edu/luci/index.html. Accessed 2005-12-19.

18. Maureen Burns, "Noble Goals/Harsh Reality: Library of University of California Images and Current Trends in Copyright Law," *Visual Resources Bulletin* 25, no. 2 (1998): 51-56.

19. See http://www.oac.cdlib.org/. Accessed 2005-12-19.

20. Encoded Archival Description (EAD) was used as the standard for the finding aids. For more information, see http://www.cdlib.org/inside/diglib/guidelines/bpgead/. Robin Chandler, "Building Digital Collections at the OAC: Current Strategies with a

View to Future Uses," *Journal of Archival Organization* 1, no. 1 (2002): 93-103. For more information about the OAC's museum collaboration, see "Museums in the Online Archive of California (MOAC): Building Digital Collections Across Libraries and Museums," *First Monday* 7, no. 5 (May 2002) at http://www.firstmonday.org/issues/issue7_5/chandler/. All URLs accessed 2005-12-19.

21. Richard Rinehart, "Museums and the Online Archive of California," *First Monday* 7, no. 5 (May 2002) at http://firstmonday.org/issues/issue7_5/rinehart/index.html. Accessed 2005-12-19.

22. For more information about the CDL's mission, see http://www.cdlib.org/glance/overview.html. Accessed 2005-12-19.

23. Time and space will not allow a more detailed discussion of all the notable UC digital projects; therefore, the focus here is on the larger image compilations. For a 2003 summary of image content being considered for digitization by UC libraries, see http://libraries.universityofcalifornia.edu/sopag/vrtf/VRTF_Appendix_IV_Sources.doc. Accessed 2005-12-19.

24. For more information about the Joint Steering Committee on Shared Collections, see http://www.cdlib.org/inside/groups/jsc/. Accessed 2005-12-19.

25. For more information about these digital image collections, see: Art Museum Image Consortium at http://www.amico.org/, Saskia at http://www.scholarsresource.com/about_saskia.aspx, and Hartill at http://www3.sympatico.ca/archimages/. All URLs accessed 2005-12-19.

26. For more information on the Systemwide Operations Planning and Advisory Group, see http://libraries.universityofcalifornia.edu/sopag/sopagcharge.html. Accessed 2005-12-19.

27. In order to keep the work manageable, only UC library collections were targeted. Archives outside the libraries, museum image collections not already in OAC, and visual resources collections would be considered later. For the full report of the SOPAG Digital Visual Resources Task Force, see http://libraries.universityofcalifornia.edu/sopag/vrtf/. Accessed 2005-12-19.

28. See Appendix VII of the SOPAG task force report for the architectural model that inspired the demonstrator project at: http://libraries.universityofcalifornia.edu/sopag/vrtf/VRTF_Appendix_VII_Architecture.pdf. Accessed 2005-12-19.

29. For more information about Luna Imaging, see http://www.lunaimaging.com/index.html . Accessed 2005-12-19.

30. Other software, such as the Madison Digital Image Database discussed below, provides some of these features, but not the full suite available in Insight.

31. Derivative file formats included MrSIDs, which support the panning and zooming functions. For more information, see http://en.wikipedia.org/wiki/MrSID. A new data structure was necessary because CDL was testing ingest of METS records, allowing for the inclusion of complex objects, such as multipage documents. For more information on the Metadata Encoding Transmission Standard see http://www.loc.gov/mets/. All URLs accessed 2005-12-19. The user training provided by Luna was given to visual resources curators and librarians selected by each UC campus.

32. Michael Ester, the founder of Luna Imaging, uses this colorful and effective way to describe the interoperability of Insight.

33. For an interesting discussion of Moore's technology adoption model with graphic, see Henry Pisciotta, "Image Delivery and the Critical Masses," *Journal of Library Administration* 39, no. 2-3 (2003): 124-127 and David J. Staley, "Adopting Digital

Technologies in the Classroom: 10 Assessment Questions," *EDUCAUSE Quarterly* 27, no. 3 (2004): 20-26.

34. The following information about the usability methods and findings was largely derived from Rosalie Lack's internal CDL report and my own experiences as an interviewer and data processor. Rosalie did an impressive job of synthesizing the data and should be duly acknowledged for her contribution. See also her article about usability testing "The Importance of User-Centered Design: Exploring Findings and Methods" in this volume, 71-88.

35. The terms informant, tester, participant, and respondent are used interchangeably to refer to the sample of faculty and graduate students mentioned above.

36. Lena Zentall took the lead on this part of the project in conjunction with the UC visual resources curators, who consulted and tested her ideas for improving the search, sort, and metadata in general.

37. For more information, see http://www.cdlib.org/inside/projects/metasearch/ and http://www.cdlib.org/inside/projects/preservation/dpr/. URLs accessed 2005-12-20.

38. The surveys can be found at http://websurveyor.net/wsb.dll/2734/images facultyta.htm and http://websurveyor.net/wsb.dll/2734/imagesstudent.htm. URLs accessed 2006-01-02.

39. Much of what is being learned from these ongoing workshops has been summarized in the following: Maureen Burns and Rina Vecchiola, "What We Want (and Don't Want) to Know about Faculty Using Digital Images: Lessons Learned at the University of California." *Art Documentation* 24, no. 2 (Fall 2005): 7-15.

40. For the Web site developed at UC Irvine see http://www.lib.uci.edu/online/ subject/subpage.php?subject=images and for UC Santa Cruz, where users also have access to ARTstor discussed below, see http://library.ucsc.edu/slides/image_resources. html. URLs accessed 2006-01-02.

41. See the project reports at http://www.cdlib.org/inside/projects/image/; contact project manager Laine Farley at laine.farley@ucop.edu to obtain more information about this password-protected site. The bibliographic references for the report are available on the Visual Resources Association Web site at http://www.vraweb.org/diag/ digitalcollbiblio.htm. URLs accessed 2006-01-02.

42. There were important earlier precedents in the Getty Information Institute sponsored Museum Educational Site Licensing Project (MESL) and Digital Library Federation's Academic Image Cooperative (AIC). See Christie Stephenson and Patricia McClung, Eds., *Delivering Digital Images: Cultural Heritage Resources for Education* and *Images Online: Perspectives on the Museum Educational Site Licensing Project* (Los Angeles: The J. Paul Getty Trust, 1998). For the AIC, see http://www.diglib.org/ collections/aic.htm. Accessed 2006-03-21.

43. Information about James Madison University can be found at http://www.jmu.edu/. For more information about the digital image database, see http://www.mdid.org/ mdidwiki/index.php?title=Main_Page. URLs accessed 2006-03-21.

44. Sharon P. Pitt, Christina B. Updike, and Miriam E. Guthrie, "Integrating Digital Images into the Art and Art History Curriculum," *Journal of Library Administration* 39, nos. 2/3 (2003): 38.

45. Ibid.,29-42 and see http://mdid.org/papers.htm. Accessed 2006-03-21.

46. For information about VIUS, see http://www.libraries.psu.edu/vius/. Accessed 2006-03-21.

47. See the extensive VIUS report at http://www.libraries.psu.edu/vius/reports. html. Accessed 2006-03-21.

48. The software for the image database is CONTENTdm by DiMeMa Inc. and more information can be found at http://contentdm.com/. Accessed 2006-03-21.

49. Pisciotta, "Image Delivery," 123-138.

50. Laine Farley, CDL, and Henry Pisciotta, PSU, also collaborated on a presentation entitled "Digital Image Systems Come of Age (But Will They Ever Grow Up?) at the Digital Library Federation meeting in New Orleans, April, 2004, see http://www.cdlib.org/ inside/projects/image/#presentations. Accessed 2006-03-21.

51. Charly Bauer and Jane A. Carlin, "The Case for Collaboration: The OhioLINK Digital Media Center," *Journal of Library Adminsitration* 39, nos. 2/3 (2003): 69-86.

52. Jennifer Trant and David Bearman, "Educational Use of Museum Multimedia: The AMICO Library," *Visual Resources Association Bulletin* 29, no. 4 (Winter 2002): 72-86.

53. The distributors of AMICO's image collections with new successor database names and URLs are as follows: Art Museum Images from Cartography Associates (AMICA) http://www.davidrumsey.com/amico/subscribe.html, the Research Libraries Group's Catalog of Art Museum Images Online (CAMIO) http://www.rlg.org/en/page.php?Page_ID=20638, and H. W. Wilson's Art Museum Image Gallery http://www.hwwilson.com/Databases/artmuseum.htm. ARTstor has also obtained AMICO images for its project. URLs accessed 2006-03-21.

54. The only reference to the dissolution found so far, beyond the distributors' messages about AMICO's new manifestations, can be found at http://www.amico.org/, it is notable that section 8 of the AMICO "Full Membership Agreement" at http://members.amico.org/docs.prev/member.9806.html discussed continuing access post-dissolution. URLs accessed 2006-03-21.

55. For more information about RLG's Cultural Materials, see http://www.rlg.org/en/page.php?Page_ID=217&projGo.x=14&projGo.y=14. Accessed 2006-03-21.

56. For more information about the Cultural Materials Alliance, see http://www.rlg.org/en/page.php?Page_ID=564. Accessed 2006-03-21.

57. For more information on the recently updated descriptive metadata guidelines, see http://www.rlg.org/en/page.php?Page_ID=214. Accessed 2006-03-21.

58. Ricky Erway, "RLG Cultural Materials Alliance–Building a Cultural Resource Together" *SCONUL Focus* 32 (Summer/Autumn 2004) at http://www.sconul.ac.uk/pubs_stats/newsletter/32/11.pdf. Accessed 2006-03-21.

59. See Guenter Waibel, "Out of the Database, Into the Classroom: Findings from the Instructional Technology Advisory Group," *RLG Focus*, no. 67 (2004) at http://www.rlg.org/en/page.php?Page_ID=17063#article2. Accessed 2006-03-21.

60. See http://www.artstor.org/info/. Accessed 2006-03-21.

61. Max Marmor, "ArtSTOR: A Digital Library for the History of Art," *Journal of Library Administration* 39, nos. 2/3 (2003): 61-68.

62. Copyright concerns are one of many unresolved issues for image services to completely address, but much of academia is relying on organizations such as the Creative Commons to help find the way. For more information, see http://creativecommons.org/. Accessed 2006-03-21.

63. Although AMICO, UC Image Service, and Cartography Associates Visual Collections (VC) use the same software (i.e., Insight), ARTstor, RLG, Wilson developed other interfaces to distribute AMICO.

64. Eileen Fry, Indiana University, presented a fascinating analysis of the PowerPoint phenomena in academia at the 2005 Visual Resources Association conference. For more information see her presentation in the session entitled "Navigating the Troubled

Waters of Discontent with Digital Imaging Technology" at http://www.arts.uci.edu/vrc/page14a.htm. The other session presentations by Pisciotta, Rockenback, and Williams are well worth looking at too and can be found at the URL above. Accessed 2006-03-21.

65. UC Berkeley, Los Angeles, San Diego, and Santa Cruz are the four campuses with access to more than one digital image service and should be the focus of future assessment.

66. Pisciotta, "Image Delivery," 127-132. Pisciotta persuasively argues that the human network of expertise is the "critical mass" in this complex, de-centered environment.

doi:10.1300/J201v04n01_07

TECHNOLOGY, PRESERVATION, AND MANAGEMENT ISSUES

Archiving Web Sites for Preservation and Access: MODS, METS and MINERVA

Rebecca Guenther
Leslie Myrick

SUMMARY. Born-digital material such as archived Web sites provides unique challenges in ensuring access and preservation. This article examines some of the technical challenges involved in harvesting and managing Web archives as well as metadata strategies to provide descriptive, technical, and preservation related information about archived Web sites,

Rebecca Guenther, MLS, is Networking and Standards Specialist, Network Development and MARC Standards Office of the Library of Congress, 101 Independence Avenue SE, Washington, DC 20540 (E-mail: rgue@loc.gov).

Leslie Myrick, PhD, is Digital Publications Manager for the Mark Twain Project, University of California, Berkeley, 2195 Hearst Avenue #330, Berkeley, CA 94720-6400 (E-mail: lmyrick@library.berkeley.edu).

[Haworth co-indexing entry note]: "Archiving Web Sites for Preservation and Access: MODS, METS and MINERVA." Guenther, Rebecca, and Leslie Myrick. Co-published simultaneously in *Journal of Archival Organization* (The Haworth Information Press, an imprint of The Haworth Press, Inc.) Vol. 4, No.1/2, 2006, pp. 141-166; and: *Archives and the Digital Library* (ed: William E. Landis, and Robin L. Chandler) The Haworth Information Press, an imprint of The Haworth Press, Inc., 2006, pp. 141-166. Single or multiple copies of this article are available for a fee from The Haworth Document Delivery Service [1-800-HAWORTH, 9:00 a.m. - 5:00 p.m. (EST). E-mail address: docdelivery@haworthpress.com].

Available online at http://jao.haworthpress.com
© 2006 by The Haworth Press, Inc. All rights reserved.
doi:10.1300/J201v04n01_08

with the Library of Congress' Minerva project as an example. It explores a possible data model for archived Web sites, including discussion of a proposed METS profile for Web sites to enable the packaging of different forms of metadata. In addition it explores how the work on metadata for long-term preservation undertaken by the PREMIS working group can be applied to Web archiving. doi:10.1300/J201v04n01_08 *[Article copies available for a fee from The Haworth Document Delivery Service: 1-800-HAWORTH. E-mail address: <docdelivery@haworthpress.com> Website: <http://www. HaworthPress.com> © 2006 by The Haworth Press, Inc. All rights reserved.]*

KEYWORDS. MODS, Metadata Object Description Schema, METS, Metadata Encoding and Transmission Standard, Web archiving, metadata, digital preservation and access

BACKGROUND: ISSUES IN WEB ARCHIVING

As the world becomes increasingly dependent upon the Web as a medium for disseminating government information, scientific and academic research, news, and any variety of general information, archivists and digital librarians are no longer asking, even rhetorically, "Why Archive the Web?"[1] but rather, how best and most expediently can we capture and manage the vast store of Web-based materials to assure preservation and access? The urgency of this question is reflected in the emergence of two major broad initiatives, the International Internet Preservation Consortium (IIPC)[2] and the National Digital Information Infrastructure and Preservation Program (NDIIPP),[3] half of whose eight recent project grants involve a Web archiving component.

Characterized by its volatility and ephemerality, Web-based material has been rightly labeled a moving target. The BBC Web site, whose banner claims that the site is updated every minute of every day,[4] is an example. Although the entry page for the BBC site may change by the minute yet continue to disseminate news for decades, the average lifespan of a Web page, according to Peter Lyman in the article cited above, is forty-four days.[5] Entire Web sites disappear at an alarming rate. A case in point is a campaign Web site for a candidate in the Nigerian elections of April 2003,[6] or any of the 135 candidates' Web sites in the California Recall campaign of 2004.[7] We will focus here on the domain of political or governmental Web sites–especially campaign and election sites–whose ephemeral nature, paired with their vital import, inspire a particular urgency. This important set of born-digital materials has attracted a number of recent Web archiving endeavors including the Library of Congress's MINERVA Project, the CRL-sponsored Political Communications Web site Archiving Project (PCWA), the California Digital Library's Web-based Government Information Project, the UCLA Online Campaign Literature archive, and, covering another genre of lost or defunct political materials, the CyberCemetery at the University of North Texas.[8]

At the same time that we, as Web site archivists, ask ourselves, "How do we collect it before it disappears or radically changes?" we also face the question, "How do we define what we are collecting?" Add to the mercurial disposition of Web materials the conundrum of delineating the boundaries of any given Web site that we choose to collect, or of fully articulating a Web site's structure: this tangle of hyperlinks cross-referenced to an essentially simple logical tree structure delivered from a heteromorphic physical file server structure, offering up a plethora of associated MIME types.[9] Then once collected, we must ask "How do we manage and provide access to this material, especially if we have harvested versions of the same site many times a week or day?" What emerges is that a Web site has to be one of the most complex and challenging of digital objects to capture, describe, manage and preserve.

This article examines some of the vexing technical issues surrounding preservation and access in the archiving of Web sites as identified by our respective work on the MINERVA project and the PCWA project, work whose overlapping concerns led to a fruitful collaboration between the two groups, partnering with the Internet Archive as the supplier of our Web content, and intent upon exploring the use of MODS and METS[10] as metadata strategies. We argue that, among the proliferation of schemas available for packaging and managing complex digital objects (DIDL, METS, IMS-CP to name a few),[11] METS is uniquely suited to encapsulate a Web site object as a Submission Information Package (SIP), Archival Information Package (AIP) or Dissemination Information Package (DIP) for use in an OAIS-compliant repository.[12] We also look forward to how experience gained from these two endeavors can be used to promulgate a set of METS Profiles for Web sites.

PROTOTYPES

Access to Web resources has evolved from Web-indexing *in situ* for discovery to a model of curation, where repositories built on the OAIS model undertake responsibility for the preservation of and access to specialized collection domains. Crawlers, agents, and robots (Excite,

Yahoo, Lycos) and their comically-monikered search engine predecessors (Archie, Gopher, Veronica, and Jughead) began scouring the Web for the purposes of indexing in the early 1990s. A later development out of Stanford, Google's indexing with limited caching, was intended not to archive pages *per se*, but occasionally the Google cache has served as a ready source of a defunct page.

The notion of depositing into a continuous archive as much of the World Wide Web as a voracious crawler could harvest was the brainchild of Brewster Kahle, co-founder and President of Alexa and the force behind the not-for-profit Internet Archive,[13] whose Wayback Machine has served since 1996 as a historical record of changes to extant Web sites as well as a museum of extinct Web sites. The quality of deposited materials culled from an eight-week broad-swath crawl by Alexa, coupled with its very limited search interface–exclusively by URL and more recently by date–has led to the indictment that the Wayback Machine achieves neither archival preservation nor access standards.[14] To the Internet Archive's credit they responded with the development of a truly archival crawler, Heritrix,[15] and partnered with the IIPC to marry Heritrix to a robust repository infrastructure.

The early impetus to construct truly archival Web crawlers and repositories came, not surprisingly, from the realm of National Deposit Libraries. Groundbreaking work was undertaken in the last decade–primarily by the National Libraries in Australia, Sweden, and France–to build preservation and access infrastructures for archiving Web materials. Two early prototypes standing at the antipodes, the National Library of Australia's (NLA) PANDORA and the National Library of Sweden's Kulturarw3 Project,[16] are interesting in many ways as paradigms of diametrically opposed approaches to capture, metadata creation, storage, and access that can be broadly construed as library-centric versus IT-centric. Both projects were and are dedicated to the long-term preservation of national digital assets, not simply the bytes but also the original look and feel of the object.

The NLA uses a combination of push and pull technology[17] and negotiates relationships with every publisher whose limited number of works from the Australian national domain have been preselected by a curator. PANDORA continues to use and improve upon an in-house Java-based application wrapped around HTTrack,[18] called PANDAS, for selection, capture, and management. The project is characterized by selective capture, MARC-centered cataloging, storage of Web site mirrors, and access primarily through the NLA's Integrated Library System, with a new full text search mechanism soon to be released.

In its early stages the Kulturarw3 Project used strictly pull processing in a broad-swath harvest of what it labeled the Swedish Web, using an altered version of the Combine harvester.[19] It depended on crawler-generated metadata for discovery and management, stored its files in multi-MIME type archive files similar to the Alexa .arc format (i.e., crawler headers, HTTP headers,[20] and file content packed into in an aggregate), and depended on full-text search for access, which was only available for use on dedicated terminals in the National Library of Sweden. A pioneer in its time, this project has since been integrated into the larger sphere of Nordic Web initiatives, specifically the NWA or Nordic Web Archive.[21]

The NWA is a collaborative effort between the National Libraries of Norway, Denmark, Finland, Iceland, and Sweden to explore issues involved in the harvesting of Web materials into national deposit libraries. Since 2000, the group has been developing an application using various programming languages to provide access to harvested Web-based materials. This NWA Toolset[22] opened the way to exposing archived Web site metadata in XML in the form of their own NWA Document Format schema,[23] which comprises descriptive and preservation metadata for a single Web page along with a list of links parsed from the page. The XML is then indexed and can be searched using either of two supported search engines: the proprietary FAST Search & Transfer ASA[24] or Jakarta's open source Lucene.[25] Although a step in the right direction, the NWA Toolkit's use of XML arguably does not go far enough on two counts: first, it is a proprietary schema, and second, it catalogs what is a discrete sub-object, i.e., it does not encompass the structure of the Web site as a complex, articulated digital object, nor does it address the inter-relations between its components. When indexing is done at the page level only, the inevitable result is that queries will return perhaps thousands of URLs from various sites, without any clear indication where to find the entry point of the site that contains that page, and thus contextualize it. In this article we suggest that indexing and navigating METS for an entire Web site may resolve this particular access puzzle.

HARVESTING AND TECHNICAL ISSUES

As a response to the need to archive, back up, or mirror Web sites, Web capture has been taking place in various scenarios, using various tools. On a large scale, a crawler such as Alexa can harvest many terabytes of files during its eight-week crawl and deposit them into a repository infrastructure such as the Wayback Machine. On a smaller scale, any like-minded Web site peruser, librarian, archivist, or Area Studies specialist can use an offline mirroring tool (e.g., HTTrack) to download mirrors of sites onto a local PC. HTTrack has been used for early prototypes such as the MINERVA testbed, and is the kernel around which the PANDORA Project's PANDAS application was built. Other tools used in the early Web site archiving projects are the freely available GNU tool wget,[26] and the Mercator crawler (until recently sponsored by Compaq and then HP),[27] both of which can mirror sites locally onto a UNIX server.

Web crawlers are applications usually written in C or Java that, working from a seed or seed list of URLs, send requests using the HTTP protocol to a Web server and then parse any hypertext links that are found in a given fetched page that point to other pages, recursively parsing the links on those pages until a specified limit is reached (perhaps a depth or breadth limit placed on the crawl, or a time or bandwidth limit). Most industrial-strength crawlers use a sophisticated system that can parse links out of various troublesome formats, such as FLASH and Javascript,[28] can apply rules to the newly discovered links and can schedule subsequent parsing to prevent duplication of effort, endless loops, or a crawl into oblivion. The crawler may follow a breadth-first or depth-first traversal algorithm, and "smarter" crawlers may apply heuristics to the selection and ordering of links to be visited. Most crawlers, from the mirroring software HTTrack to the Internet Archive/IIPC-sponsored Heritrix, provide fine-grained control over parameters defining and limiting the capture process to make the harvest as complete and "polite" or unobtrusive (to the Web server being harvested) as possible.

Crawling is half the picture. Archival crawlers generally collect the files specified by crawl parameters into either a physical mirror of the site, as does HTTrack or wget, or into some aggregate archive file typified by the Alexa or Heritrix .arc file. Each storage paradigm presents its own challenges. A Web site mirror simply replicates the physical structure of the captured site, rewriting all hyperlinks to relative internal links to keep the archived site hermetically sealed within the archive. Accompanying metadata from mirroring crawlers must generally be mined from logs, for example those recording the HTTP headers sent by the host, error logs, information about the client and host machines, download time, and size of files. An .arc file, on the other hand, is a large multi-MIME type file containing all the material from a Web harvest, usually compressed into a 100 MB package. A typical Alexa .arc file consists of four categories of metadata: a file header with information about the .arc file itself, a crawler-generated header for each file collected from the Web harvest, the HTTP response headers sent by the Web server to accompany each file, and then the files themselves, often containing metadata along with the data they comprise.

A full discovery and preservation metadata set for Web archiving would thus include not only descriptive and technical information about the individual files but also technical metadata about the host server that delivered the files, the capture event itself, and the archive into which the files are deposited. The Heretrix crawler's packaging of this information into a single file, the .arc file, presents a certain economy. HTTrack can now also archive into a single .arc-like file rather than spreading its metadata through the five or six logs it generates by default. Can any single metadata schema encompass this range of information?

To date a great amount of energy has been expended hashing out the issues around standardized descriptive metadata (e.g., MARC, MODS, Dublin Core) and its role in discovery of Web materials archived in repositories such as national libraries and archives. The earliest impulse has generally been to apply MARC at the collection or Web site level: the NLA PANDORA project led the way, building a complex harvesting and management application around a MARC cataloging module. In the summer of 2000 the Association for Library Collections and Technical Services (ACLTS) Preconference on Metadata for Web Resources meeting also tackled this issue.[29] The title of the volume of published papers, *Cataloging the Web: Metadata, AACR and MARC*, indicates a certain amount of corroboration of the accepted best practice at the time. When the Library of Congress undertook its testbed Web harvest of the 2000 Election, they elected to use a MARC record describing the collection as a whole for management and discovery, but description was not provided at the more granular level of the individual sites in the collection.

METADATA FOR WEB SITES:
THE MINERVA EXPERIENCE

The MINERVA Web Preservation Project at the Library of Congress (LC) was established to collect and preserve "born-digital" materials, specifically open-access primary source materials on the World Wide Web.[30] The project's multidisciplinary team of library staff (representing cataloging, legal, public services, and technology services) studied methods to evaluate, select, collect, catalog, provide access to, and preserve these materials for future generations of researchers. Initially the project sought to establish archived thematic collections of Web sites. The first prototype was a Web archive for Election 2000, followed by the Election 2002 (see Figure 1), September 11th, and 107th Congress Web archives, among others. Library of Congress staff provided seed lists of Web sites to be included in the collection, along with specifications about how often they should be collected, and the Internet Archive and Webarchivist.org collected the material.

Descriptive Metadata

For the Election 2000 Web Archive, the only descriptive metadata created was a collection-level MARC record that describes the Election 2000 Web Archive as a whole. The record is in the Library of Congress' Online Public Access Catalog with links into the Web archive homepage. Library of Congress Control Number 2001561915 illustrates this approach.[31] For the Election 2002 Web archive, LC collaborated with the SUNY Institute of Technology and WebArchivist.org for descriptive metadata for each Web site in the collection using the Metadata Object Description Schema (MODS).[32] In this case the object described is the intellectual object rather than the specific snapshot of that Web site on a certain day, although each Web site was collected multiple times between July and December 2002. A link from the MODS record for the intellectual object allows users to access the various captures within the archive itself. Some of the metadata was generated from the Web pages themselves (e.g., titles), some from features that were evaluated and entered into a database developed by Webarchivist.org (e.g., producer type, party affiliation), and some created by humans. XML MODS records were created with a subset of MODS fields that were deemed useful for description of Web sites,[33] which included the following: Title, Name, Abstract, Date Captured, Genre, Format, Collection Title, Identifier, Language, Access Condition, and Subject.

In addition, WebArchivist.org developed a browse/search system that utilized the metadata to allow navigating through the collection[34] or through categories assigned to the individual Web sites (Candidate, Citizen, Civic/Advocacy Groups, Government, Political Party, Press, Public Opinion, and Miscellaneous).

Each category allows the user to drill down to more specific browsing, for example under Candidate through party, office, geographic area, and name. The selection of an access point results in a MODS record that describes the particular Web site and allows the user to link into that

FIGURE 1. The Election 2002 Web Archive Browse Page

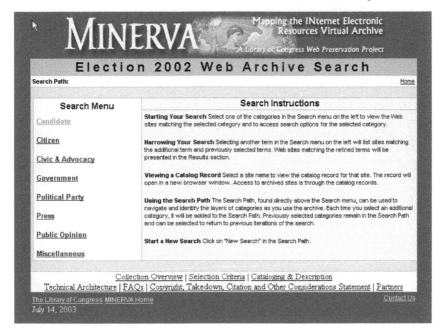

particular archived Web site in the archive itself, where all snapshots that were captured may be acessed by date of capture (see Figure 2).

The MODS record is in XML (see Figure 3) and is transformed into an HTML display using an XSLT stylesheet.

The September 11th Web Archive,[35] which includes approximately 2,300 sites with metadata (about 30,000 Web sites exist in the entire archive), follows the same approach for its descriptive metadata, except that the categories for the drill-down browse are necessarily different. These include: Producer Name, Producer Type, Producer Country, Language, and Subject. In this case, categories use both the Webarchivist.org database categories (e.g., Producer Type) as well as metadata in the MODS records (e.g., Language, Subject).

Because much of the metadata for each site was generated either from the site itself or from the database of features that Webarchivist.org had established, the metadata were not always accurate and required additional quality control. The experience showed the difficulty of generating

FIGURE 2. Sample Metadata Record Display with Access to Archived Web Site

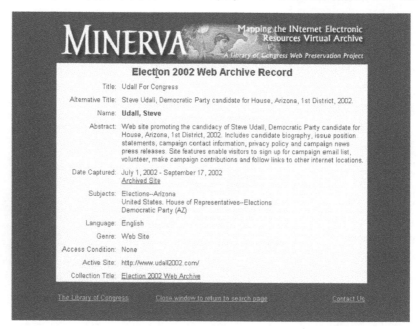

descriptive metadata from Web sites or the Internet Archive files. Consequently, the LC Minerva Team decided to experiment with having LC staff create metadata for the 107th Congress Web Archive in-house using XML tools.

The 107th Congress Web Archive includes 583 one-time captures of Web sites for members of Congress and committees. Descriptive metadata generally includes the same MODS elements as for Election 2002, except that there is enhanced subject analysis with the use of standard Library of Congress Subject Headings and Library of Congress Classification numbers. Some of the metadata was provided as defaults, and some by cataloging staff. Records for the Web sites, which, as with Election 2002, also include a link into the Web archive itself, may be searched using the Lucene search engine, and Apache Cocoon[36] provides an open-source XML Web publishing framework for the archive.

In addition, LC began a new project in 2005 to provide descriptive metadata for the Web sites captured as the Iraq War, 2003 Web Archive and to take it a step further by capturing some metadata from the

FIGURE 3. Sample MODS XML Record for One of the MINERVA Project's Archived Web Sites

```xml
<?xml version="1.0" encoding="utf-8"?>
<mods xmlns="http://www.loc.gov/mods/" xmlns:xsi="http://www.w3.org/2001/XMLSchema-instance"
xmlns:xlink="http://www.w3.org/TR/xlink">
<!--2073-->
<titleInfo>
<title>Udall For Congress</title>
</titleInfo>
<titleInfo type="alternative">
<title>Steve Udall, Democratic Party candidate for House, Arizona, 1st District, 2002.</title>
</titleInfo>
<name type="">
<namePart>Udall, Steve</namePart>
</name>
<genre>Web Site</genre>
<originInfo>
<dateCaptured point="start" encoding="iso8601">20020701203928</dateCaptured>
<dateCaptured point="end" encoding="iso8601">20020917070025</dateCaptured>
</originInfo>
<language authority="iso639-2b">eng</language>
<physicalDescription>
<internetMediaType>text/html</internetMediaType>
</physicalDescription>
<abstract>Web site promoting the candidacy of Steve Udall, Democratic Party candidate for House, Arizona,
1st District, 2002. Includes candidate biography, issue position statements, campaign contact information,
privacy policy and campaign news press releases. Site features enable visitors to sign up for campaign email
list, volunteer, make campaign contributions and follow links to other internet locations.</abstract>
<subject>
<topic>Elections</topic>
<geographic>Arizona</geographic>
</subject>
<subject>
<name type="corporate">
<namePart>United States.</namePart>
<namePart>House of Representatives</namePart>
</name>
<topic>Elections</topic>
</subject>
<subject>
<topic>Democratic Party (AZ)</topic>
</subject>
<relatedItem type="host">
<titleInfo>
<title>Election 2002 Web Archive</title>
</titleInfo>
<identifier type="uri">http://www.loc.gov/minerva/collect/elec2002/</identifier>
</relatedItem>
[record continues]
```

Internet Archive files to minimize the amount of metadata provided by catalogers. The project is also an attempt to mainstream the workflow of cataloging archived Web page using professional staff, primarily for subject analysis. LC developed a cataloging template using the XMLSpy's Spyvision and Authentic software[37] that allows catalogers to modify harvested metadata as well as add controlled subject headings quickly and easily. Metadata captured from the source files themselves (the captured HTML files and the Internet Archive format files) include: Title (if available in HTML tag), Date(s) captured, File format, Keywords and Abstract (if available), and URL of both the active site and the archived site. A few elements are generated by the input template: genre (always "website"), type of resource (always "text"), collection title (the title and a link to the Iraq War 2003 Web Archive as a collection), and two broad subject headings. The record identification number, identifier, and location are generated on the basis of the handle registration file (each intellectual object is assigned a handle to ensure persistence in identification). A statement of restrictions on access is generated if applicable on the basis of information in one of LC's management systems.

Catalogers use the template developed in-house to complete the record and supply additional language and subject access. The cataloger evaluates the extracted title, keywords, and abstract to determine whether they are appropriate to the Web site and makes any revisions if necessary. In addition he/she selects a language from a short list of languages if the site is not in English, as well as appropriate subjects from a drop-down list of about thirty possible controlled Library of Congress Subject Headings. A subject specialist analyzes the Web sites in advance to determine which languages and subject areas are present in the collection. The template supplies the appropriate language code for the language selected, and the subjects reflect the form as established in LC authority files. The cataloger may also fill in a personal or corporate name if readily available and appropriate.

A collection level MARC record in the Library of Congress Online Catalog will provide collection-level access to the archive and link to the archive homepage. The resulting XML MODS records will be searchable using the same search system (Lucene) as for the 107th Congress Web Archive. Bibliographic control will be implemented for additional collections using this model. In the future, consideration will be given to encoding the objects as METS documents to bring together various forms of metadata that will be needed to access and preserve Web pages into the future. This approach would allow for the inclusion of both descriptive metadata and administrative metadata intended to support long term preservation.

ENTER METS

The METS XML schema for packaging the descriptive, administrative and structural metadata, file inventory and, optionally, the data content of complex digital library objects is, by design, a model of flexibility and extensibility holding out a minimum of constraints against the content model of any given object. The heart of a METS object, and the only required component, is the structural map (<structMap>). This element delineates, using nested <div> elements, the logical or physical structure of a complex digital object.[38] Insofar as an effective <structMap> element would in most cases contain internal pointers to any files that comprise a given <div> element in the structure, the <fileSec> with its file inventory is by implication also an integral part of most METS documents. Around this core, users can plug in as extension schemas appropriate XML schemas for descriptive, administrative, and technical metadata, and/or they can create pointers to external metadata files in an <mdRef> (see Figure 4). Libraries describing book or Web site objects, for instance, might use MODS as an embedded descriptive metadata schema, or point to an external MARC record in an OPAC, while museums or archives describing visual materials might prefer to embed VRA Core.

METS's flexibility is both its strength and its onus. Using only the METS XML schema (mets.xsd) as an encoding guide, two encoders or programmers from the same digital library team charged with the task of producing METS documents for a digitized monograph, a seemingly simple object in its logical structure and description, would most likely produce two very different instances. Posting a model METS instance document as a paradigm for encoding a particular digital object would be a stop-gap normalization technique, but what happens when that METS file leaves the library for inclusion in another repository? From its inception METS was intended not only for managing objects archived in-house, but also for use as a transfer syntax, for the generation of Submission Information Packages and Dissemination Information Packages traveling into and out of archives. How, then, to foster interoperability in so elastic a format? This is where METS profiles come into play.

FIGURE 4. Sample METS Document with Embedded MODS Description

```
<?xml version="1.0" encoding="UTF-8"?>
<mets:mets PROFILE="lc:patriotismSongCollection" OBJID="loc.natlib.ihas.200000012"
xsi:schemaLocation="http://www.loc.gov/METS/ http://www.loc.gov/standards/mets/mets.xsd
http://www.loc.gov/mods/ http://www.loc.gov/standards/mods/mods.xsd"
xmlns:mets="http://www.loc.gov/METS/" xmlns:p="http://www.loc.gov/mets/profiles/patriotism"
xmlns:lc="http://www.loc.gov/mets/profiles/" xmlns:xlink="http://www.w3.org/1999/xlink"
xmlns:xsi="http://www.w3.org/2001/XMLSchema-instance" xmlns:mods="http://www.loc.gov/mods/">
  <mets:dmdSec ID="DMD">
    <mets:mdWrap OTHERMDTYPE="MODS" MDTYPE="OTHER" ID="MODS1">
      <mets:xmlData>
        <mods:mods>
          <mods:titleInfo>
            <mods:title>My country 'tis of thee</mods:title>
          </mods:titleInfo>
        </mods:mods>
      </mets:xmlData>
    </mets:mdWrap>
  </mets:dmdSec>
  <mets:fileSec>
    <mets:fileGrp>
      <mets:file ID="BLURB1">
        <mets:FLocat
xlink:href="http://lcweb2.loc.gov/natlib/ihas/patriotism/collection/200000012/200000012.xhtml"
LOCTYPE="URL"/>
      </mets:file>
    </mets:fileGrp>
  </mets:fileSec>
  <mets:structMap>
    <mets:div DMDID="MODS1" TYPE="p:songCollection">
      <mets:div TYPE="p:blurb">
        <mets:fptr FILEID="BLURB1"/>
      </mets:div>
      <mets:div TYPE="p:collectionMembers">
[record continues]
```

A METS profile is an XML schema that permits the specification of constraints beyond those required by the METS XML schema itself. This complement of further limitations serves to define a specific document class whose properties are predictable. The METS schema proper can validate three categories of constraints in an instance: structural validation of the document and the elements' content model, referential and identity integrity, and datatype validity. Beyond these basic conformances, a METS profile might require, for instance, the use of particular extension schema, rules for description, and controlled vocabularies; it may specify the arrangement and use of METS elements and attributes, or the technical characteristics of data files within a METS object. A profile may also prescribe particular tools or applications to be used to validate or display the METS object, or to create other METS objects that conform to the profile. In this way the profile as a class definition whose intention is primarily to promote interoperability also, on a pragmatic level, guides metadata creators and implementers in the generation and deployment of METS.

The marshalling of descriptive, administrative/technical, and structural metadata–whether through programmatic extraction, human cataloging, or some combination thereof–to describe and manage an archived Web site presents significant challenges. First and foremost is the intellectual and structural problem of the delineation of the boundaries of the object that is being archived and defined; where precisely do the boundaries of a Web site lie? Should a repository also archive pages or graphics (e.g., banner ads) referenced by external hyperlinks from the archived site? The term "near files" has been coined to account for files such as these that may reside on another domain or server but are necessary to fully render the site. Should the metadata schema record those links, but not archive the pages or graphics? Or simply ignore the links altogether?

The complex nature of a Web site as a digital object presents a related puzzle, granted that one accepts that a site rather than a page should be the basic unit of capture, deposit, and description. Indeed, a component Web page itself reveals its own complexity in its simultaneous rendering of an HTML page that may be hard-coded or may have been dynamically generated, with any combination of embedded scripting, graphics, multimedia, applets, or hyperlinks. The structure of a Web site presents a number of different facets: one could model it as an essentially flat logical tree structure, designating the index.html page as a root node and all other pages as leaf nodes; or as the navigational or hyperlink structure; or as the host Web server's physical directory and file structure, as replicated by capturing a physical mirror of the harvested site. When a Web site becomes an archived artifact, which of these structures should be recorded?

Web site archivists' lack of influence over the production of captured content, and more importantly its embedded metadata, is another issue. Most large- and small-scale Web archiving projects to date, even large European Deposit Library initiatives, have depended almost entirely upon pull processing. Only recently have archivers reported some progress in establishing push processing models for content deposit. Some organizations, e.g., the Library of Congress (MINERVA) and the National Library of Australia (PANDORA), have gone to great lengths to establish contacts, at least on a copyright clearance level, with the owners of each of the sites they archive. Others, such as the Swedish National Library's Kulturarw3 project or the Internet Archive, have undertaken hit-and-run broad-swath capture for the most part without prior notification or negotiation. Often, until an owner of a site complains about a crawler or opts out of an archive, the relationship of archivists with producers of content is spectral at best. Thus the notion of a repository's possible influence over the creation of content or metadata is not on the table.[39]

This lack of control over creation presents its own challenges in the generation of metadata. File-specific technical metadata (e.g., file name, file size, MIME type, and date modified) we can entrust to machines to extract with some fidelity. The descriptive metadata that can be harvested from the content of an HTML Web page, on the other hand, is fraught with difficulties: template-generated repetitions of the same <title> tag for every page on a site; incorrect or non-existent <title> tags; description and keyword <meta> tags that read more like graffiti or ads; even the charset attribute, which indicates the character set used in the <meta> tags possibly incorrectly. The PCWA archive, for instance, contains a homepage from a French Marxist site whose creator had copied wholesale not only the Javascript he wished to purloin but the entire <meta> description and keyword set from a German sports site, thus rendering his own site, to a <meta>-tag harvester such as Alta Vista, a curious hybrid of a Marxist political archive and a German sporting goods outlet.

If at times untrustworthy, the metadata set for an archived Web site is, for the most part, sufficient in scope for management, preservation, and discovery thanks to advances in crawler application programming. An archiving crawler of the caliber of Alexa, Heritrix, Mercator, or the NEDLIB harvester [40] in Europe will generate and/or extract a fairly rich metadata set from the capture itself, the host server's HTTP response headers, and in some cases from <meta> tags in the HTML pages that are archived. A subset of the same metadata can be mined with some effort from log files produced by more humble crawlers like the GNU project's wget and the offline browser HTTrack. Post-processing of archived multimedia files using freely available metadata extraction tools such as JHOVE, ImageMagick and mp4ip can add even further information.[41] But until we have international standards for file-specific technical metadata, such as audio, video, and vector graphics, much of this information has only a temporary slot in local schemas. One example of locally developed METS schemas is the Library of Congress A/V Prototype.[42]

Once Web sites have been deposited and the metadata provided on ingest has been extracted or cataloged, yet another challenge lurks in the mechanisms of version management amongst successive captures of a changing Web site, whether the added material comes wholesale through repeated snapshots, or piecemeal through incremental harvest(s) of only those files that have been modified since last capture. Given the difficulty in managing the complexity of tracking changes made by the creators, how then does one trace the digital provenance of files once they have been deposited and undergo refreshing or migration to new formats, or are otherwise altered by the repository?

PREMIS (PRESERVATION METADATA: IMPLEMENTATION STRATEGIES)

These questions were examined as part of the work of an international working group that developed a list of core elements and a data dictionary for metadata to support long-term digital preservation.[43] The Preservation Metadata: Implementation Strategies Working Group (PREMIS)[44] released its data dictionary in May 2005 along with XML schemas for encoding element values, and follow-up projects will attempt to implement the element set. In addition, a maintenance activity and implementers' group has been established, hosted by the Library of Congress.[45] The XML schemas are based on the PREMIS data model and include technical metadata to support the preservation process that is applicable to all file format types (not specific technical metadata for certain types of files, e.g., still image, video, audio), event-based metadata addressing the digital processes undergone by objects in the repository in their life cycle, information about agents related to the objects by events and/or rights statements, and rights statements concerning preservation. These XML schemas may be used as METS extension schemas to provide critical metadata to support the preservation of digital objects; as of this writing, details on how to use these as extension schemas in the METS document are being established.

In developing the PREMIS data dictionary, the working group established a data model to provide structure for arranging entities and to promote a better framework for understanding and applying the semantic units. There are five types of entities: intellectual entities, objects, agents, rights, and events. Technical metadata relates to objects, while digital provenance metadata relates to events. Both of these entities interact with agents, rights and intellectual objects. The technical metadata considered in scope for the PREMIS data dictionary is that which is applicable regardless of file format. Technical metadata for specific file formats, such as video and audio files, are developed by experts outside of the

PREMIS effort. The object entity is divided into subtypes for purposes of indicating applicability of particular semantic units (elements in the data dictionary are referred to as "semantic units"): file, bitstream, and representation. Types of metadata included are identifiers, information about the environment in which the object was created, storage information, fixity, size, format information (including a link to a format registry), significant properties, inhibitors, creating application information, digital signature information, and relationships to other objects.

Digital provenance metadata is centered on events that have acted upon objects and is intended to record processes in the life of the digital object. Semantic units include event identifier, event type (e.g., compression, fixity check, migration, validation), event outcome, event date/time, and related agents.

Additional work is needed to experiment with the application of the PREMIS data dictionary to Web sites. Because of the complex nature of Web sites and the possibilities for extensive linking, the PREMIS semantic units may need to be recorded at a variety of levels. The PREMIS report includes a section on implementation issues with a summary of issues on preservation metadata for Web sites and how to view relationships between various objects that make up a Web site.[46] Specific guidance for implementers using PREMIS for preservation-related metadata could be recorded in a METS application profile for Web sites.

DEVELOPING A METS PROFILE FOR WEB SITES

An outgrowth of the collaboration between the MINERVA and PCWA projects has been the exploration of the development of a METS data model for Web sites and a set of METS Profiles for Web site object description. For continuous archives of Web materials, an immediate and fully predictable management and access crux presents itself: many versions of a given Web site must coexist in the archive and will need to be searched and delivered as discrete yet interrelated entities through an access mechanism. Ideally this should be achieved through some combination of full-text search and metadata management, especially when so all-encompassing a schema as METS is available to undertake the task. What emerged from our exploration, then, is that it is not sufficient to create a single profile to describe a snapshot of a Web site, when there is a conceptual aggregation implied in collecting a Web site and all its versions. Furthermore, as repositories of Web-based materials have begun to evolve and are being utilized, repositories have responded to the way researchers use these materials. Responses to use patterns by refactoring Web materials into collections has led to a further refinement of the profile model for Web materials in order to account for various levels of "artificial" aggregation, for example into Internet Libraries or theme-based projects such as MINERVA.

Some Web sites' structure and general content remains fairly stable throughout the lifespan of those sites. The John Kerry Campaign site, for instance, as captured on November 1, 2004 and November 3, 2004–the days straddling the election–would not differ vastly, but users would benefit if each snapshot offered its own level of description and management. Say a researcher wanted to locate information on last-minute campaign stops in the campaign of 2004 and a copy of Kerry's 2004 concession speech. A top level MODS record would not contain this specificity of information, but MODS records at the snapshot level on the days in question could describe the content of a specific version if staff resources were available to analyze particular captures. Some Web sites by nature change content so drastically from one date to the next that they most closely resemble serials or a monograph series. For instance, LC staff is beginning to provide MODS descriptions for the Iraq War, 2003 Web Archive, although the sites are still being captured. Due to its ongoing nature, dates of capture will include a start date and will be left open until capture is completed, similar to the cataloging of a serial publication.

A METS object may be created at any level of aggregation with links to lower-level METS objects. The METS structure allows for associating metadata at any level, which is critical for future use of the objects. Thus, one can associate descriptive metadata at the intellectual object level and technical at any of the levels, particularly the single capture level. A top-level aggregation might be a MINERVA theme-based Internet Library such as Election 2002, with an intermediary aggregation such as the Web site of Bernie Sanders, the Independent Candidate for the House of Representatives from Vermont. Under that aggregation would stand the 172 snapshots captured between July 2, 2002 and December 2, 2002.

The profiles that constrain how the respective instances should be encoded have been labeled Aggregate and Single Capture. The former is considerably sparer than the latter in that the <div> elements in its structural map generally consist of pointers (<mptr> elements) or links to lower-level METS objects. For descriptive metadata the Aggregate Level profile specifies that an instance contain at least a single MODS record describing the site as an intellectual object. Description rules specify a data dictionary identifying the source for each of the MODS fields, e.g., title from the <title> tag in the archived HTML (in most cases) and ISO standards for date and language formats. At this aggregate level there is no file-based technical metadata to record, no file inventory, no link structure, while the structural map simply nests a <div> for each archived version within the root <div> for the abstract website. The Administrative Metadata section (<amdSec>) of the aggregate-level METS record may be the most appropriate site for managing digital provenance metadata and other preservation metadata that pertain to versions subsumed under the aggregation. As institutions gain experience with the PREMIS schemas, they may find that it is desirable to include preservation-related metadata at the intellectual object level as well as at the file level. These sorts of issues will be considered as part of the PREMIS Implementers' Group testbeds. Some of the participants in the National Digital Information Infrastructure Preservation Program (NDIIPP) cooperative partnerships will be experimenting with using METS for Web archives.[47]

The Single Capture profile can be conceived as a child of Aggregate Level when more than one version of a Web site is archived, or, it can serve to guide the description of a single capture. Descriptive metadata description rules in the emerging METS profile specify a top-level MODS record for the entry page that describes the focus, purpose, or content of the Web site at the time of capture, while subsidiary page-level descriptive metadata should be rendered in MODS and be page-specific. These page-level MODS descriptions, which will easily number in the hundreds or thousands, will, by necessity, be programmatically extracted and, judging from the scarcity of descriptive metadata that can be culled from a combination of HTTP headers and <title> tags, will probably contain title, date, and identifier information only. Administrative metadata description rules in the Single Capture profile specify the METS textMD schema for HTML page files[48] and the NISO Metadata for Still Images in XML (MIX) schema[49] for raster image metadata.[50] Other standards are emerging for technical metadata for additional file types, and the PREMIS Object schema may be used for technical metadata that applies to all file formats. Metadata-schema gaps remain for vector graphics, which make up a fair percentage of content (e.g., FLASH, SVG, PDF files), or binary text formats such as Microsoft Word. In addition, the PREMIS Event schema may be used in the Digital Provenance section (<digiprov>) of the METS record to track changes undergone by the object in its digital lifecycle.

As previously indicated, the heart of a METS instance is the structural map. The particular strength of METS in describing the structure of Web sites lies in the easily navigable cross-references between the structural map of the page files and the hyperlink structure that is expressed in the <structLink> element. Of the possible choices for modeling the Web site structure enumerated above in the description of the METS profile for Web sites, the PCWA archive has elected to record a simplified tree structure in the <structMap> complemented by a cross-referenced representation of the hyperlink structure in the <structLink> section. The profile prescribes an essentially flattened, three-level <div> structure, where the root <div> for the Web site subtends a <div> for each HTML page, and each page <div> nests a <div> for each hyperlink it contains.

A Web page can be described as essentially an HTML wrapper embedding other files (e.g., stylesheet, images, applets. mp3s) or hyperlinks that "symphonically" render in parallel a single effect. This second-level <div>, then, delineates the page's parallel components by subtending a filepointer (<fptr>) element containing a subsidiary parallel element (<par>) with an <area> element for each file that is necessary to render the Web page, i.e., the HTML page itself and all embedded image, .css, scripting, and multimedia files. Any material that is not rendered as an embedded file but requires a link transversal (usually another HTML page) is assigned its own <div> at the third level.

In addition to refining constraints against the content model, METS profiles can also encapsulate technical specifications that would extend to the crawler application by prescribing content file requirements. For instance, in the PCWA single capture profile all dynamically generated Web page files (e.g., php) must have their file extensions converted to .html by the crawler or a post-processing script. In a similar vein, through relative link rewriting, all ingested HTML pages should contain no links pointing to the live archived site, but may contain links to live external sites. In these ways profile requirements provide content constraints to hermetically seal the site within the archive. Although a container format is clearly needed and several are available, the METS content packaging standard for complex digital objects, with its facility for representing complicated nesting relationships and intricate cross-referencing, appears to offer an effective solution to the tangle of relationships that is an archived Web site. It is an open, nonproprietary standard (unlike DIDL[51]), geared towards the encapsulation of a wide array of digital objects and their metadata (not merely Learning Objects as is the case with IMS-CP).

CONCLUSION

Web archiving as an art and a vocation is still new enough to be fraught with numerous questions any time a new enterprise takes it up: How do we collect it before it changes or disappears? How do we manage these hundreds or thousands of snapshots of a single site (times however many sites we are curating)? How do we manage the huge variety of MIME types captured in a single snapshot? How do we provide effective, sufficient metadata for management and discovery? And finally how do we guarantee that this material can be preserved in order to make it available for the foreseeable future to a community of users? Many empirical studies are beginning to offer bits of answers.[52] The kaleidoscopic quality of the questions and answers as they are passed from one project team to another in pursuit of this moving target–Web-based materials–is what gives the pursuit its allure, and its promise that the pieces will someday fall perfectly into place.

NOTES

1. See the Problem Statement that introduces Peter Lyman's article "Archiving the World Wide Web" in *Building a National Strategy for Preservation: Issues in Digital Media Archiving* (Washington, DC: Council on Library and Information Resources, Library of Congress, April 2002: 38-51). Available online (CLIR Reports 106) at http://www.clir.org/pubs/reports/pub106/web.html. Accessed 2005-12-01.

2. IIPC membership consists of the National Libraries of France, Italy, Finland, Sweden, Iceland, Canada, Norway and Australia, the British Library and the Library of Congress. They are working closely with the Internet Archive to develop the Heritrix crawler according to their specifications. See their Web presence at http://netpreserve. org/about/index.php. Accessed 2005-12-01.

3. The NDIIPP Program along with its partners has a mandate to "develop a national strategy to collect, archive and preserve the burgeoning amounts of digital content, especially materials that are created only in digital formats, for current and future generations." See their Web site at http://www.digitalpreservation.gov/. Accessed 2005-12-01.

4. See http://news.bbc.co.uk/default.stm. Accessed 2005-12-01. It could be argued that any site containing dynamic scripting that updates the timestamp function could safely make this claim.

5. See Cathy Smith's report from the Digital Preservation Coalition seminar Web Archiving: Managing and Archiving Online Documents and Records, held in March 2002. http://www.dpconline.org/graphics/events/presentations/pdf/Smith.pdf. Accessed 2005-12-01.

6. Under the auspices of the Andrew W. Mellon Foundation and the Center for Research Libraries, the recently completed initial phase of Political Communications

Web Archiving Project (PCWA) explored issues surrounding the archiving and management of mostly nongovernmental organizations (NGO), radical political Web sites from Southeast Asia, Sub-Saharan Africa, Latin America and Western Europe. The project team comprised archivists, librarians, metadata specialists, preservationists, area specialists, and programmers from Cornell, Stanford, University of Texas, Austin, and New York University, and benefited greatly from mentoring by members of the Library of Congress' MINERVA team and NDMSO. Archived content came from Alexa through the intermediation of the Internet Archive, who culled sites from a seedlist of roughly 400 URLs and processed the material into somewhat customized .arc and .dat files. In addition they undertook a focused crawl using Mercator of 38 sites documenting the historic Nigerian Election of April 2003. For more information see the PCWA website at http://www.crl.edu/content/PolitWeb.htm. Accessed 2005-12-01.

7. For more information, see http://www.cdlib.org/inside/projects/preservation/recall/. Accessed 2005-12-01.

8. MINERVA (http://www.loc.gov/minerva/), PCWA (http://www.crl.edu/content/PolitWeb.htm), Web-Based Government Information (http://www.cdlib.org/programs/Web-based_archiving_mellon_Final_corrected.pdf), CyberCemetery (http://govinfo.library.unt.edu/), and UCLA Online Campaign Literature (http://digital.library.ucla.edu/campaign/). All URLs accessed 2005-12-01.

9. The Multipurpose Internet Mail Extensions (MIME) is defined by the Internet Request For Comments RFC 2046, originally to allow for textual message bodies in character sets other than US-ASCII, and extensible set of different formats for non-textual message bodies and for multiple part message bodies. See: ftp://ftp.rfc-editor.org/in-notes/rfc2046.txt. Accessed 2005-12-01. Essentially it is a standard for the format of e-mail and a large number of file formats have MIME types registered as RFCs by the Internet Assigned Numbers Authority (IANA). The combination of type and subtype is called a MIME type.

10. Metadata Object Description Schema (MODS) is an XML schema for rich descriptive metadata that is compatible with the MARC format commonly used in libraries; the Metadata Encoding and Transmission Standard (METS) is an XML schema for encoding various types of metadata (e.g., descriptive, administrative, structural) regarding objects in a digital library. For more information see http://www.loc.gov/mods/ (MODS) and http://www.loc.gov/mets/ (METS). Accessed 2005-12-02.

11. Two emerging XML schema-based standards for packaging the metadata and content of digital objects are the Digital Item Declarative Language (DIDL) which comprises Part II of the proprietary MPEG-21 standard, and the Content Packaging Standard for Learning Objects, IMS-CP, part of the SCORM initiative. A copy of the DIDL Standard may be purchased from the ISO website: http://www.iso.ch/iso/en/CatalogueDetailPage.CatalogueDetail?CSNUMBER=35366&ICS1=35. For a study of the use of the DIDL standard at the Los Alamos National Laboratory, see http://www.dlib.org/dlib/november03/bekaert/11bekaert.html. For the IMS-CP specification, see http://www.imsglobal.org/content/packaging/index.html. A promising endeavor using IMS-CP to package its content is the CWSpace project at MIT: http://cwspace.mit.edu/. All URLs accessed 2005-12-01.

12. For the OAIS reference model, see http://www.ccsds.org/documents/650x0b1.pdf. Accessed 2005-12-01.

13. See http://www.archive.org/. Accessed 2005-12-01.

14. Until recently the only access to this trove of materials was through URL search. An experimental full-text search engine named Recall was introduced for a short period; a more robust full-text search engine is in the works.

15. The Heritrix homepage is found at http://crawler.archive.org/. Accessed 2005-12-01. The project has also been submitted to SourceForge hosting.

16. For PANDORA see http://pandora.nla.gov.au/, and for Kulturarw3 see http://www.kb.se/kw3/ENG/Description.htm. Accessed 2005-12-01.

17. Most Web harvesting is done using pure "pull" technology, where a crawling agent makes a request over http and pulls the content down onto the remote host. "Push" technology in the realm of Web archiving would involve negotiations where providers agree to actively push content to the collector, whether it be packaging and sending database dumps or actual files from the server. These transfers would not necessarily use the http protocol, but some form of portable media.

18. HTTrack is "a free and easy to use offline browser utility." For more information see http://www.httrack.com/. Accessed 2005-12-01.

19. The COMBINE harvester, an open-source Web crawling application, was originally developed as a Web indexer for the DESIRE project: http://www.lub.lu.se/desire/. It was later adapted to harvest and store Web sites for early Nordic Web archiving projects such as the Kulturarw3 project in Sweden. See http://www.lub.lu.se/combine/. All URLs accessed 2005-12-01.

20. The HyperText Transfer Protocol (HTTP) is a stateless client-server protocol for transmitting messages over the internet using TCP (Transmission Control Protocol) connections. Clients transmit requests for information using a standard set of fielded request headers and receive files prefixed by standard response headers from the server. On the HTTP 1.1 Protocol see RFC 2616 at http://www.w3.org/Protocols/rfc2616/rfc2616.html. Accessed 2005-12-01. An explanation of request and response headers can be found in sections 5.3 and 6.2 respectively.

21. Their minimalist Web site at http://nwa.nb.no/ is well supplemented by the 2003 ECDL Paper by Thorsteinn Hellgrimsson and Sverre Bang, "Nordic Web Archive," available at http://nwatoolset.sourceforge.net/docs/nwa@ecdl2003.pdf. Accessed 2005-12-01.

22. See http://sourceforge.net/projects/nwatoolset/. Accessed 2005-12-01.

23. See http://nwatoolset.sourceforge.net/docs/nwadocformatxmlschema.php. Accessed 2005-12-01.

24. See http://www.fastsearch.com/. Accessed 2005-12-01.

25. See http://jakarta.apache.org/lucene/docs/index.html. Accessed 2005-12-01.

26. See http://www.gnu.org/software/wget/wget.html. Accessed 2005-12-01.

27. See http://crawler.archive.org/. Accessed 2005-12-01.

28. Links embedded in pages encoded in FLASH are difficult for Web crawlers' parsing modules to parse because FLASH pages are compiled binaries; dynamically scripted links in Javascript contain enough obfuscation to be difficult to recognize by simple parsing algorithms.

29. For the ACLTS, a division of the American Library Association, see http://www.ala.org/ALCTSTemplate.cfm?Section=alcts. Accessed 2005-12-01. The papers were published in Wayne Jones, Judith R. Ahronheim, and Josephine Crawford, eds., *Cataloging the Web: Metadata, AACR, and MARC 21*, Series: ALCTS Papers on Library Technical Services and Collections #10, Scarecrow Press, 2002.

30. See http://www.loc.gov/minerva/. Accessed 2005-12-01.

31. To view record in LC's online catalog see: http://catalog.loc.gov/cgi-bin/ Pwebrecon.cgi?v3=1&DB=local&CMD=010a+2001561915 &CNT=10+records+per+page. Accessed 2005-12-01.

32. See http://www.loc.gov/standards/MODS. Accessed 2005-12-01.

33. See http://www.loc.gov/minerva/collect/elec2002/mods-elements.html. Accessed 2005-12-01.

34. See http://lcweb4.loc.gov/elect2002/. Accessed 2005-12-01.

35. See http://www.loc.gov/minerva/collect/sept11/. Accessed 2005-12-01.

36. See http://cocoon.apache.org/2.1/. Accessed 2005-12-01.

37. See http://www.altova.com/products.html. Accessed 2005-12-01.

38. A METS instance may contain more than one <structMap> element; the METS for a digitized monograph may contain a physical structural map describing the page structure and a logical structural map describing the breakdown of the monograph into front matter, chapters, sections, and back matter. An application could navigate <div>s for either page or logical structure to allow for concurrent access by physical and logical components.

39. The default model for Web archiving would be a "pull" model, wherein the consuming archive sends crawling agents to harvest files from the host servers of with little or no interaction with Web site producers. In this scenario the crawler is responsible for recognizing and adding new content The "push" model is predicated upon a negotiated relationship between producer and consumer, where, for example, as a service, the producer might "push" new content as is it produced. The legal deposit system has depended fairly heavily upon pull processing, but can in many cases depend upon deposit from creators. See for instance the Royal Library of the Netherlands' argument for push processing: http://www.kb.nl/hrd/dd/dd_links_en_publicaties/publicaties/Washingtonmaart2003.doc. Accessed 2005-12-02.

40. The Networked European Deposit Library NEDLIB produced a Java-based open-source harvester, developed by the National Library of Finland. For information on its specifications and use see http://www.rlg.org/preserv/diginews/diginews5-2.html#feature2. It is maintained by the Finnish Center for Science http://www.csc.fi/sovellus/nedlib/. URLs accessed 2005-12-02.

41. Metadata extraction tools of this ilk extract embedded file metadata from files using various parsing algorithms. The JSTOR/Harvard Object Validation Environment (JHOVE) is an application that can identify and validate file formats for a given object and extract information embedded in a file into a text or XML report. For more information about these tools, see http://hul.harvard.edu/jhove/ (JHOVE), http://www.imagemagick.org/ script/index.php (ImageMagick), and http://mpeg4ip.sourceforge.net/documentation/ index.php (mp4ip). URLs accessed 2005-12-02.

42. See http://www.loc.gov/rr/mopic/avprot/metsmenu2.html. Accessed 2005-12-02.

43. See http://www.oclc.org/research/projects/pmwg/premis-final.pdf. Accessed 2005-12-02.

44. See http://www.oclc.org/research/projects/pmwg/. Accessed 2005-12-02.

45. See http://www.loc.gov/standards/premis. Accessed 2005-12-02.

46. See pages 6-4 through 6-8 of the PREMIS final report: http://www.oclc.org/ research/projects/pmwg/premis-final.pdf. Accessed 2005-12-02.

47. See http://www.digitalpreservation.gov. Accessed 2005-12-02.

48. See http://dlib.nyu.edu/METS/textmd.htm. Accessed 2005-12-02.

49. See http://www.loc.gov/standards/mix. Accessed 2005-12-02.

50. For the Library of Congress Audio Visual Prototype, including schemas, see http://www.loc.gov/rr/mopic/avprot/avlcdocs.html. Accessed 2005-12-02.

51. Many articles explaining the Digital Item Description Language (DIDL) are available online. See, for example, O'Reilly's xml.com site (http://www.xml.com/pub/a/2001/05/30/didl.html) and OASIS' Cover Pages site (http://xml.coverpages.org/mpeg21-didl.html). URLs accessed 2005-12-02.

52. See, for instance, any of the Proceedings of the ECDL Web Archiving Workshops for the past four years. The homepage for the International Web Archiving Workshops (IWAW) provides links to reports and proceedings for each of the four events. http://bibnum.bnf.fr/ecdl/. Accessed 2005-12-02.

doi:10.1300/J201v04n01_08

Video Preservation
and Digital Reformatting:
Pain and Possibility

Jerome McDonough
Mona Jimenez

SUMMARY. The digital library community is increasingly concerned with long-term preservation of digital materials. This concern presents an opportunity for strategic alliances between digital library units and preservation departments confronting the difficulties inherent in preservation reformatting of moving image materials. However, successful collaboration between digital library and preservation departments may require adjustments to the work practices of each group, including their creation and management of metadata and their definition of acceptable practice with respect to preservation reformatting. doi:10.1300/J201v04n01_09 *[Article copies available for a fee from The Haworth Document Delivery Service: 1-800-HAWORTH. E-mail address: <docdelivery@haworthpress.com> Website: <http://www.HaworthPress.com> © 2006 by The Haworth Press, Inc. All rights reserved.]*

Jerome McDonough, MLIS, PhD, is Assistant Professor, Graduate School of Library & Information Science, University of Illinois at Urbana-Champaign, 501 East Daniel Street, MC-493, Champaign, IL 61820-6211 (E-mail: jmcdonou@uiuc.edu).

Mona Jimenez is Associate Professor and Associate Director of the Moving Image Archiving & Preservation Program, Cinema Studies Department, Tisch School of the Arts, New York University, 721 Broadway, Room 600, New York, NY 10003 (E-mail: mona.jimenez@nyu.edu).

[Haworth co-indexing entry note]: "Video Preservation and Digital Reformatting: Pain and Possibility." McDonough, Jerome, and Mona Jimenez. Co-published simultaneously in *Journal of Archival Organization* (The Haworth Information Press, an imprint of The Haworth Press, Inc.) Vol. 4, No.1/2, 2006, pp. 167-191; and: *Archives and the Digital Library* (ed: William E. Landis, and Robin L. Chandler) The Haworth Information Press, an imprint of The Haworth Press, Inc., 2006, pp. 167-191. Single or multiple copies of this article are available for a fee from The Haworth Document Delivery Service [1-800-HAWORTH, 9:00 a.m. - 5:00 p.m. (EST). E-mail address: docdelivery@haworthpress.com].

Available online at http://jao.haworthpress.com
© 2006 by The Haworth Press, Inc. All rights reserved.
doi:10.1300/J201v04n01_09

KEYWORDS. Moving image preservation, metadata, preservation reformatting, digital preservation, moving image archives, MARC, EAD, METS

INTRODUCTION

The digital library community is increasingly focused on the issue of preservation. Within the past few years, numerous institutions have created programs devoted to research and development on digital preservation issues, including the National Archives and Records Administration's research program in the preservation of electronic records, the National Digital Information Infrastructure for Preservation Program, the Digital Preservation Coalition and the new Digital Curation Centre in the United Kingdom, the Preserving Access to Digital Information (PADI) initiative at the National Library of Australia, and the OCLC/RLG sponsored PReservation Metadata Implementation Strategies (PREMIS) effort on preservation metadata.[1] Given the enormous outlay of mental and financial capital on digital preservation issues, it would be safe to characterize digital preservation as one of the defining issues for digital library research at the moment.

The use of digital technologies may present the archival and library communities with a unique opportunity to enhance the preservation of video recordings. All tape, whether analog or digital, suffers from the same issues of media instability and obsolescence of playback equipment that worry many preservationists with respect to data formats. Tapes require periodic reformatting, and in the case of analog materials, the signal inevitably degrades with transfer. While initial reformatting from analog to digital is certainly costly, future reformatting, properly executed, may prove less costly (as it is more amenable to automation) than continuing a tape-to-tape process. Also, digital reformatting holds the promise of preserving the electronic signal intact, rather than subjecting it to decay at each future migration. These and other predictions need to be tested, but we must remain open to the possibility that the use of digital technologies may actually improve the odds of the long-term sustainability of analog, tape-based recordings.

An awareness of the potential for digital technologies to play a significant role in the preservation of works has been present in digital library research and development for over a decade.[2] Early work on digital image libraries pointed out that a sufficiently high-quality digital image could provide a surrogate for, and hence reduce wear on, an original item; that such a high-quality image could replace an item in certain circumstances; and that given the expense of producing *any* digital copy of an item, libraries and archives might as well try to produce as high a quality image as feasible.[3] The time is right for testing whether the potential of digital preservation can be realized for videotape formats. The success of our research will depend in large part on our ability to meld concepts and practices between the digital library community, library preservation departments, and the broader community of audio-visual preservationists. The remainder of this article will take a closer look at some of the problems with existing practices with regards to video recordings, outline some possible solutions to these problems using digital technologies, and discuss some of the economic issues surrounding digital preservation of video materials.

PARADIGM SHIFTS

The library preservation community has been quick to recognize the value of digital reformatting to produce surrogate preservation copies to reduce wear on fragile original material. Its application to create *replacement* preservation copies, however, has been a matter of much greater debate. While the Association of Research Libraries has recently endorsed the use of digital reformatting as an acceptable preservation strategy, others within the preservation community still view this as a highly suspect move, given the unproven status of digital technologies as a preservation medium.[4] The potentially high costs associated with the use of digital storage for replacement preservation copies have also provoked concerns about the viability of digital reformatting as a preservation strategy.[5]

Despite the concerns raised about the use of digital reformatting technologies for preservation, however, several factors are influencing the library and archival community towards greater acceptance of their use. Demonstrated user demand for electronic resources combined with librarians' desire to enhance access to library materials is a potent combination driving the digitization of libraries' special collections. While these concerns focus on access, the economics of any digitization effort tend to favor preservation-quality capture. As Stephen Chapman and Anne Kenney observe in advocating for full informational digital capture of materials, "it seems clear that the costs of creating high-quality images that will endure over time will be less than the costs associated with creating lower-quality images that fail to meet long-term needs."[6]

Since there is an economic argument to be made for creating digital copies that are sufficient to serve as both surrogate and replacement preservation copies, further discussions of whether analog or digital media should be used for preservation surrogates tend to focus not on which is preferable, but whether it is economically justifiable to pursue both strategies simultaneously. Given the costs involved in digitization, there is an obvious pressure to rely on digital copies for both access and preservation, rather than to add to costs by performing separate preservation reformatting to analog media.

There are certainly other economic factors that work counter to the use of digital technologies for preservation reformatting. The argument for the efficacy of simultaneous digital conversion of videotapes for both access and preservation may have merit, but the realities of such a workflow have not been tested. Economic arguments for digital preservation of video materials are being advanced, such as by the company Media Matters in relation to the System for Automated Migration of Media Assets (SAMMA) mass transfer system utilizing robotics,[7] but for the most part libraries and archives see the economics of the digital preservation of video as an obstacle, due to the extraordinary current costs of storage required for high quality video and the still unknown costs of the conversion process itself.

However, there are issues beyond the economic that are also driving the consideration of digital files as a preservation medium for video. Obsolescence of equipment and media presents a far greater risk to longevity than deterioration of the media itself. Given proper storage conditions, deterioration in many cases can be arrested or prevented, but obsolescence is out of our control. While there are certainly unknowns regarding the costs of employing digitization and digital storage for preservation reformatting, these must be weighed against the costs that would be incurred in supporting tape-based reformatting in the face of rapid change in videotape formats that the commercial video industry has exhibited in the past. Moreover, the economics of the commercial broadcasting sector–the formats used for production and distribution of television–undermine an archivist's choice in high-quality videotape formats. Radical shifts are occurring: changing acquisition formats from tape to data, the proliferation of computer-based editing systems, and the trend toward file-based distribution systems. The pressure toward digitization is intense, as predictions are made about the wholesale disappearance of videotape as a storage medium.

In fact, changes in audio preservation practices are foreshadowing those in the video field. Historically, the preferred format for audio has been analog 1/4″ audio reels. However, there is currently only one tape manufacturer of audio reels, and reel-to-reel decks are going out of production. Audio preservationists have settled on broadcast .wav as the file format of choice, and metadata standards are being codified.[8] While there are certainly still skeptics about digital as a preservation format, most will agree that digital capture simultaneous with any analog transfer makes sense, for the reasons noted above.

Complicating matters, many libraries and archives are beginning to confront the painful reality that with the increase of 'born-digital' materials, the question of whether to engage in preservation of digital content is being taken out of their hands, in some cases, quite literally. In the case of *Public Citizen, Inc. et al. v. John Carlin, in his official capacity as Archivist of the United States et al.*, the United States District Court found that the use of paper to preserve electronic records was not an acceptable practice in all cases. The court's reasoning in this case is worth noting:

> ...the administrative record in this case demonstrates that electronic records often have a number of other unique and valuable features not found in the paper printouts of the records. For example, records in electronic recordkeeping systems have searching, manipulating and indexing capabilities not found in paper records, an advantage recognized by NARA itself.... In addition, electronic records can be transmitted over telephone or communication lines and therefore can be distributed or made available to the public more readily than paper copies. Finally and most importantly, electronic records often contain information that is not preserved in a print-out record or even in other computerized systems of records.
>
> For example, paper printouts of computer spreadsheets only display the results of calculations made on the spreadsheet, while the actual electronic version of the spreadsheet will show the formula used to make the calculations.... Some word processing systems allow users to annotate a document with "a summary" or "comments" that contain information on the author of the document, its purpose, the date that it was drafted or revised, and annotations by authors or reviewers.... These comments, however, usually do not appear on a printed copy of the record.... Such differences between electronic and paper records illustrate the fact that the administrative, legal, research and historical value of electronic records is not always fully captured indeed, is usually not captured–by paper or microfiche copies.[9]

The court clearly recognized that in this case, preservation required preserving the functionality of the original document, and not simply the text. The factors recognized by the court are equally relevant to archives confronting preservation of ephemera such as Web pages. If they are to fulfill their traditional mission of collecting and preserving the intellectual heritage of society, they must make the significant investment required to establish systems to preserve digital material. If libraries and archives must create and maintain costly systems in order to preserve born-digital material, then there is certainly an economic argument to be made that they should maximize the benefits they receive from these investments by using them to support preservation of analog material, in addition to digital.[10] Efforts to preserve digital information thus tend to fuel the movement towards using digital technologies to preserve non-digital information.

CONVERGING GOALS

The factors leading to the growing support for the use of digital technologies in support of video preservation are in turn leading to a growing convergence of preservation and digital library departments at many institutions. At the Elmer Holmes Bobst Library (Bobst) at New York University (NYU), the new Video Preservation Lab provides convergence in the sense of a shared resource. The Preservation Department and the Digital Library Development Team merged their equipment resources for reasons of economy, but this resulted in a far better equipped lab than either party could have created separately. This comingling of analog and digital technologies, in a system where reformatting to both tape and digital files is possible, broadens format options for both groups and creates a space for shared learning that will benefit not only the departments, but the library as a whole.

While convergence of this sort may be worrisome to some in both the preservation and the digital library communities, there are advantages to both in such a move. As Hannah Frost (2004) noted in a recent talk, programs that ally and coordinate with related programs tend to be more effective.[11] Perhaps more importantly, preservation programs may be unsuccessful in arguing for additional funding when seeking to do preservation for its own sake, and therefore may enjoy greater success in fundraising when preservation work also serves to vastly enhance access.

While preservation and digital library units may now find themselves more closely allied than ever before, they are allies facing a powerful and intractable foe when confronting the long-term survival of video materials. In confronting this foe, both types of departments may need to adjust their practices in order to succeed. Issues of adequate and appropriate metadata, encoding practices, and cost are among the most salient points of negotiation for preservation and digital library units; we will try to provide an overview of these issues and outline some of the approaches that NYU is taking with respect to digital video preservation.

DESCRIPTIVE METADATA AND VIDEO PRESERVATION

Lack of adequate description severely impedes access to materials and makes selection and appraisal for preservation nearly impossible. Unfortunately, video in most archival collections has been largely ignored and lacks the most basic intellectual and physical control. The majority of libraries and archives are just beginning to address the preservation of video, whether in special or general collections. For those trying to remedy these problems, the inadequacies of current descriptive practices, or the lack of practices altogether, has become glaringly obvious. The relative lack of preservation-related description traditionally created in libraries and archives, contrasted with the extensive user-oriented metadata associated with digital libraries, is striking.

Traditional archival processing techniques do not generate sufficient information for long-term management of video collections. Placing item-level description of moving image materials into a searchable database is not commonly part of archival processing. In a 2003 survey of media materials in Bobst special collections, it was found that fewer than 15 percent of the items had descriptive metadata in searchable databases, and the two existing databases were incompatible and available only to a few staff.[12] Archive databases that do exist are often not centralized, existing outside of the scope of Information Technology departments (preventing routine back-ups and the provision of standard office-level software). This lack of ability to perform item-level searching within collections makes management of video materials nearly impossible.

Even institutions that do perform item-level description generally do not record technical information essential for selection and prioritization of materials for preservation. For example, because videotape is a machine-readable format and playback decks for a given tape format may not be available, knowledge of the exact format of a tape is a key piece of information in determining whether reformatting of a tape must be prioritized. Information contained in finding aids is often too vague to be helpful, or is simply incorrect. For example, items may be listed as "reels," without any additional information to identify them as audio or video recordings. There are numerous ways data could be manipulated to aid in preservation selection. Recording tape brands, so that preservation staff could search for tapes associated with a particular brand known to have problems with sticky shed syndrome, would be an example of such an enhancement.

Even those institutions with the desire and resources to collect the full range of information needed for long-term management of video materials, however, are confronted with the problem that library and archival data structure standards such as MARC and EAD are not useful tools for life-cycle management of video collections. Again, one should not be surprised; these tools were developed as access tools. EAD reflects the emphasis in archival management on the collection and other high-level aggregations and is tied to the finding aid as the primary tool for description. Container lists contain very limited information, and one can question whether, without basic physical description, they are in the most useful form for researchers, particularly those wishing to access footage. Understandably, archivists need descriptive tools that fit within a collection management system, recording relationships between audiovisual items and the larger collections in which they reside.

One sensible and efficient approach to archival processing—one that we have tested and plan to implement in Bobst—is to describe the video items in our media database, and then generate a container list by exporting a smaller set of data into the finding aid, which is marked up in EAD. Thus, the archive maintains full records for the item for management and access, and fulfills the format of the finding aid without doing double work. However, at Bobst, this type of integration is being promoted by the Media Preservation Specialist and has not yet led to a concerted effort by the archivists themselves to adopt new workflows.

Of course, obstacles to proper description are not solely a lack of systems, tools, and integration. Most archivists are generalists, and will have limited experience with the specifics of media conservation and preservation. Archival training programs do not currently prepare archivists specifically to handle media materials; specialized programs such as NYU's new Moving Image Archiving and Preservation Program have been designed to fill this gap. Up until this point, media specialties have been developed largely through apprenticeship, informal mentorships, and workshops offered by such organizations as the Association of Moving Image Archivists (AMIA).[13] In particular, there is a lack of training to help archivists with identification, appraisal and selection, which would help to stem the tide of materials that have little research value. However, most archives do not have the machines necessary to support the basic tasks of appraisal and selection. Also, collection-surveying tools are just beginning to be adapted for media collections.

For library general applications, the problems are similar in nature, but have as much to do with mining the data as creating it. Media-specific technical data is limited in MARC, but is generally richer than in a container list. However, extracting data that would aid in preservation planning and selection is very difficult, as integrated library management and cataloging systems were not designed with this in mind. For example, the date of publication, an easily obtained field in MARC, is not a reliable indication of the age of a tape. Yet age, like format, is a key predictor of condition. Sorting video titles by date of acquisition would be helpful, but since this date is maintained in a local field and dates were not consistently entered, Bobst staff finds it impossible to sort video titles by age. With over 12,000 video titles, manual examination of the tapes is not feasible.

Local methods for video description in archival collections have been shared through such organizations as AMIA, but that organization's cataloging and documentation initiatives fundamentally simply expand on the MARC model. Efforts to develop descriptive tools that map to the MARC standard, but expand its scope and offer an easier interface, such as the cataloging template offered by Independent Media Arts Preservation (IMAP),[14] have not gained acceptance in national forums such as AMIA or the Society of American Archivists (SAA).[15] Adopting item-level description that supports the conservation of audiovisual materials is essential as a first step for preservation, whether or not digital reformatting is deemed appropriate. However, digital preservation is not feasible without full description, beyond MARC standards, of the items to be digitized. An even larger issue emerges: how can born analog, born digital, and digitally reformatted copies be properly tracked and described across library departments to serve preservation *and* access?

NEW METADATA FOR DIGITAL VIDEO PRESERVATION

In discussing the multiple factors responsible for the short lifespan of digital information, Howard Besser observed, "extensive metadata is our best way of minimizing the risks of a digital object becoming inaccessible."[16] As we seek to extend the useful life of video, metadata provides the essential information we need to insure our ability to provide our users with access to this information. One of the unavoidable realities of libraries and archives, however, is that metadata is expensive to produce and maintain, and with the explosive increase in new information resources over the past several years, memory institutions have been hard-pressed to keep up with their traditional forms of metadata production, let alone produce vast amounts of metadata of the new types needed to manage and preserve digital information. A framework establishing what metadata is essential to record and what is merely useful would assist libraries and archives in determining where to apply their scant resources for metadata production.

We believe that a user-centered design perspective can provide such a framework. As Dr. Besser's quote above indicates, the fundamental purpose of preservation is ultimately access; there is no reason to invest the resources necessary to preserve an item that will never be used. The criteria for determining whether any piece of metadata is essential is whether the information it conveys is absolutely necessary for someone to make use of the information that the metadata describes.

This is by no means an easy determination to make. Previous work on digital library design has demonstrated that the value of any piece of metadata varies with both the nature of the digital object being retrieved and the purpose for which a user intends to employ that object.[17] *A priori* determinations regarding the value of a particular piece of metadata are thus difficult at best. While participatory design practices can assist a given institution in determining what is essential for their user community, this knowledge is by necessity localized and not likely to be of general applicability. To a great extent, a devotion to user-centered design principles is incompatible with an effort to make general statements about the value of particular forms of metadata.

The remainder of this discussion of metadata needed for preservation of digital video should not therefore be considered a recommendation for general practice. Our practices with respect to metadata are still developing in response to the needs of NYU's faculty, students and staff, and our experience may not be directly translatable to other institutions. Moreover, our work on identifying needed metadata to support preservation activity is not complete, and our efforts to formalize schema for recording this metadata are still in flux. Despite this, we do have some experience both with our patrons' expectations regarding access and with the technological complexities of managing video streams, and we hope that our experience may help inform others who are developing programs for video preservation.

The Making of America II Testbed Project identified three major categories of user need with regards to metadata: "It was agreed that the purpose of metadata was (a) to help the user discover or locate resources; (b) to describe those resources in order to help users determine whether the resources would be useful; and (c) to provide physical access to the electronic resource."[18] Category (a) above covers the traditional realm of descriptive metadata discussed in the last section. Categories (b) and (c), however, cover the newer realms of administrative and structural metadata needed to work with digital resources, and cover a large scope. We can further subdivide these categories to identify several narrower areas of user need, and the associated forms of metadata:

- to assist users in understanding the intellectual property rights and permissions applicable to an electronic resource so that they may determine whether they may use the resource and the uses to which they may put it [intellectual property rights metadata];
- to assist users in understanding the technological nature of an electronic resource so that they know what facilities they need to make use of it [technical metadata];
- to enable users to determine the integrity and authenticity of an electronic resource [digital provenance metadata];
- to facilitate users' navigation of an electronic resource [structural metadata]; and
- to provide an intellectual and physical context for the electronic resource by making explicit its relationship to other electronic resources, whether content or metadata [structural metadata].

In addition to the descriptive metadata previously discussed, these four classes of metadata–intellectual property rights, technical, digital provenance, and structural–provide the major categories of information to which patrons and librarians[19] at New York University must have access if they are to be successful in their respective tasks of scholarship and information management.

Intellectual Property Rights Metadata

For both scholars and archivists, the fundamental need with respect to intellectual property rights metadata is the same. We need to know what we are legally permitted to do with any given video resource; for scholars this is a matter of knowing whether they have sufficient use rights to accomplish and report on their studies, while for archivists this is a matter of knowing whether they have sufficient use rights to engage in the activities necessary to keep the resource accessible. Essential rights information, then, consists of knowing whether a copyright still applies to the material or whether it has entered the public domain (either through lapse of copyright or an affirmative dedication of a work to the public domain); if still in copyright, who holds the copyright; what, if any, explicit permissions the copyright holder may have already granted regarding use of the material; and finally, contact information for an individual or organization who may assist in determining whether permission may be obtained for uses not explicitly granted by the copyright holder.

It should be noted at this point that there is a fundamental difference between informing a user regarding the copyright status of a video resource (including the granting of permissions over a work's use), and trying to enforce limitations on a work's use. Unfortunately, the digital rights expression languages that have been developed for communicating rights and permissions information in the past few years, such as XrML[20] and ODRL,[21] are all fundamentally concerned with the problem of trying to enforce limitations on usage. This makes them poorly suited for recording the full spectrum of rights information that libraries and archives need to convey to their users. However, these languages are extensible to varying degrees, and there have been interesting recent developments trying to extend digital rights expression languages to record rights information beyond the merely restrictive, such as the effort to extend ODRL to express Creative Commons[22] licenses. At NYU, we are currently investigating whether an extension of ODRL might allow us to record the range of rights information we need for both scholars and librarians.

Technical Metadata

While scholars' and archivists' needs with respect to intellectual property rights information are quite similar, there is a more fundamental difference in their needs with respect to technical metadata. Scholars have two principal concerns with regards to a video resource. The first is access; they simply want to be able to examine the content. The information necessary to support that function may be very minimal indeed. In some cases, just providing a MIME[23] type will suffice; at most, a reference to currently available software to display the file may be required. The second area of concern is quality; scholars need enough information regarding the technical nature of the resource to judge whether it is of sufficient quality for their purposes. The metadata necessary to evaluate this will vary depending on the audience, but typical information will include the bit depth of the sampling used to create the digital video stream, the frame rate and frame size, the color space employed in the video stream, and the type and extent of compression applied to the video.

In addition to supporting their patrons' desires for obtaining access and evaluating the quality of a video resource, archivists also must address the potential need to migrate video content from its current format to a new one if applications for dealing with that format are no longer available. This requires far more extensive and detailed information regarding the format of a video resource, what the *Open Archival Information System Reference Model* refers to as a "representation network."[24] This constitutes the full set of information needed to interpret a bitstream, including the basic file format definition and any further specification documents that may be necessary to understand the basic definition. This has a clear implication for selecting a file format for preservation purposes: the complete specifications for that format must be publicly available. This has led the NYU Digital Library Team to focus on standardized file formats for video preservation, and we are currently investigating the use of the Motion JPEG 2000 format (standardized by ISO in ISO/IEC 15444-3:2002/Amd 2:2003,[25] with reference to the file format specified by the ISO Base format, ISO/IEC 15444-12[26]) for preservation of digital video.

For technical metadata, then, NYU has decided to record the minimal information required to provide scholars with the information they need to view a video resource, and to evaluate its quality. This includes an identifier for the format (which will also be used to locate an appropriate representation network of documentation when needed), bit depth and sampling rates for audio and video streams, video frame rate and frame size, and any form of subsampling employed on the video signal. Separately, we are seeking to work with others through such initiatives as the Digital Library Federation's Global Digital Formats Registry[27] to see if there are ways to minimize the costs involved in maintaining the detailed information required for a representation network of documentation for video formats.

Digital Provenance Metadata

Previous work has addressed the need to establish integrity and authenticity of digital information within the library and archives context, and mechanisms for doing so.[28] There have also been several efforts to try to define a metadata set adequate to the task of recording a digital object's provenance and any preservation processes applied to the object in the course of its lifecycle.[29] Despite this, we still know very little about scholars' real needs for information regarding the provenance of digital information, and less about the range of information that we will need to manage digital information ourselves. Thus, while we are investigating various proposed solutions for preservation and digital provenance metadata at New York University, we are currently collecting only a limited amount of metadata within this area. An MD5 checksum is recorded for all video files, and automated processes on our repository periodically regenerate those from the files and compared the result to the stored checksum to verify the continuing integrity of the files.[30] When a digital video file has been created from an analog source, we try to record technical characteristics of the source video, such as signal format and the type of carrier (tape format) used, but we are not capturing any significant information about digitization processes, beyond the technical metadata recorded for the digital video file (bit depth, sampling rate and structure, etc.). While we hope to eventually employ the PREMIS preservation metadata model as the basis for recording information on the events in a video stream's lifecycle and the agents acting on it, we need to have more extensive discussions with our users, and with preservation staff, to determine the level of detail of information that is appropriate and affordable for us to record.

In evaluating how best to start recording preservation and digital provenance metadata, one of the difficulties NYU and other institutions confront is that such metadata is fundamentally different in nature from the descriptive metadata that libraries and archives typically produce. Libraries are accustomed to metadata that describes an individual asset. Although the individual asset may be a journal run consisting of hundreds of volumes, for the purposes of description, it is considered as a single entity, and it is atypical for libraries to record extensive information relating any cataloged item to other items in their holdings. Archives do record information relating the various items within a collection in their finding aids, but in traditional archives this information is relatively static. An archival collection, once described, will add material slowly if ever, and the relationships between items will not typically change. The principle of *respect des fonds* encourages a practice in which the described relationships between items in a collection are fixed and unvarying.

Digital provenance metadata by its nature describes the relationships among multiple items and is of necessity dynamic; as material is refreshed or migrated, details regarding the old and new incarnation of an item, and the process from which the new is produced from the old, must be recorded. Further, the process is never completed until such time as a library or archive decides to dispose of an item (and its history) permanently. If digital provenance metadata were to be compared to any other form of metadata that libraries and archives already produce, the closest cousin would be holdings records for serials, which are also continually changing for any active title, and which also involve recording the relationship of items being added to a collection to an existing body of material. It is worth noting that cataloging of serials holdings is one of the more difficult and expensive forms of cataloging for libraries. While digital provenance metadata for any item will probably not be as dynamic as serials holdings information, the amount of information needing to be recorded for any change in an item's status is likely to be far more extensive. Finding ways to reduce the costs of producing digital provenance metadata will be vital if libraries are going to retain sufficient information regarding an item's origins and history for scholars to evaluate the item's authenticity.

Structural Metadata

The problem of recording complex inter-relationships of items only multiplies when we consider structural metadata. For video resources at NYU, there are three major classes of structure that we need to record to support patrons' use of video assets:

- the logical structure of a given work;
- the relationship of this logical structure to the individual digital video assets we retain for a work; and
- the relationships that the logical structure and video assets may have with descriptive, intellectual property rights, technical and digital provenance metadata.

There have been several efforts to devise schemes for recording complex structural metadata for multimedia materials, including standards efforts such as MPEG7, MPEG21 and SMIL,[31] and more experimental efforts such as the Universal Preservation Format.[32] At NYU, we are using the Metadata Encoding and Transmission Standard (METS)[33] for recording the complex set of relationships between logical structure, assets, and associated metadata. METS, an XML document format for recording multiple forms of metadata for digital library objects, provides the facilities needed to track a fairly complicated set of relationships and structures.

Consider the following hypothetical example: The library possesses a video recording of a performance. The performance is logically structured into four sections. We possess a Motion JPEG 2000 file that is our preservation master; this file derives from a Betacam SP videotape, which we still possess, and was used to produce a DVD, which the library makes available for circulation, as well as a streaming MPEG4 file. We have a MARC record in our library catalog for the video recording, as well as small Dublin Core records describing each section of the performance. We have technical metadata for all of the various assets (Betacam SP tape, Motion JPEG 2000 file, DVD, and MPEG4 file), and we have also recorded digital provenance information regarding the derivation of the Motion JPEG 2000 file from the Betacam SP tape. Graphically, we'd have the situation shown in Figure 1.

Here we see the complex set of relationships that can occur for even a relatively straightforward video resource. We need to establish an abstract logical structure for the work (a video resource with four subsections); each of the pieces of that structure needs to be linked to the matching portion of each of the various video assets for that resource (using time code values, for example, to indicate that section 1 begins at particular points in the Motion JPEG 2000, DVD and MPEG4 instances). The logical structure needs to be linked with descriptive metadata

FIGURE 1. Example METS Schematic[34]

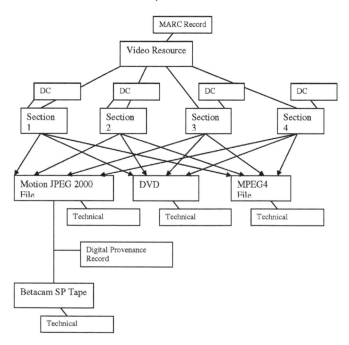

appropriate to its various components, the physical assets need to be linked with their respective technical metadata, and digital provenance information needs to be linked to the originating Betacam SP tape and the Motion JPEG 2000 file. Fortunately, METS handles this sort of complexity well. It facilitates recording an abstract, logical, hierarchical structure for a resource, and then indicates how that structure may be mapped on to various different instantiations of the video material. It also records the various forms of descriptive metadata associated with the parts of the video resource, as well as the technical metadata records associated with the physical assets. It can also record digital provenance information regarding the agents and processes involved in translating the Betacam SP video stream into a Motion JPEG 2000 file. While we are still exploring the exact forms of technical, intellectual property and digital provenance metadata that we wish to record, METS provides an overarching structural framework into which we can easily place the various forms of information we decide are needed to support our users.

Digital Artifacts

The experience of the digital library community during the last decade has clearly demonstrated that while digital reformatting may be acceptable as a preservation strategy, not all digital files are equally preservable. A variety of factors must be weighed in determining a particular file format's suitability as a long-term carrier of information.[35] Two of the most salient factors which have emerged in discussions among digital library developers have been what Arms and Fleischhauer[36] refer to as "disclosure," the ready accessibility, now and in the future, of technical specifications necessary to understand how the digital information in a file format is encoded; and what we may call survivability, the ability of information recorded within a file to be successfully migrated to a new format without corruption. While there are a variety of standards-based file formats for digital video that adequately fulfill the requirement of disclosure, survivability is a somewhat different matter. The evolution of video technology over the years has resulted in a situation where the standards for digital video that have been adopted by those manufacturing video processing equipment work counter to a need to produce digital video that lends itself to long-term survival. A brief history of video technology and its handling of color is necessary to understand why this is so.

A standard video signal consists of luma and chroma information. Luma (which has the standard abbreviation of Y') is commonly understood as the lightness component of an image, indicating how bright or dark any given pixel should be. Chroma conveys color information independent of the luma portion of the signal, and consists of a pair of color difference signals in which the value for luma is subtracted from the gamma corrected blue and red portions of the video signal ($B'-Y'$ and $R'-Y'$); these color difference signals are then typically scaled, and different mechanisms (depending on whether the signal is analog or digital) applied to reduce their data rate for transmission. For those accustomed to the video systems employed in computer graphics, where video is conveyed as a set of red, green, and blue tristimulus components, the use of luma and chroma might seem a bit overcomplicated, but there were several good reasons for adopting this approach in the early history of television. Dividing a video signal into luma and chroma made it easier to reduce the bandwidth necessary to transmit a video signal and still retain acceptable video quality. It also made it feasible for broadcasters in the 1950s to transmit a single signal which could be used by both the large installed base of black-and-white television sets (which simply discarded the chroma component and displayed the luma component), and gave the new color television receivers the ability to display both color and black-and-white broadcasts.[37]

One of the keys to reducing the amount of bandwidth used to transmit a video signal was the fact that human beings have relatively poor visual acuity for color detail compared to their ability to perceive detail presented by variations in brightness.[38] Separating the luma component of a video signal from the chroma components allowed video engineers to separately process the chroma portion of the signal to reduce the amount of visual detail it carried, and hence, the bandwidth required to transmit that portion of the signal. If the luma portion of the signal was preserved intact, the loss of detail in the chroma portion was not noticeable. This practice of reducing the amount of bandwidth used by the chroma portion of the video signal was preserved in the transition from analog to digital video technologies by the use of chroma subsampling. In digitizing a video signal, it is standard practice to sample the luma portion of the signal at every pixel. Chroma, however, is typically sampled at a lower rate. In production and broadcast equipment, the two color-difference signals are sampled at half the rate of the luma (referred to as 4:2:2 sampling); while luma is sampled at every pixel, the color difference samples are only taken every other pixel. This cuts the number of bits needed to represent the signal by a third. Consumer video equipment, including digital video cameras and DVD players, use digital video signals with even lower sampling rates for chroma, cutting the bandwidth requirements for the video signal in half.

The reduction of bandwidth enabled by chroma subsampling is significant. If we sample the active portion of a video frame at a resolution of 720 by 480 pixels, and sample the luma and the two color-difference signals at every pixel, we will take 1,036,800 samples per frame. If we use 10 bits for each sample, we will need 10,368,000 bits for each frame. NTSC video has a frame rate of 29.97 frames per second, so a single second of video would require 310,728,960 bits, or about 38.84 megabytes. A full hour would require nearly 140 gigabytes. Even today, the equipment required to support a data rate of 310 megabits per second is rather expensive. Reducing that data rate by a third or a half makes life much easier for engineers designing video equipment as well as providing significant cost savings to consumers purchasing it.

Unfortunately, what is a boon for video engineers and consumers is the bane of video preservationists. Jettisoning color information to lower the data rate of a video signal is a form of lossy compression. Color information present in the original scene is being sacrificed in order to obtain a lower data rate for the video signal. When we need to display the video signal to a user, the missing information must be substituted through a process of interpolation; typically, either the missing chroma values for pixels where no chroma sampling occurred are copied from a neighboring pixel where the information is present, or new chroma values are created by averaging the chroma values of the linearly adjacent pixels. While the result will be a video image indistinguishable from the original scene for most viewers, the interpolated information is not a match for what was originally there.

Interpolating this information once for display purposes is not problematic. Successive sampling and interpolations, however, will cause visible artifacting of the video image. This problem is familiar to those working in video post-production, where successive renderings of a digital video stream may require repeated applications of a video codec. This can result in noticeable blurring and smearing of chroma within the image.[39]

If preservationists could be certain that they would never have to interpolate missing chroma information during migration of digital video files, this might not be a problem. Unfortunately, this may not be the case. Consider the possible example of the widespread adoption of high-definition television (HDTV) and the consequent demise of standard definition television (SDTV) as a result. If software support for manipulation of digital SDTV signals appears likely to become unavailable, archivists will need to consider migrating to HDTV standards. The Society of Motion Picture and Television Engineers has set slightly different standards for the mechanisms for encoding luma and chroma information in SDTV and HDTV. Migrating between SDTV and HDTV thus involves a process of mapping from the SDTV version of the $Y'CbCr$ color space into the HDTV version.[40] This is problematic, as Charles Poynton notes, "$Y'CbCb$ data cannot be accurately exchanged between these flavors of coding without undergoing a mathematical transform of comparable complexity—and comparable susceptibility to artifacts—as resampling for the correction of pixel aspect ratio. (If the mathematical transform is not performed, then dramatic color errors result.)"[41] Migrating from SDTV to HDTV thus requires a color space conversion involving re-interpolation of the chroma information, one susceptible to error. Again, the results of a single reinterpolation are unlikely to be dramatically obvious. But long-term preservation of digital video materials will almost certainly require multiple migrations. If each of these migrations imposes a degradation resulting from reinterpolation of data, then digital migration may prove to be nearly as damaging a process to a video stream as high-quality analog migration.

Some of the potential migration problems for digital video can be avoided by choosing the appropriate encoding parameters and file format for a digital master file. At NYU, we are considering the storage of 4:4:4 video using the Motion JPEG 2000 standard (ISO /IEC 15444-3:2002) in lossless mode and using an XYZ color space as one possibility for a digital video file format which both lends itself to long-term sustainability and for which the necessary disclosure of technical specifications has occurred. There are also indications that this choice of file format and encoding parameters may see adoption outside the digital library community, including its application in such industries as digital cinema, which would mean that hardware and software to support this standard is more likely to be forthcoming. While this choice is by no means a settled issue for NYU, it does appear to be a promising direction.

COSTS

While the availability of standards such as Motion JPEG 2000 opens up the technical possibility of creating digital video that is amenable to long-term preservation, archivists must also consider the economic feasibility of such a move. The economic issues are somewhat more problematic at the moment. As described earlier, a standard definition television signal, digitized at its full frame rate and resolution using 4:4:4 capture, requires 38.84 megabytes per second of storage, or nearly 140 gigabytes per hour. Storing one video at this level of quality may be economically feasible; unfortunately, few archives have the option of preserving only one video. At NYU, a recently completed survey of the video holdings in our special collections indicated that we have over 30,000 hours of moving image material. If 5 percent of this material is on videotape requiring preservation reformatting, and were we to decide on digital reformatting as our preservation strategy, we would need to digitize 1,500 hours of video, requiring 210 terabytes of storage. For a high-availability server environment such as we are using at NYU's digital library, a terabyte of storage currently costs about $10,000; storing 1,500 hours of video would thus require about $2,100,000. At the moment, such costs are beyond our ability to support.

However, all indications are that this will be a temporary dilemma. Between 1992 and 2000, disk storage costs fell at an average rate of 45 percent per year.[42] If a similar rate continues to hold, by the year 2010, the terabyte of disk storage which cost NYU $10,000 in early 2004 should cost approximately $276. This would mean that storing 210 terabytes of information would cost a far more reasonable $57,960. While those costs are certainly high, they are well within the ability of an institution such as NYU to support. While preservation reformatting of video to lossless digital files on disks may not be economically feasible at the moment, it promises to be so in the very near future. Archives currently considering whether to use digital technologies for preservation reformatting may wish to consider the likely availability of affordable, lossless reformatting in the near future when making such decisions. For some institutions, it might make more sense to continue existing reformatting practices for the short period until lossless digital reformatting is available. Other institutions wishing to investigate the possibility of digital reformatting might consider using high-quality digital videotape formats, such as Digital Betacam, as a temporary and more cost effective solution until lossless digital video on disk is an economically viable approach.

CONCLUSION

The rise of digital technologies and the convergence of digital library and preservation departments present the library and archival world with unique opportunities to improve both access to and preservation of video materials. To fully realize this vision, however, we must be willing to examine and revise many of our traditional practices with respect to metadata and preservation reformatting. While a move towards digital preservation of video requires careful analysis of costs and a thorough understanding of the technologies employed, it holds the promise of significantly improving the long-term survivability of video materials.

Some of the most significant cultural works of the last century have been recorded on videotape. If future generations of scholars are to be able to view this material, we must consider how best to exploit digitization as a mechanism for the preservation of video materials.

NOTES

1. For more information on the National Archives and Records Administration's research program in the preservation of electronic records, see http://www.archives. gov/era/index.html. The National Digital Information Infrastructure for Preservation Program's Web site may be found at http://www.digitalpreservation.gov. Information about the Digital Preservation Coalition can be found at http://www.dpconline.org/ and about the new Digital Curation Centre in the United Kingdom at http://www. dcc.ac.uk/. The Web site location for the PADI initiative at the National Library of Australia is at http://www.nla.gov.au/padi/, and for the OCLC/RLG sponsored PREMIS project at http://www.oclc.org/research/projects/pmwg/. All Web sites accessed 2005-07-28.

2. See, for example, M. Lesk, *Image Formats for Preservation and Access: A Report of the Technology Assessment Advisory Committee to the Commission on Preservation and Access* (Washington, DC: The Commission on Preservation and Access, 1990); and A. R. Kenney and L. K. Personius, *The Cornell/Xerox/Commission on Preservation and Access Joint Study in Digital Preservation: Report: Phase I.* (Ithaca, NY: Dept. of Preservation and Conservation, Cornell University Library, 1992).

3. A. Kenney and S. Chapman, *Digital Imaging for Libraries and Archives,* (Ithaca, NY: Dept. of Preservation and Conservation, Cornell University Library, 1996).

4. For an argument supporting the former position, see K. Arthur, S. Byrne, E. Long, C. Q. Montori, and J. Nadler, *Recognizing Digitization as a Preservation Reformatting Method* (Washington, DC: Association of Research Libraries, 2004), available online at http://www.arl.org/preserv/digit_final.html. Accessed 2006-01-06. For an argument supporting the latter position, see Y. De Lusenet, Y., "Microfilm and Digitization as Choices in Preservation," *Liber Quarterly: The Journal of European Research Libraries* 13:2 (2003).

5. S. Chapman, "Counting the Costs of Digital Preservation: Is Repository Storage Affordable?" *Journal of Digital Information* 4, no. 2 (2003), available online at http://jodi.ecs.soton.ac.uk/Articles/v04/i02/Chapman/chapman-final.pdf. Accessed 2006-01-06.

6. S. Chapman, and A. R. Kenney, "Digital Conversion of Research Library Materials: A Case for Full Informational Capture," *D-Lib Magazine* 2, no. 10 (1996), available online at http://www.dlib.org/dlib/october96/cornell/10chapman.html. Accessed 2006-01-06.

7. More information is available at http://www.media-matters.net/. Accessed 2005-07-28.

8. The Wikipedia entry on the WAV file format provides a good summary, along with links to additional information. See http://en.wikipedia.org/wiki/WAV. Accessed 2006-01-06.

9. *Public Citizen, Inc. et al., Plaintiffs, v. John Carlin, in His Official Capacity as Archivist of the United States et al., Defendents* (Filed Oct. 22, 1997), U.S. District Court, District of Columbia, Civil Action No. 96-2840 (PLF). Available online at http://lw.bna.com/lw/19971111/962840.htm. Accessed 2006-03-14.

10. It is important, however, not to further confuse matters by conflating of two types of born-digital materials–digital tape and data files. There is an increasing tendency to define conversion processes involving digital tape *or* data files as "digital preservation," when in fact the technical features and the demands of tape and data are quite different.

11. H. Frost, "Growing a Program in Media Preservation," *Barbara Goldsmith Preservation Lecture Series*, The Fales Library & Special Collections, New York University, October 28, 2004.

12. The situation at Bobst has improved. Staff in the Fales Library and Special Collections and the Preservation Department have described an estimated additional 4,000 items using a compatible template.

13. Additional information about AMIA is available at http://www.amianet.org/. Accessed 2006-03-14.

14. The template can be obtained at http://www.imappreserve.org. It has been a very valuable tool for a range of organizations–in particular smaller organizations that have significant video collections but lack archive staff.

15. Additional information about SAA is available at http://www.archivists.org/. Accessed 2006-03-14.

16. H. Besser, "Digital Longevity," in Maxine K. Sitts, ed., *Handbook for Digital Projects: A Management Tool for Preservation and Access* (Andover, MA: Northeast Document Conservation Center, 2000). Available online at http://www.nedcc.org/digital/dighome.htm (Besser chapter at http://www.nedcc.org/digital/ix.htm). Accessed 2006-03-15.

17. N. A. Van House, M. H. Butler, V. Ogle, and L. Schiff, L., "User-centered Iterative Design for Digital Libraries: The Cypress Experience," *D-Lib Magazine* 2:2 (February 1996). Available online at http://www.dlib.org/dlib/february96/02vanhouse.html. Accessed 2006-03-15.

18. B. J. Hurley, J. Price-Wilkin, M. Proffitt, and H. Besser, *The Making of America II Testbed Project* (Washington, DC: The Digital Library Federation), 1999, 32. Available online at http://www.clir.org/pubs/reports/pub87/pub87.pdf. Accessed 2006-03-15.

19. As librarians, we tend to forget that we are also users of the resources we collect for our patrons, although we put them to somewhat different uses.

20. Information on XrML, "the digital rights language for trusted content and services," is available at http://www.xrml.org. Accessed 2006-03-15.

21. Information on the Open Digital Rights Language initiative is available at http://www.odrl.net. Accessed 2006-03-15.

22. For more information on the Creative Commons project, see http://www.creativecommons.org. Accessed 2006-03-15.

23. MIME is an abbreviation for Multipurpose Internet Mail Extensions, a standard for the encoding of digital content other than 7-bit ASCII text within mail messages defined in RFCs 2045-2049, which is available at the Internet Engineering Task Force's Web site, http://www.ietf.org. Accessed 2006-03-15. The MIME type registry has become a defacto classification system for content formats used on the Internet.

24. Consultative Committee for Space Data Systems, *Space data and information transfer systems–Open Archival Information System–Reference Model* (ISO 14721:2003), Geneva: International Organization for Standardization, 2003.

25. International Standards Organization/International Electrotechnical Commission, *ISO/IEC 15444-3:2003. Information Technology–JPEG 2000 image coding system–Part 3: Motion JPEG 2000–AMENDMENT 2: Motion JPEG 2000 Derived from ISO Base Media File Format* (Geneva: International Standards Organization, 2003).

26. International Standards Organization/ International Electrotechnical Commission, *ISO/IEC 15444-12:2005. Information technology–JPEG 2000 Image Coding System–Part 12: ISO Base Media File Format* (Geneva: International Standards Organization, 2005).

27. For more information the Global Digital Formats Registry see http://www.diglib.org/preserve.htm. Accessed 2006-03-15.

28. See Council on Library and Information Resources, *Authenticity in a Digital Environment* (Washington, DC: CLIR, 2000); D. Bearman. and J. Trant, "Authenticity of Digital Resources: Towards a Statement of Requirements in the Research Process," *D-Lib Magazine* 4, no. 6 (June 1998), available online at http://www.dlib.org/dlib/june98/06bearman.html; and A. J. Gilliland-Swetland and P. B. Eppard, "Preserving the Authenticity of Contingent Digital Objects: The Interpares Project," *D-Lib Magazine* 6:7/8 (July/August 2000), available online at http://www.dlib.org/dlib/july00/eppard/07eppard.html. All URLs accessed 2006-03-15.

29. The InterPARES Project (http://www.interpares.org), the National Library of Australia's Preservation Metadata for Digital Collections (http://www.nla.gov.au/preserve/pmeta.html), the Cedars Project (http://www.leeds.ac.uk/cedars/), the National Library of New Zealand's preservation metadata data model (http://www.natlib.govt.nz/files/nlnz_data_model.pdf) and the OCLC/RLG PREMIS effort (http://www.oclc.org/research/projects/pmwg/) are some of the more notable examples. All URLs accessed 2006-03-15.

30. The MD5 message digest algorithm is a cryptographic hash function, which can be used to generate a unique 128-bit value for a file based on its contents. Even a small change in the contents of a file will cause it to generate a different MD5 digest value. By recording an MD5 digest value for a file, and then periodically regenerating it and comparing the new value to the previously recorded one, it is possible to detect when a file has been changed. The MD5 algorithm is documented in R. Rivest, *The MD5 Message-Digest Algorithm: Request for Comments 1321 (RFC 1321*, (Reston, VA: Internet Engineering Task Force, 1992). Available online at http://www.ietf.org/rfc/rfc1321.txt. Accessed 2006-03-15.

31. MPEG7, the Multimedia Content Description Interface, is a set of ISO standards (ISO/IEC 15938, parts 1-11) developed by the Motion Picture Experts Group (MPEG) to provide a mechanism to create detailed descriptions of multimedia content; an excellent overview of the standard can be found at http://www.chiariglione.org/mpeg/standards/mpeg-7/mpeg-7.htm. MPEG21, the Multimedia Framework, was also developed by MPEG and formalized in ISO/IEC 21000, parts 1-12, and seeks to provide a complete framework for the creation and delivery of multimedia content; see http://www.chiariglione.org/mpeg/standards/mpeg-21/mpeg-21.htm for an overview. SMIL, the Synchronized Multimedia Integration Language, is a standard of the World Wide Web Consortium and provides a language for authoring simple, interactive multimedia resources; see the W3C's Web site at http://www.w3.org/AudioVideo/ for more information. All URLs accessed 2006-03-15.

32. T. Shepard and D. MacCarn, *The Universal Preservation Format: a Recommended Practice for Archiving Media and Electronic Records* (Boston, MA: WGBH Educational Foundation), 2003.

33. See http://www.loc.gov/standards/mets for more information on the METS standard. Accessed 2006-03-15.

34. Note that the diagram in Figure 1 is not complete, and has been simplified for reasons of space. A complete diagram would also indicate derivation relationships between the original source material and the DVD and MPEG4 instances, as well as the existence of digital provenance metadata for those derivations.

35. For discussions of the factors involved in deciding the suitability of a file format for long-term preservation use see G. W. Lawrence, W. R. Kehoe, O. Y. Rieger, W. H. Walters, and A. R. Kenney, *Risk Management of Digital Information: a File Format Investigation* (Washington, DC: CLIR, 2000), available online at http://www.clir.org/pubs/reports/pub93/pub93.pdf; Frey, F., "File Formats for Digital Masters," in *Guides to Quality in Visual Resource Imaging* (Washington, DC: CLIR, 2000), available online at http://www.rlg.org/legacy/visguides/visguide5.html; A. Brown, *Digital Preservation Guidance Note 1: Selecting File Formats for Long-Term Preservation* (Kew, Richmond, Surrey, UK: The National Archives, 2003 June 19), available online at http://www.nationalarchives.gov.uk/preservation/advice/pdf/selecting_file_formats.pdf; and C. R. Armsand C. Fleischhauer, *DigitalFformats for Library of Congress Collections: Factors to Consider when Choosing Digital Formats* (Washington, DC: Library of Congress, 2003 November 7), available online at http://memory.loc.gov/ammem/techdocs/digform/DigForm_Intro_v04.pdf. All URLs accessed 2006-03-15.

36. See citation in endnote 35.

37. C. Poynton, *Digital Video And HDTV Algorithms and Interfaces* (New York: Morgan Kaufman Publishers, 2003).

38. C. Poynton, *Merging Computing with Studio Video: Converting between R'G'B' and 4:2:2* (Montreal, Canada: Discreet Logic, 2004). Available online at http://www.poynton.com/PDFs/Merging_RGB_and_422.pdf. Accessed 2006-03-15.

39. For an excellent visual demonstration of this, see the example images provided by OneRiver Media at their Web site http://codecs.onerivermedia.com. Accessed 2006-03-15. In particular, an examination of tenth generation renderings provided by 4:2:2 'uncompressed' codecs and those provided by 4:4:4 codecs clearly show the problems that chroma subsampling may pose for preservation. Repeated interpolation of missing color information in successive renderings of 4:2:2 video causes significant degradation of the video; codecs which use 4:4:4 sampling demonstrate none of these artifacts.

40. For a discussion of the color space and other issues faced in upconverting from SDTV to HDTV see S. Ackerman, *Issue Faced in DTV Up-conversion* (Orlando, FL: Teranex, Inc., 2002). Available online at www.siliconoptix.com/teranex/resources/whitePapers/IssueFacedinDTVUp-Conversion/. Accessed 2006-03-15.

41. Poynton, *Merging Computing*, 8.

42. S. Gilheany, *Projecting the Cost of Magnetic Disk Storage over the Next 10 Years* (Manhattan Beach, CA: Archive Builders, 2003). Available online at http://www.archivebuilders.com/whitepapers/22011p.pdf. Accessed 2006-03-15.

doi:10.1300/J201v04n01_09

Digital Archiving and Preservation: Technologies and Processes for a Trusted Repository

Ronald Jantz
Michael Giarlo

SUMMARY. This article examines what is implied by the term "trusted" in the phrase "trusted digital repositories." Digital repositories should be able to preserve electronic materials for periods at least comparable to existing preservation methods. Our collective lack of experience with preserving digital objects and consensus about the reliability of our technological infrastructure raises questions about how we should proceed with digital-based preservation practices, an emerging role for academic libraries and archival institutions. This article reviews issues relating to building a trusted digital repository, highlighting some of the issues

---

Ronald Jantz, MA, MLS, is Government and Social Sciences Data Librarian, Scholarly Communication Center, Rutgers University Libraries, Alexander Library, 169 College Avenue, New Brunswick, NJ 08901 (E-mail: rjantz@rci.rutgers.edu).

Michael Giarlo, MLIS, is Senior Computer Specialist in Information Technology Services University of Washington Libraries, and a Graduate Student in Computational Linguistics, University of Washington, (E-mail: leftwing@alumni.rutgers.edu).

A more detailed treatment by these authors of several of the issues covered in this article was published previously in *D-Lib Magazine* 11:6 (June 2005), available at: http://www.dlib.org/dlib/june05/jantz/06jantz.html.

[Haworth co-indexing entry note]: "Digital Archiving and Preservation: Technologies and Processes for a Trusted Repository." Jantz, Ronald, and Michael Giarlo. Co-published simultaneously in *Journal of Archival Organization* (The Haworth Information Press, an imprint of The Haworth Press, Inc.) Vol. 4, No.1/2, 2006, pp. 193-213; and: *Archives and the Digital Library* (ed: William E. Landis, and Robin L. Chandler) The Haworth Information Press, an imprint of The Haworth Press, Inc., 2006, pp. 193-213. Single or multiple copies of this article are available for a fee from The Haworth Document Delivery Service [1-800-HAWORTH, 9:00 a.m. - 5:00 p.m. (EST). E-mail address: docdelivery@haworthpress.com].

Available online at http://jao.haworthpress.com
© 2006 by The Haworth Press, Inc. All rights reserved.
doi:10.1300/J201v04n01_10

193

raised and possible solutions proposed by the authors in their work of implementing and acculturating a digital repository at Rutgers University Libraries. doi:10.1300/J201v04n01_10 *[Article copies available for a fee from The Haworth Document Delivery Service: 1-800-HAWORTH. E-mail address: <docdelivery@haworthpress.com> Website: <http://www.HaworthPress.com> © 2006 by The Haworth Press, Inc. All rights reserved.]*

KEYWORDS. Digital preservation, digital libraries, trusted repositories, architecture, Fedora, authentication, digital objects, persistent identifiers, digital signatures, roles

INTRODUCTION

In order to understand the tasks of digital preservation, we need to devise some working definitions for the concepts of "document" and "digital object." David Levy[1] has offered some useful intuitive definitions: "Documents are talking things. They are bits of the material world–clay, stone, animal skin, plant fiber, sand–that we have imbued with the ability to speak." As paper and printing technologies have matured, people have grown to expect a document to hold human verbal communication fixed so that it can be repeated. This notion of fixity, however, is a relative term that takes on greater meaning and challenges in the world of digital documents. The fixity of microfilm and paper is generally considered to be much greater than any of the digital media. The great advantage of digital media, the ease of copying and modification, also becomes a major liability. Clearly, we are dealing with a situation that requires active management, one in which many digital objects that are not given migration attention will become inaccessible within a few short years. Further, since the digital object or digital surrogate is not a document, it cannot "speak" to humans without a technological infrastructure that transforms the object into a representation of the original. Hence, we must find ways to "fix" both the digital object and the infrastructure in order to engender trust in digital preservation. Similarly, we will encounter other questions of definition with traditional preservation concepts. What, for example, is the "digital original"? This concept in the digital realm, in its strictest interpretation, makes little sense in an environment where files are routinely copied for purposes of system administration, digital library maintenance, and migration. How do we interpret concepts such as fidelity and stability, and are these useful digital preservation concepts?

DEFINITIONS

The phrase "digital preservation" creates confusion since readers, familiar with traditional approaches, assume that "preservation" involves the use of well-defined techniques to prevent the original artifact from deteriorating further and, perhaps even to improve it to the point where it can be used again. Digital preservation involves quite different methods, skills, and outcomes and can complement traditional preservation services, while simultaneously providing unique and dynamic new uses of information. In this article, we will use the following definition of digital preservation as proposed by Research Libraries Group (RLG):

> *Digital preservation* is defined as the managed activities necessary: (1) For the long term maintenance of a byte stream (including metadata) sufficient to reproduce a suitable facsimile of the original document and (2) For the continued accessibility of the document contents through time and changing technology.[2]

Although this definition provides an intuitive understanding of what we must do to digitally preserve, it should be noted that the definition requires further development and explanation. In particular, the phrase "sufficient to reproduce a suitable facsimile" suggests that that an original exists in some physical form and that somehow the archivist can deduce, perhaps by visual inspection, that the facsimile is "suitable." How do we account for the situation in which the original has been destroyed? Perhaps a more serious flaw in this definition is the implication that an original document did, at some point, exist. The definition therefore does not apply to virtually all of the born-digital resources that have no corresponding physical representation. For example, a database of numeric data containing thousands or even millions of records has no physical, non-electronic counterpart, and we cannot apply the criteria of "suitable facsimile" to these types of resources. For the purposes of this article, the authors will limit the discussion to those information resources that in fact do have a physical, non-electronic representation from which the digital surrogate is derived. The problem of preserving and providing long-term access to born-digital science data is receiving considerable attention.[3] Although much of our infrastructure will support the activities of a curator of science data, the large sizes of these datasets, uniqueness of format, and the absence of a physical counterpart suggest that different approaches will be required.

The RLG report on trusted digital repositories provides a starting point and framework for explaining and demonstrating the important concepts of digital preservation. In particular, the concept of a "trusted digital repository" is based on two major requirements: (1) the repository with associated policies, standards, and technology infrastructure provides the framework for doing digital preservation, and (2) the repository is a trusted system, i.e., a system of software and hardware that can be relied upon to follow certain rules. The following is a proposed definition of a reliable digital repository, also from the RLG report:

> A reliable digital repository is one whose mission is to provide long-term access to managed digital resources; that accepts responsibility for the long-term maintenance of digital resources on behalf of its depositors and for the benefit of current and future users; that designs its system(s) in accordance with commonly accepted conventions and standards to ensure the ongoing management, access, and security of materials deposited within it; that establishes methodologies for system evaluation that meet community expectations of trustworthiness; that can be depended upon to carry out its long-term responsibilities to depositors and users openly and explicitly; and whose policies, practices, and performance can be audited and measured.[4]

We are clearly in uncharted waters when we try to operationalize concepts such as "community expectations of trustworthiness." Over the years, libraries and archives have built up considerable trust within the communities that they serve; however, the accumulated trust derives from traditional services. How do we transform these institutions to become trusted repositories of digital information?

TRUSTED REPOSITORIES

Proper stewardship of our cultural materials suggests responsible management, balancing risks and expense, and extending our time focus across human generations and technological epochs. At the core of stewardship is the concept of trust. For academic libraries and archives involved with digital repositories, the trust issues are somewhat different than those encountered in e-commerce. In both academic and commercial organizations, a climate of trust must be established. However, users of e-commerce are typically concerned about financial fraud or identify theft. In contrast, for the digital repository, trust involves scholarship, authenticity, reliability, and persistence over time and has little relationship to immediate financial rewards. There appear to be no universally accepted definitions of trust, however working definitions are evident within the research literature. Grabner-Kraeuter[5] suggests that within an economic framework trust is viewed as "a risky advance concession in the expectation of a positive outcome without any explicit contractual security or control measure against opportunistic behavior." According to Grabner-Kraeuter, both system- and transaction-specific uncertainties can be minimized by policies in the three categories of guarantees, information, and reputation. Schneiderman[6] offers the following definition of trust: "The positive expectation a person has for another person or an organization based on past performance and truthful guarantees." The *Oxford English Dictionary*[7] defines trust as "confidence in or reliance on some quality or attribute of a person or thing, or the truth of a statement." Although the "thing" we are most concerned about is the underlying digital preservation technology, these definitions suggest that trust is a multifaceted issue, involving people, organizations, and technology. Trust is a major obstacle to getting started in the digital preservation process, and similar trust issues have been with us since the ancient times. Casson[8] describes how the Athenian government of the third century BCE passed a decree to set up a repository of trustworthy copies. The Athenians were actually confronted with a very similar problem to our current digital environment in which every copy was made by hand and was therefore unique. Actors and scribes began taking liberties with the plays of Sophocles and Euripides, and a city clerk was appointed to read the copies for purposes of comparison and to identify copies that departed from the original. In today's environment it is easy to copy and modify a file; however, automated and technological approaches must supplant manual procedures if we are to protect against the unauthorized changes such as those found by the city clerks of Athens.

Preservation of a Historic Newspaper

Researchers have been examining the issue of trust in electronic commerce and many of the same issues will plague digital repositories in executing the digital preservation role. Many of us have experienced concerns about using a credit card for online purchases, or believing that an airline's electronic ticket is really as valid or reliable as the traditional printed ticket. Trust can become a significant long-term barrier and considerably increases the complexity of the digital preservation task.

A typical example raises some very interesting questions about trust and decisions that are made by librarians and archivists. *The Poultryman* is a weekly newspaper that was published in Vineland, New Jersey from 1931 to 1969. Most of the earlier editions are very brittle and access to the collection is by request only in the Rutgers University's Special Collections and University Archives. Figure 1a below depicts an excerpt of an issue of *The Poultryman* from 1937. On the right, in Figure 1b, is a text-only rendition of the short article on the Hightstown Auction. Intuitively, the reader will likely put more trust in the page image of Figure 1a, which has the discoloration of an old, original newspaper and even a marking from some previous reader (the arrow pointing to the article). The text-only version on the right is more legible, but suffers from uncertainties that are surely lodged in the reader's mind. How was the text created and could the text have been altered in the process of human markup and error correction? To deliver advanced features, optical character recognition (OCR) techniques can be applied to the images of the newspaper so the user can do full-text searching. OCR software will produce some errors, and the plain text, corrected version in Figure 1b will likely offer better full-text searching results and require less management and technical overhead for long-term preservation. It is possible, perhaps likely, that a preservationist will make a decision in the future to simplify digital holdings by retaining the text-only version,

FIGURE 1a. Page Image

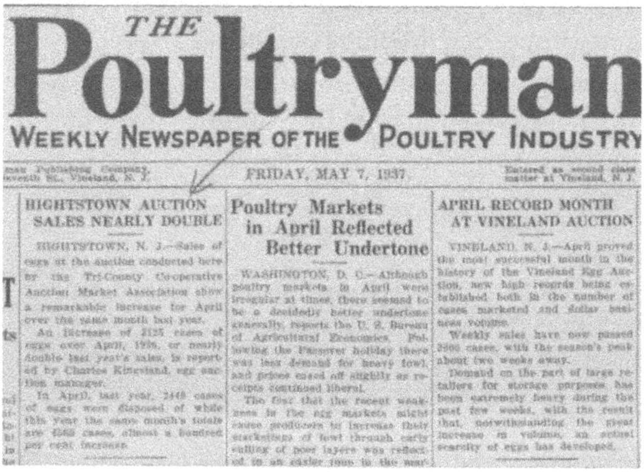

THE Poultryman

WEEKLY NEWSPAPER OF THE POULTRY INDUSTRY

FRIDAY, MAY 7, 1937

HIGHTSTOWN AUCTION SALES NEARLY DOUBLE

Poultry Markets in April Reflected Better Undertone

APRIL RECORD MONTH AT VINELAND AUCTION

FIGURE 1b. Text-Only

Hightstown Auction Sales Nearly Double

Sales of eggs at the auction conducted by the Tri-county Co-operative Auction Market Association show a remarkable increase for April over the same month last year.

An increase of 2125 cases of eggs over April, 1936, or nearly double last year's sales, is reported by Charles Kingsland, egg auction manager.

. . . .

- The Poultryman, May 7, 1937

abandoning the digital surrogate forever and subtly suggesting that only the information content of the newspaper is worth preserving. Assuming we have offered full-text searching of the digital surrogate, we realize that different indexing and search algorithms will produce different results. This complex issue suggests that we cannot preserve the digital object without also preserving the corresponding software that delivers full-text search results to the user.

The archival and preservation community has yet to embrace the concept and practice of digital preservation, and we are properly cautious about abandoning our traditional methods. Because *The Poultryman* is very brittle, it is unlikely that Rutgers University Libraries (RUL) will retain the original print material after all newspaper issues have been digitized. Do we have sufficient trust in our digital preservation process to forego the added step and added expense of microfilming the newspaper collection? In a sense, microfilming technology lulls us into a false sense of security suggesting that the preservationist can just store the microfilm masters in a safe place and forget about them. The results of a study at the University of Kentucky clearly suggest that any institution with large microfilm collections must also dedicate significant time to active management and preservation of the microfilm.[9] Can we answer basic questions about our microfilm collections such as the inventory of master negatives and the types of deterioration that are identifiable? What policies and standards were used in the microfilming process? The Kentucky study found that less than 1 percent of their film masters produced in forty-eight years are truly of archival master quality, and that this situation is likely to be typical for many institutions. As we shall see in the following discussion, the digital world may present more risk to archival masters being modified or lost; nonetheless, in addition to the obvious benefits of access and flexibility, the same underlying digital technology offers much greater assistance in managing a large collection.

In implementing a digital preservation process, how do we balance risk and expense? At RUL we have debated these issues without reaching any clear institutional decisions as yet. Digitization is only the front-end of a process that requires a stable technological infrastructure and life-cycle management. How do we garner trust in this process? The authors suggest that we can only render the process "trusted" by embracing it and doing it with continuous refinement and improvement. The following sections describe some of the components that will ultimately culminate in a trusted system.

DIGITAL PRESERVATION PROCESS AND ARCHITECTURE

New technology cannot be deployed into an organization without clearly defining the new and altered processes that are associated with the technology. Unfortunately, most organizations ignore process design or give it short shrift. These process designs not only specify what is to be done but also clearly identify how work should flow smoothly across different organizations within the institution. Once the process design is developed, semiautomated techniques can be deployed to minimize human errors and labor.

Human Processes and Workflow

We not only have trust issues related to the digital object and infrastructure but also with the human aspects of competency and trustworthiness. Lynch[10] suggests that we are really concerned more about human behavior than human identity, and behavior can be properly directed through well-defined processes. How do we ascertain the quality of metadata, or detect some intentional or inadvertent effort that results in alteration of the digital object? How do we provide for consistency and a high level of quality? Digital preservationists and archivists will be confronted repeatedly with decisions on what to retain and what constitutes the preservation master, requiring many trade-offs among issues such as administrative support, storage costs, dynamic features, and more fluid concepts such as avoiding risk and engendering trust in the repository. During the life cycle of the digital object, the preservationist will need to follow best practices. These human processes and associated workflow can be well defined and deployed into the organization. To most readers, the object-level process as shown in Figure 2 will be intuitive and rather self-evident; however, each major step (P1.0-P3.0) requires

FIGURE 2. Object-Level Capture, Ingest, and Life-Cycle Management

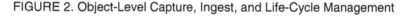

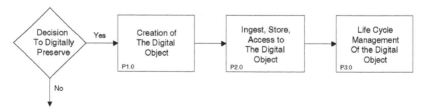

further decomposition, documentation, and deployment throughout the organizations that are charged with digital preservation. Depending on the policies and infrastructure, each institution will need to carefully decompose each of these tasks (P1.0-P3.0) so they can be consistently executed throughout the organization.

The Digital Preservation Architecture

A digital repository is simply a "place" to store, access, and preserve digital objects. The RUL repository architecture is based on Fedora (Flexible Extensible Digital Object Repository Architecture), a framework and implementation funded by a grant from the Andrew W. Mellon Foundation and available at no cost through an open-source Mozilla Public License.[11] Figure 3 below illustrates Fedora's architecture. At RUL, we have complemented this basic architecture by developing both management and end-user applications and integrating critical technologies required for digital preservation.

Digital objects can be quite complex, reflecting the structure of the physical artifact and including multiple content byte streams and special

FIGURE 3. Generic Fedora Repository Architecture

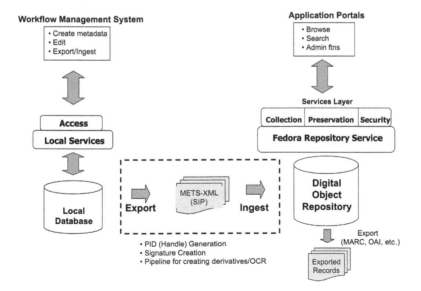

software used to deliver dynamic results to the user. A flexible digital repository should allow us to store all types of digital objects along with the appropriate descriptive and administrative metadata. A digital object might be a newspaper article, an electronic journal article, a digitized image of a photograph, numeric data, a digital video, or a complete book in digital form. Although our emphasis here is on digital preservation, the RLG definition implies that preservation and access are inextricably linked. As a result the repository not only provides for preservation, but also creates an environment for access to the objects that have been preserved.

The left-hand side of the chart shown in Figure 3 illustrates how the Workflow Management System (WMS) is used to create the metadata and associated data streams for each object and to ingest the object into the repository. The "export" function (shown within the dotted box) provides the capability to export the encapsulated object as a METS-wrapped XML Submission Information Package (SIP). The SIP, as defined in the Open Archival Information System (OAIS) reference model, is the information package to be delivered to the repository for ingest.[12] The repository can now serve as a preservation platform for those projects that have been ingested through the WMS. At RUL, we are using this approach to preserve major digital content, such as numeric data from the Eagleton Poll Archive,[13] electronic journals published by the libraries, and digital dissertations. On the right-hand side of Figure 3, application portals provide unique, customized access to the various collections within the repository. Two major application portals are the New Jersey Digital Highway (http://www.njdigitalhighway.org), an IMLS grant funded project, and Rutgers University Community Repository (RUcore) (http://rucore.libraries.rutgers.edu/). The services layer of the architecture provides technological assistance to those who are charged with managing and preserving digital objects. These special services, focused on collections, preservation, and security, can reduce the risk of what sometimes appears to be the inherent fragility of the digital object.

The Digital Object

From a digital preservation perspective, perhaps the single most important design process is to define the architecture or "model" of the digital object. We will further define the digital object as the basic unit of both access and digital preservation, and one that is considered to be the most granular from a preservation management perspective. The digital object contains all of the relevant pieces of information required to reproduce the document, including metadata, byte streams, and special scripts that govern dynamic behavior. This data is encapsulated in the digital object and should be managed as a whole. If our archive is organized in such a way that bits and pieces of the object are scattered throughout the storage system, it becomes difficult, perhaps impossible, to maintain the integrity of the digital object.

Each format to be preserved (e.g., book, newspaper, journal) will have an architecture appropriate for the unique characteristics of that format. Taking the historic newspaper from Figure 1 as an example, presentation (or access) images, digital masters, and OCRed text are all encapsulated in the digital object. In this case, we have made a preservation decision to preserve the digital masters (TIFF images) and the uncorrected, OCRed text in XML format. Each newspaper issue is exported in a METS file and the resulting file becomes the SIP as shown in Figure 3. The object architecture for a newspaper issue is shown in Figure 4 below.

Given the bibliographic data supplied by the archivist or librarian, the SIP for each object is generated and ingested automatically into the repository. In addition to the metadata, there are five data streams[14] in Figure 4 required for the presentation object:

1. A METS-XML structure map (SMAP1) that specifies the logical and physical structure of the newspaper issue
2. A presentation file in Djvu format (DS1)
3. A presentation file in PDF format (DS2)
4. The text of the newspaper issue in XML format (DS3), and

FIGURE 4. Digital Object Architecture for RUL's Historic Newspapers

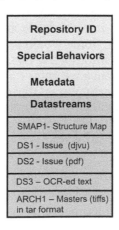

Repository ID
Special Behaviors
Metadata
Datastreams
SMAP1- Structure Map
DS1 - Issue (djvu)
DS2 - Issue (pdf)
DS3 – OCR-ed text
ARCH1 – Masters (tiffs) in tar format

5. The archival digital masters (TIFF images) encapsulated in a widely available archival format such as a tar file or zip file (ARCH1)

These images provide the digital preservationist with a non-proprietary version of the original source content, which is used in the event that the presentation formats need to be regenerated or migrated to new formats or platforms. Although we will not discuss in detail the special behaviors (Fedora disseminators) shown in Figure 4, it should be noted that these special objects provide the ability to create services for unique content transformations and presentation of objects, thus allowing for the preservation of the object behavior as well as the content of the digital object.

At this juncture it is important to highlight a process, supported by the underlying Fedora framework, that is critical for managing and preserving digital objects for long periods of time. The process, referred to generally as "encapsulation," is simply a way to group together all the relevant material for the digital object and to manage the resulting digital object as one. As can be seen from Figure 4, we have encapsulated all the relevant information about the newspaper to be preserved into one digital object. One can easily imagine easily rendering a digital book object, consisting of several hundred files, into a similar object structure. Encapsulation is an essential technology enabling the preservationist to keep all an object's files together and to migrate, delete, purge or perform other similar operations on the object as a whole.

TRUST AND TECHNOLOGY-ASSISTED PRESERVATION PROCESSES

In this section, we will review several technologies and processes that have been integrated into the RUL architecture to help improve trust in digital repositories. Some would say that the act of digitization commits us to preserving information that, by its very form, is fragile and transitory. However, once we enter this digital world, we also can take advantage of special technologies that will help us manage both the volume and inherent mutability of our digital resources. In developing this architecture, our focus has been on using existing or emerging standards and open source software.

Digital Signatures

Once we ingest a digital object into a repository, we want a high degree of assurance that the object has not been modified either accidentally or fraudulently. A digital signature is a critical technology that must be operational in a digital preservation repository to guarantee the integrity of the digital object. Our policy is to compute a digital signature for the archival masters (ARCH1 in Figure 4) and to store this signature in the technical metadata of the object. As part of our security service, a background process periodically re-computes the signature for each byte stream and compares it with the originally computed signature. Any differences are reported to the collection manager, and backups or offline storage are used to restore the integrity of the object.

Persistent Identifiers

It is surprising that the scholarly community has not risen up to protest loudly against instances of citation failures in the digital realm. For scholars to cite with confidence a digital object, they must be assured that the object will be accessible via the citation for many years, a process sometimes referred to as "referential integrity" or "citation persistence." The rapidly evolving environment in which digital objects reside suggests that references to these objects have a high probability of becoming inoperable in a few short years. To address this problem, the concept of a persistent identifier (PID) has been developed.[15] The concept is fairly simple. We want to assign a globally unique name to a digital object, a name that can be used, in perpetuity, to refer to and retrieve the digital object. In developing the RUL repository infrastructure, we examined two PID technologies: the CNRI (Corporation for National Research Initiatives) Handle[16] and the Archival Resource Key (ARK).[17] We believe that both the Handle and ARK approaches have advantages and that the associated organizational and technological approaches will continue to mature. At this juncture in our digital preservation architecture, we have chosen to implement the CNRI Handle solution. Referring to the export/ingest process in Figure 3, each PID is generated automatically from the metadata submitted by the user. The handle is stored in the descriptive metadata as an identifier and is available for harvesting via the OAI Protocol for Metadata Harvesting.[18]

Given that we have a digital object stored in the repository, how do we guarantee its persistence in original form over time? How can we assure the scholar that she is using a surrogate that has been faithfully created from the original? To better understand and answer these questions, it is useful to examine traditional preservation and archival concepts and their meaning and interpretation in the digital realm.

Originality: Validating Object Integrity

What is the digital original? In the traditional print world, the original is the artifact that has not been copied or derived. This concept in the digital realm, in its strictest interpretation, makes little sense in an environment where files are routinely copied for purposes of system administration, digital library maintenance, and migration. In the case of the newspaper cited above and other digital objects, it is likely over time that thousands of digital copies will be made, so "oneness" and "uniqueness" have little significance in the digital context. However, we can reinterpret "originality" with some technological and process assistance. Each page in an issue of the newspaper is associated with a digital master TIFF image carrying the date/time stamp in the header, a stamp that is inserted in the scanning process. Further, as previously noted, in the creation of the master digital object a unique digital signature is computed and inserted in the metadata for the object. At this point, we have some criteria for reinterpreting the meaning of originality in the digital context. The original digital object is one in which the digital signatures for the TIFF images and the digital object are being continuously re-verified, via automated processes, to insure content has not changed. A combination of technologies–including encapsulation, simple date/time stamps, and digital signatures–have enabled us to reinterpret the concept of originality. If a copy was made of the object that retained the original date/time stamp and the content was inadvertently modified, the signature authentication process would fail. In effect, we are providing reasonable assurance to the scholar that the byte streams of the TIFF images have not changed since the time the images were scanned and stamped. We can follow the process of copying a file to its logical conclusion to determine the possible consequences for both the scholar and the repository. If the repository allows a user to download the digital surrogate for personal use, it is conceivable and even likely that multiple copies will be made. Why would someone want to modify the digital object that has been created faithfully to represent the original? Unfortunately, there are many reasons including hackers acting merely on their nihilistic impulses, and those who would alter content and ownership for financial or political gain. In the example of a rare book, someone might want to copy the byte stream, edit out a watermark, and print and bind the document for commercial purposes. Although we are not at this juncture addressing the more complex issues of copyright, these technologies allow us to verify that in fact the digital object has been modified. Our task here is simply to demonstrate that current tools and technologies, assembled as part of the digital preservation infrastructure, can provide reasonable levels of assurance to the scholar and the owner of the digital object.

Fixity

The traditional concept of fixity suggests that the underlying substrate and the content do not deteriorate over time. We can continue to build on the definition of originality above to develop concepts related to fixity and which are important for the trusted digital repository. If the digital signature for the content can be verified, then we are assured that the digital content (i.e., the byte stream) has not changed. As the digital object "grows old" in our repository, we can use scheduled tasks (using commands such as "cron" in UNIX/Linux[19]) and simple alerting mechanisms to notify the preservationist if there have been any modifications to the byte stream. Although this will not solve the problem of fixity, the technology can be a tool to create a framework in which someone can take action to restore or correct a problem that has been detected by a signature failure.

The reader should note that the RLG definition of digital preservation uses the phrase "maintenance of the byte stream," suggesting that human intervention is required. We would prefer to fix the byte stream so that we can preserve the same configuration of bits across time and multiple migrations. Lynch[20] has suggested this concept of digital fixity might be possible by developing canonical forms for each object. Each of these forms would have a definition that is open and not dependent on proprietary software and the technological infrastructure. Although we are beginning to see software for validating object formats,[21] there is considerably more research and standardization required before we will be able to develop these canonical forms. In the meantime we must rely on a suite of technological assists and services to maintain the byte stream over the many migration events that will occur in the life cycle of the digital object.

Fidelity: Versioning, Audit Trails, and Alerting Services

The concept of fidelity relates to the faithful reproduction, maintenance, and repair of the original. In a large repository with millions of objects, collection managers will want to be aware of the activity in their specific collections. For example, in a large institution there could be a sizable staff responsible for ingesting, maintaining, and purging digital objects from the repository. The services layer in the architecture shown in Figure 3 provides the archivist and preservationist with technological assists in managing the life cycle of the object. The audit trail is critical for maintaining an uninterrupted record of the life cycle of the digital object. The audit trail, a feature of the Fedora platform, records two essential pieces of information that are inserted automatically into the digital object metadata whenever authorized personnel edit the object. For example, if an edit is made to the descriptive metadata, the old copy of the metadata is saved, the new descriptive metadata receives a version number, and a record for this transaction is inserted into the digital provenance metadata for the object, indicating that an edit transaction has occurred. If this change to the object is conducted through the authorized management interface, the digital signature for the object is updated to reflect the new content. Alerting services inform via e-mail the responsible managers of critical events that have occurred on specific objects, including actions such as ingesting, editing, signature failure, and purging. This area of using intelligent agents and semiautomated processes is growing rapidly and one that is the focus of considerable research.[22]

Stability: Storage Management

In the traditional archival world, stability relates to the physical characteristics of the substrate (e.g., clay tablet, papyrus, microfilm) and the tendency of these materials to deteriorate over time. In the digital arena, we can look at similar concepts relative to compact discs (CDs) or magnetic disk systems. All of our digital recording media require active management in order to avoid problems due to media degradation and failure. The only approach to this generic problem is for the repository manager to put in place policies for routine backups, off-site backup, and the use of mirrored sites or other types of redundancy options to ensure that there is always another digital "place" where one can find the original object. From a digital preservation perspective, redundancy of content is perhaps the most critical consideration.

While the selection and installation of software components–for example, applications for creating and managing digital signatures and persistent identifiers–are crucial to building a digital repository, perhaps the core of the repository is the storage infrastructure. Likewise, the sometimes-fragile trust that is placed in a repository may ultimately hinge upon the development of effective storage management policies. Even in instances where some ideal combination of software technologies has been incorporated into a repository (let us for now assume that such an objectively ideal combination exists), the last line of defense against fraudulent or accidental loss or alteration of data is indeed the hardware. While hardware decisions do not begin or end with those concerning storage management, they are beyond the scope of this article.

Returning for a moment to the RLG definition, digital preservation is defined as "the *managed* activities necessary ... for the long term maintenance of a byte stream ... *sufficient to reproduce a suitable facsimile* of the original document." Emphasis has been added to the definition to convey two points. First, a digital repository that is designed to provide digital preservation per the RLG definition must be able to produce a copy of the source content stored within that is "suitable," that displays the same text or image, for example, or generally provides the same experience. Since software cannot make this provision without some sort of underlying storage hardware, careful providers of digital preservation will consider storage hardware as a key component of a repository. Second, if the definition is extended to cover the broader spectrum of tasks related to digital preservation, it is not sufficient to allocate vast amounts of storage space for a digital repository without regard for the *management* thereof.

In order to meet the requirements of digital preservation, the Rutgers University Libraries have chosen for our digital repository a storage management solution based on the open architecture of a Storage Area Network (SAN). Hierarchical Storage Management (HSM) software running on the SAN allows the repository servers to address a high-capacity disk array and a tape library as though they are connected disks. The HSM software permits repository administrators to more effectively manage the storage system, optimizing usage of the disk space and ensuring data is backed up in full. HSM policies have been created to store all presentation-form data streams on disk and release rarely accessed archival data streams to tape, though they still appear to be on disk, due to the HSM software, and are automatically staged back from tape to disk upon access. The hardware and software work together to ensure lost or mangled data may be regenerated, and easily accessed, to form a "suitable facsimile" should such an event occur.

All of our digital recording media require active management in order to avoid problems due to media degradation and failure. For several reasons, we ultimately want to have a network of interoperating digital library repositories. From a digital preservation perspective, redundancy of content is perhaps the most critical consideration. Although we have a data persistence strategy that includes RAID technology, daily backups, and weekly offsite delivery of backup tapes, we also want to replicate all object content in a mirrored server configuration. This type of configuration not only provides redundancy of content but also insures higher availability of the content. Although RUL has not yet implemented a mirrored repository configuration, this capability is planned as part of the ongoing Fedora development, and is available in other implementations such as the LOCKSS (Lots of Copies Keep Stuff Safe) system.[23]

Though we have supported the notion that digital preservation ought to be wholeheartedly embraced by archives and libraries, we do not intend to forward the thesis that technology in and of itself is a solution for the problems of data persistence and continuous access to Web-based resources. Without an organizational commitment to digital preservation practices, and development of policies and human processes, technology will be of little use. Policies must be established to determine how storage will be used, how files will be backed up, how long backed-up files will be retained, and how often backup tapes will be transferred to and from off-site safety vaults. These are the types of policies that information technologists are usually expected to create and enforce, though the perspective and knowledge of archivists should be brought to bear on them in the context of digital archives. Archivists and information technologists will need to work closely together in order to ensure that realistic, effective policies are put in place and efficient processes are designed. For instance, archivists and information technologists might collaborate to tackle questions such as how off-site back-up tapes will be transferred to safe vaults, how tapes will be swapped out of the tape library and who will be responsible, and what processes are in place to increase storage capacity without impacting mission-critical services? Information technologists will need to be made aware of the archivists' preservation requirements in order for digital preservation to become a widespread reality and, more importantly, archivists will need to embrace the notion that digital preservation is a responsibility that archives ought to assume.

CONCLUSION

It seems that we have been at similar transition points in our preservation history. In 1880, *The Library Journal* reported on the destruction by fire of Professor Theodor Mommsen's personal library of rare books and manuscripts. In addition, rare books from the Vatican Library that were on loan to Professor Mommsen were also destroyed. The article suggests that perhaps these rare artifacts could have been preserved by making a photographic replica.[24] Some 100 years later in 1990, Michael

Lesk suggested that the digitization process and storage technology have reached a practical threshold in terms of capacity and costs.[25] In our current environment, we realize that the volume of material which must be preserved is not manageable with traditional processes. In a review of David Bearman's writings, James Gerhlich points out that Bearman's analysis suggests that for every archival function there is an order of magnitude (ten times) more work to be done than the current professional staff can manage with existing methods. Bearman further points out that improvements in existing methods rarely yield more than double the improvement.[26] The message is that we must, as an archival and preservation community, adopt new methods.

Despite the many challenges, academic libraries and archival institutions must begin to assemble and integrate the policies, standards, methods and technologies for doing digital preservation. There is much research yet to be done. For example, we can't yet easily discern if two digital objects are equivalent in structure and semantics.[27] Libraries and archives will have to deal with these types of uncertainties in addition to such active management issues as migration of data, an area that is largely indeterminate given the unknowable technology in the future. Although there certainly are risks in undertaking digital preservation, our cultural heritage institutions must begin to establish a trusted reputation simply by deciding to get started in this new role. The Association of Research Libraries has recently published a discussion draft suggesting, in the context of using digitization as a reformatting strategy, that "libraries cannot wait for long-term solutions to be completely settled before testing the water."[28] Finally, it must be said that the importance of the element of trust will always remain for the organization that takes on the role of "trusted digital repository." We rarely doubt the accuracy and validity of our bank statements although many of us perform quick little sanity checks to see if our balance approximates what we think it should be. We want to have at least this same level of trust with digital repositories, and ultimately, we will have to trust the people and organizations that have the responsibility for managing the processes and technologies of digital preservation.

NOTES

1. D. Levy, "Heroic measures: reflections on the possibility and purpose of digital preservation," in I. Witten, R. Akscyn, and F. M. Shipman, III, eds., *Digital libraries 98: the Third ACM Conference on Digital Libraries, June 23-26, 1998, Pittsburgh, PA* (New York: Association for Computing Machinery, 1998), 152-161.

2. *Attributes of a Trusted Digital Repository: Meeting the .Needs of Research Resources: an RLG-OCLC Report* (Mountain View, CA: RLG, 2001), available online at http://www.rlg.org/longterm/repositories.pdf. Accessed 2006-03-18.

3. M. Duke, M. Day, R. Heery, L.A. Carr, and S.J. Coles, "Enhancing Access to Research Data: the Challenge of Crystallography," *Proceedings of the 5th ACM/IEEE Joint Conference on Digital Libraries: Denver, CO, USA, June 7-11, 2005* (New York: ACM Press, 2005), 46-55. See also C. L. Palmer, "Scholarly Work and the Shaping of Digital Access," *JASIST* 56:11 (September 2005), 1140-1153.

4. *Attributes of a Trusted Digital Repository.*

5. S. Grabner-Kraeuter, "The Role of Consumers' Trust in Online-shopping," *Journal of Business Ethics* 39, no. 1/2 (2002), 43-50.

6. B. Schneiderman, "Designing Trust into Online Experiences," *Communications of the ACM* 43, no. 12 (2000), 57-59.

7. *The Oxford English Dictionary*, 2nd ed. (New York: Oxford University Press, 1989).

8. L. Casson, *Libraries in the Ancient World* (New Haven, CT: Yale University Press, 2001), 30.

9. T. Teper, "A Collection Assessment of University of Kentucky's Newspaper Negatives," *Microfilm & Imaging Review* 30, no. 4 (2001), 113-126.

10. C. Lynch,"When Documents Deceive: Trust and Provenance as New Factors for Information Retrieval in a Tangled Web," *JASIST* 52, no. 1 (January 2001), 12-17.

11. T. Staples, R. Wayland, and S. Payette, "The Fedora Project: an Open-Source Digital Object Repository Management System," *D-Lib Magazine* 9, no. 4 (April 2003), available at http://www.dlib.org/dlib/april03/staples/04staples.html. More information on Fedora is available at http://www.fedora.info/. URLs accessed 2006-03-18.

12. Information on METS is available at the official Web site at http://www.loc.gov/standards/mets/. Information on SIPs and other aspects of the OAIS (Open Archival Information System) and its reference model for the long-term preservation of digital information is available at http://ssdoo.gsfc.nasa.gov/nost/isoas/. URLs accessed 2006-03-18.

13. R. Jantz, "Public Opinion Polls and Digital Preservation: an Application of the Fedora Digital Object Repository System," *D-Lib Magazine* 9, no. 11 (November 2003), available at http://www.dlib.org/dlib/november03/jantz/11jantz.html.

14. The term data streams is used in the Fedora architecture and can be considered roughly equivalent to the concept of byte streams as used in the RLG definition of digital preservation.

15. R. Jantz and M. Giarlo, "Digital Preservation: Architecture and Technology for Trusted Digital Repositories, *D-Lib Magazine* 11:6 (June 2005), available at http://www.dlib.org/dlib/june05/jantz/06jantz.html. Accessed 2006-03-18.

16. For more information, see the Handle System Web site at http://www.handle.net. Accessed 2006-03-18.

17. Kunze, J., and R.P.C. Rogers, *The ARK Persistent Identifier Scheme*, February 2006, available at http://www.cdlib.org/inside/diglib/ark/arkspec.pdf. Accessed 2006-03-18.

18. For more information, see the OAI website at http://www.openarchives.org. Accessed 2006-03-18.

19. Additional information on the UNIX command "cron" can be found at http://en.wikipedia.org/wiki/Cron. Accessed 2006-03-18.

20. C. Lynch, "Canonicalization: a Fundamental Tool to Facilitate Preservation and Management Of Digital Information," *D-Lib Magazine* 5, no. 9 (September 1999), available at http://www.dlib.org/dlib/september99/09lynch.html.

21. See, for example, JHOVE, a format-specific digital object validation tool, available at http://hul.harvard.edu/jhove. Accessed 2006-03-18.

22. J. Hunter and S. Choudhury, "A Semi-automated Digital Preservation System Based on Semantic Web Services," *JCDL 2004: Proceedings of the Fourth ACM/IEEE Joint Conference on Digital Libraries: Global Reach and Diverse Impact, Tucson, Arizona, June 7-11, 2004.* New York: ACM Press, 2004, 269-278.

23. V. Reich and D. Rosenthal, "Lockss: a Permanent Publishing and Web Access System," *D-Lib Magazine*, 7:6 (June 2001), available at http://www.dlib.org/dlib/june01/reich/06reich.html. Accessed 2006-03-18.

24. "The Loan of Rare Books," *The Library Journal* 5, no. 6-7, 217.

25. M. Lesk, *Image Formats for Preservation and Access: a Report of the Technology Assessment Advisory Committee to the Commission on Preservation and Access*, July 1990, available at http://palimpsest.stanford.edu/byauth/lesk/lesk.html. Accessed 2006-03-18.

26. J. L. Gehrlich, "The Archival Imagination of David Bearman, Revisited," *Journal of Archival Organization* 1, no. 1 (2002), 5-18.

27. A. Renear and D. Dubin, *Towards Identify Conditions for Digital Documents*, available at http://www.siderean.com/dc2003/503_Paper71.pdf. Accessed 2006-03-18.

28. Association of Research Libraries, *Recognizing Digitization as Preservation Reformatting Method*, June 2004, available at http://www.arl.org/preserv/digit_final.html. Accessed 2006-03-18.

doi:10.1300/J201v04n01_10

The Complexities of Digital Resources: Collection Boundaries and Management Responsibilities

Joanne Kaczmarek

SUMMARY. The boundaries that define a discrete collection of intellectual or informational resources have never been precise or immutable. With the proliferation of born-digital and digitized analog materials, these boundaries are becoming even less well defined. Supporting users' information needs in the current digital environment requires redefining the responsibilities of persons responsible for executing traditional library collection development practices and archival appraisal strategies. Developing and supporting the necessary technical and organizational infrastructure for long-term sustainability of digital collections will require intentional collaboration among information professionals. This article explores these issues in the context of both academic and state government entities, clarifying the need for a shift in roles for information professionals. doi:10.1300/J201v04n01_11 *[Article copies available for a fee from The Haworth Document Delivery Service: 1-800-HAWORTH. E-mail address:*

Joanne Kaczmarek, MLIS, is Archivist for Electronic Records, University of Illinois at Urbana-Champaign, 1408 West Gregory Drive, Room 19 Library, Urbana, IL 61801 (E-mail: jkaczmar@uiuc.edu).

The author wishes to acknowledge the insight offered by many colleagues, and the excellent editorial support of Jean Ascoli.

[Haworth co-indexing entry note]: "The Complexities of Digital Resources: Collection Boundaries and Management Responsibilities." Kaczmarek, Joanne. Co-published simultaneously in *Journal of Archival Organization* (The Haworth Information Press, an imprint of The Haworth Press, Inc.) Vol. 4, No.1/2, 2006, pp. 215-227; and: *Archives and the Digital Library* (ed: William E. Landis, and Robin L. Chandler) The Haworth Information Press, an imprint of The Haworth Press, Inc., 2006, pp. 215-227. Single or multiple copies of this article are available for a fee from The Haworth Document Delivery Service [1-800-HAWORTH, 9:00 a.m. - 5:00 p.m. (EST). E-mail address: docdelivery@haworthpress.com].

Available online at http://jao.haworthpress.com
© 2006 by The Haworth Press, Inc. All rights reserved.
doi:10.1300/J201v04n01_11

215

<docdelivery@haworthpress.com> Website: <http://www.HaworthPress.com>
© *2006 by The Haworth Press, Inc. All rights reserved.]*

KEYWORDS. Collection management, digital libraries, collaboration, collection boundaries

INTRODUCTION

The boundaries that define a discrete collection of intellectual or informational resources have never been precise or immutable. With the proliferation of born-digital and digitized analog materials, these boundaries are becoming even less well defined. This blurring of the boundaries is apparent in libraries and archives that support education and scholarship as well as those that support government information management mandates. Understanding digital collections and their unique management needs is paramount to successfully supporting persistent access to the resources within such a collection.

Questions to be considered include:

- How are the boundaries of digital collections to be defined?
- Who is responsible for developing and providing access to digital collections?
- What management strategies are most likely to be successful?

In the 1980s the concept of library collection development was placed into the broader discussions of collection management, focusing on the systematic, efficient, and economic stewardship of library resources.[1] Library collections have been developed and maintained through policies that articulate relatively well-defined priorities. These priorities vary according to the type of library and its objectives, the clientele, the extent and condition of materials already in a collection, and preferred format types (based on the ability of the library to support access to these formats.) With the promulgation of digital resources, collection development and management librarians have been encouraged to redefine their roles once again, this time as "knowledge managers."[2] In the case of academia, Clifford Lynch notes that libraries are moving from the role of "passive collections of knowledge to spaces that encourage active learning."[3]

The suggested shift in the role of librarians is strikingly similar to the shift in roles archivists have been advised to make in the digital environment. Archives have acted as passive receptacles of records worthy of accessioning after they have been created and are no longer actively used. Appraisal of these records (by North American standards) is usually based upon classical appraisal strategies that consider the evidential and informational value of records.[4] It is now generally accepted that appraisal of records must occur as close to the records' creation as possible to ensure that electronic records are properly managed over time, keeping their authenticity intact and keeping them accessible.[5]

Librarians and archivists in general share the goal of managing information for the purpose of supporting users' needs. Despite this commonality, fundamental differences in how the daily activities of each group are executed to support this goal have limited constructive collaborations.[6] The nature and proliferation of digital resources raises fundamental issues regarding the roles and activities of both professions. Supporting users' information needs in the current digital environment requires redefining the responsibilities of those responsible for executing traditional library collection development practices and archival appraisal strategies.

These issues must be addressed and agreed to across institutional and organizational lines and in consideration of the needs of known current, and as yet unknown future users of the digital resources. Developing and supporting the necessary technical and organizational infrastructure for long-term sustainability of digital collections will require intentional collaboration among information professionals. This article explores these issues in the context of both academic and state government entities, clarifying the need for a shift in roles for information professionals.

DIGITAL COLLECTION BOUNDARIES

Boundaries can define a parcel of land, an intellectual domain, the scope of responsibilities of a person's work, or a collection of digital images. Defining boundaries gives a sense of limit and context to places, people, things, and ideas. In the realm of information resources, librarians and archivists have played key roles in identifying and defining logical boundaries for collections as part of their responsibilities for collection management and archival appraisal and acquisition. But in the digital environment, identifying and expressing logical boundaries is not always straightforward. Determining the ownership and access rights as well as a discrete subject of a collection's functional or intellectual domain can be very difficult.

Expanding the Concept of Collection

Hur-Li Lee expands the concept of a collection to include the continuity and interconnectivity characteristics of information.[7] This concept is similar to the steps taken by an archivist during arrangement and description. The similarity indicates a potential point of synergy between these archival functions and this new suggested direction for library collection development and management. It is also generally accepted that the organic nature of records received and managed by archives have their primary significance in relation to activities rather than to particular subjects, representing a functional approach to description rather than a subject approach.[8] This type of information represents the context or "interconnectivity characteristics" of the information resource described by Lee. Context enriches information the way knowing the historic context for Shakespeare provides a deeper experience of his sonnets. Context is also an essential component of digital resources if the value of a collection is to be fully realized.

As more information resources are created and distributed digitally, this expanded archival concept of a collection may prove even more useful when assigning responsibilities for managing or describing a collection. For example, it will be easier to create search interfaces designed to customize result sets based upon user profiles or the historical origins of a resource if contextual information is maintained and available online alongside the actual information.

Librarians working with faculty in support of classroom instruction are secondary users of faculty course content. This arena is one in which librarians and archivists might work more closely together to help support the teaching needs of faculty. If the assumption is that faculty papers continue to contain course content and lesson plans and that these university resources will continue to be appraised, accessioned, described, and managed by archivists, then facilitating long-term management and appropriate access will require identification of crossover boundary areas and an explicit articulation of procedures for managing the materials. This may require a shift or sharing in responsibilities for collecting or accessioning.

State Government Digital Collection Boundaries

Another example of the complexity of digital resource boundaries can be seen when attempting to define the boundary of a digital collection for a state government agency. When collecting digital resources from agency Web sites, decisions must be made about how many levels of links to follow and include as part of the agency's Web content. The Preserving Electronic Publications (PEP)[9] project was funded to develop "a national model for monitoring changes made to electronically published state government documents on the Internet to ensure public access." The project findings note the difficulty in drawing distinct collection boundaries around records and publications in the digital environment.[10]

The lack of clarity defining collection boundaries of state agency Web sites is due in part to the nonstandard use of the Web by government agencies. With some Web sites, information is presented in a way that is similar to library serials. Each month a new report may be posted to a state government agency Web site, leaving old reports up, providing easy access to back issues. In other instances old content is not kept online for viewing once new content has been posted. Even new content is sometimes posted in a way that does not make clear the nature of the content. Because wide variations in strategies for posting content to the Web may exist between and even within state agencies, it is difficult to deploy simple Web crawling scripts to particular Web domains and expect to get predictable results. This means the boundaries of what is collected (and therefore the scope and extent of the collection) may vary from one month to the next.

The convenience of tools used to generate digital resources, such as desktop publishing tools and Web authoring tools, has created massive quantities of content, making it particularly difficult to apply clear collection development and appraisal strategies to Web content. It becomes increasingly difficult and not necessarily useful to attempt to identify the official publications of organizations when these materials are posted to agency Web sites. It is still more difficult to distinguish documentary evidence or historically significant records if there are no systematic controls in place that prescribe the management of official records and summary reports of data.

Does the unpredictable variation in collection boundaries of Web content matter? Since this variation creates the possibility for overlapping collections, or gaps in collections, it represents inefficient collection development efforts and introduces a factor of unreliability in the completeness of any given collection.

Academic Digital Collection Boundaries

In the traditional university setting the boundaries of a collection of faculty papers are determined in part by the faculty member, with the long-term management of these materials being assumed by the university archivist. Faculty papers are often rich with correspondence, working papers, student papers, course materials, and lesson plans. Until recently, outside the archives, universities have had little general interest in collecting resources of this nature and archivists have acquired them only through the passive process of accessioning faculty papers upon their retirement or after they are deceased.

The nature of faculty papers creates a sense of fuzzy boundaries, as some components of these resources may also be considered departmental records. Take the example of a faculty member who is also a department head. He or she will no doubt correspond with colleagues about research, with students about grades, and with support staff about administrative activities. This may demonstrate why university archives are often charged with collecting both faculty papers and administrative records. Within the context of correspondence that occurs primarily in a digital environment (e-mail), drawing boundaries and separating the collection to distinguish correspondence that is primarily about research and teaching versus administrative activities is nearly impossible, thereby making the distinction between administrative records and faculty papers even more obscure. Complicating the definitions of faculty papers are the self-publishing avenues of personal Web pages and blogs.[11] These materials risk being lost to the historical record if intentional effort is not expended to consider them for inclusion in some formalized collection.

Another difficulty in the academic arena arises with course materials and lesson plans. In the current digital era, these components of a faculty's work may no longer be stored in filing cabinets but instead reside on departmental or campus computers. Now that more courses are developed and delivered online using courseware applications,[12] some universities are finding an interest in collecting these materials to provide them for reuse in future courses and for general reference purposes. Decisions must be made regarding whether or not a separate boundary should be drawn to define a collection of reusable (digital) course content as compared to non-digital course content. Is it reasonable to assert that these resources are still part of an archival collection of faculty papers, regardless of their location or the department that may have routine stewardship responsibilities over them? Determining and articulating ownership of, and stewardship responsibilities for these materials is essential when defining the collection or collections to which they belong.

DIGITAL COLLECTION RESPONSIBILITIES

Another challenge when attempting to manage digital information resources lies in determining the lines of responsibility for collecting and managing materials. How are the roles of information professionals shifting, and if so, how does this affect the responsibilities for collecting and managing digital resources? The ubiquitous and ephemeral nature of digital resources and the dynamic technical infrastructures used to create and support them demands a careful re-evaluation of the responsibilities of information professionals in this environment.

Sharing Collection Responsibilities

Who should be responsible for digital collection development and management decisions? Within the context of any single institution or organization, particular responsibilities for digital resources will vary depending upon many factors. Fulfilling responsibilities for digital collection management will likely need a shared approach. In the case of libraries and archives a variety of digital resources may be collected for a variety of reasons. In some instances resources are collected to document significant historical events, which may be used in conjunction with teaching or conducting research. Since archivists often work with records managers, some digital resources may be collected to document actions taken in the course of executing business functions or reaching administrative decisions. The proliferation of digital resources provides an opportunity to share infrastructures and to understand better the mutable and reusable nature of information.

Shifting responsibilities will also require coordination with an organization's information technology staff, as well as the creators and primary users of these resources. Current practices used to create and collect digital resources are subject to change frequently, driven by a rapidly shifting technology landscape and sophisticated marketing techniques used to encourage quick adoption of new technologies. It is unlikely that this paradigm will be replaced by a more static one in the near future. This state of nearly constant change imposes unique challenges in the development of collection and management policies.

Grey Literature and Faculty Papers Collecting Responsibilities

At the University of Illinois at Urbana-Champaign efforts are now underway to establish an institutional repository. This initiative has been launched as a collaboration between the department of Campus Information Technologies and Education Services (CITES)[13] and the University Library.[14] The project is initially planning to focus on "… collecting scholarly output–and more specifically, the 'grey literature'–publications, reports and working papers that emanate from scholars and programs at the University."[15] Collecting these types of grey literature has traditionally been the responsibility of the University Archives, a department supported by the University Library. The publications and reports of university programs are gathered and kept as a series within a record group or subgroup representing the publishing unit. Working papers of scholars often have been part of a collection of "faculty papers" gathered and managed by the university archives. The Illinois Digital Scholarship Repository project is engaged in defining shared collection management responsibilities for digital resources that may belong to a collection split between formats (digital and analog) and between stewardship lines (University Archives, University Library, or CITES).

State Agency Publications Collection Responsibilities

Within state government it is not always clear where the lines of responsibility are drawn between the state libraries, archives, or other agencies indicating which one should execute what activities for the purpose of collecting state government records and publications that are posted on agency Web sites. If both the state archivist and the state librarian begin to collect digital resources that fall within their jurisdiction to collect, using commonly available "Web crawling" tools, it is plausible some records will be included in multiple collections. While multiple copies of resources may be considered a good practice for ensuring long-term availability,[16] without intentional coordination and ongoing communication there are no guarantees that the full scope and proper context for the materials will be captured.

It is possible that responsibilities for both collecting and managing digital resources are already being shared in some organizations. What may not be in place is a clear expression of these management responsibilities through policies and plans that can account for a dynamic technological environment. Whether addressing shared responsibilities within one organization or across institutional borders, participation from as many stakeholders as possible is also essential. Broad participation will reduce unnecessary duplication of effort and will help assure that responsibility for long-term stewardship of various collections of materials is effectively addressed. Defining management responsibilities must become an ongoing and shared activity, due to the continuing state of change imposed by the digital environment.

NDIIPP:
A MODEL FOR SHARED MANAGEMENT
OF DIGITAL COLLECTIONS

NDIIPP Background

The United States Congress launched the National Digital Infrastructure for Information Preservation Program (NDIIPP)[17] in 2000 with a financial commitment of $99.8 million. This program authorized the Library of Congress to develop an overall strategy for collaborating with a multitude of stakeholders having responsibilities for collecting and maintaining digital materials. This collaboration includes developing policies, protocols, and sustainable strategies for long-term preservation of selected digital materials. The mission statement of NDIIPP reads: "Develop a national strategy to collect, archive, and preserve the burgeoning amounts of digital content, especially materials that are created only in digital formats, for current and future generations."[18]

The notion of a national strategy suggests collection management decisions will be made across institutional borders, taking into consideration the perspectives of multiple stakeholders. This will require extraordinary efforts to sustain functioning partnerships. As such, engaging the creators of digital resources in conversations regarding the role they inherently play in the success of such a national strategy will be essential.

Testing Archival Principles with Web Crawling Techniques

In September 2004, eight awards under NDIIPP were announced.[19] One award was given to the University of Illinois at Urbana-Champaign (UIUC), in partnership with the Online Computer Library Center (OCLC), the Arizona State Library and Archives, the Connecticut State

Library, the Illinois State Library, the North Carolina State Library, the Wisconsin State Library, the Tufts University Perseus Project, and the Michigan State University Library.

One of the four UIUC project goals focuses on finding manageable ways to capture and provide long-term access to Web site content that represents state government reports and publications. The overlap of librarian, archivist, and IT personnel responsibilities is being examined within the context of this goal. An obvious challenge of this goal is the sheer volume of material posted to the Web by state agencies. Finding and classifying all state government reports and publications by sifting through this volume is impossible with human effort alone. To address the challenge, software tools are being developed to "crawl" state agency Web sites to aid state librarians charged with the responsibility collecting these resources. Development of these software tools has been influenced by a Web crawling model based on archival concepts.[20] This model stems from the observation that Web sites are often organized similarly to archival collections, following the principle of original order.[21] Original order assumes that the order in which the document creator or owner originally put materials may have had some functional purpose, which if preserved, can be meaningful to future users of those materials. The model assumes that content posted on Web sites has more often than not also been stored in some intentional order, represented by the directory structure of the file system into which the content is aggregated. Based on this assumption, the materials automatically harvested from state government Web sites will be assumed to reflect their original order. As such, they will automatically be given classification terms that were pre-assigned to various levels within the directory structure, similarly to how archival folders in the analog environment inherit the classifications of the series, subgroups and groups to which they belong. While not specifically noted as a project outcome, project participants are interested in assessing the validity of the assumptions made by this model as well the utility of tools built to accommodate these assumptions. Feedback will be sought from state library project participants and materials collected by the tools, and the classifications they have inherited, will be examined.

CONCLUSION

Scholars as well as the general public are turning to online digital resources at an ever-increasing rate with the expectation that their information needs will be satisfied.[22] If these expectations are to be met, reliable digital information must be made readily available. To meet these expectations the library and archives communities, in tandem with information technologists, computer scientists, and digital resource creators, must cooperate on many levels. Flexibly defining digital collection boundaries and building new models for sharing collection management responsibilities are key areas in which information professionals would benefit by intentional collaboration. Digital collection boundaries that are flexible will also require a shifting of collection management responsibilities to more effectively present and preserve these resources.

Coordinating efforts between librarians and archivists is not a novel concept, nor has it always been well received.[23] Nonetheless, librarians and archivists are key stakeholders in the development of digital repositories being designed to support scholarly research, teaching, and historical documentation, and without coordination the potential of these initiatives will not be fully realized. Working together and working broadly across departmental and institutional borders is necessary to develop and drive the strategies and partnerships that will enhance digital collection management and ensure persistent access.

Opportunities to test theories and create partnerships are underway through ongoing initiatives such as NDIIPP, expressly created in response to the challenges of digital resource preservation. Among other things, NDIIPP is addressing the challenge of determining the appropriate organization or organizational level at which digital collection management decisions should be made. This in turn will influence how agreed-upon standard partnerships should be designed for sharing responsibilities across departments, organizations, jurisdictions, and even across international borders. These and many other ongoing efforts hold the promise of providing a sustainable backdrop for the future information landscape.

NOTES

1. Joseph J. Branin, "Collection Management and Development: Issues in an Electronic Era," Introduction, *Fighting Back Once Again: Collection Management to Knowledge Management* (Chicago, IL: Advanced Collection Management and Development Institute, 1993), xii.

2. Ibid., xiv.

3. Clifford Lynch, "Future of Libraries: Six Dimensions on How Libraries, Librarians, and Library Patrons Will Adapt to Changing Times: The New Dimension of Learning Spaces," available online at: http://www.ciconline.org/NR/rdonlyres/

e3tajgvi7abumq4zkmo6suje6ycarvh4ztnjlu2wetf3eb4rocmvefveqmi5qofoogibcj7fzb qixt5jdrwwfrbljkb/W04-futurelibraries.pdf. Accessed 2005-11-28.

4. T. R. Schellenberg, *Modern Archives* (Chicago, IL: The University of Chicago Press, 1956), 139.

5. Barbara Craig, *Archival Appraisal: Theory and Practice* (Morlenbach, Germany: Strauss Offsetdruck, 2004), 74-79.

6. William J. Maher "Improving Library-Archives Relations: User Centered Solutions to a Sibling Rivalry," *Journal of Academic Librarianship*, 15 (1990), 356.

7. Hur-Li Lee, "What is a Collection?" *Journal of the American Society for Information Science*, 51, no. 12 (October 2000), 1111.

8. T. R. Schellenberg, *The Management of Archives* (New York, NY: Columbia University Press, 1965), 120.

9. More information about the Preserving Electronic Publications (PEP) project is available online at: http://www.cyberdriveillinois.com//departments/library/who_we_are/pep.html.

10. Ibid.

11. A definition of blogs is available at: http://www.matisse.net/files/glossary.html#B. Accessed 2005-11-28.

12. Examples of currently popular courseware applications include WebCT (http://www.webct.com/), Blackboard (http://www.blackboard.com/) and the Sakai Project, a community source software development effort being led by a consortium of higher education institutions with funding from the Mellon Foundation (http://www.sakaiproject.org/). All URLs accessed 2005-11-30.

13. Information about the University of Illinois at Urbana-Champaign Campus Information Technologies and Educational Services is available online at: http://www.cites.uiuc.edu/. Accessed 2005-11-28.

14. Information about the University of Illinois at Urbana-Champaign Library is available online at: http://www.library.uiuc.edu/. Accessed 2005-11-30.

15. Information about the University of Illinois at Urbana-Champaign Illinois Digital Scholarship Repository is available online at: http://www.cites.uiuc.edu/. Accessed 2005-11-28.

16. "...let us save what remains: not by vaults and locks which fence them from the public eye and use in consigning them to the waste of time, but by such a multiplication of copies, as shall place them beyond the reach of accident." Thomas Jefferson to Ebenezer Hazard (Philadelphia), 1791 February 18. In *Thomas Jefferson: Writings: Autobiography, Notes on the State of Virginia, Public and Private Papers, Addresses, Letters*; ed., Merrill D. Peterson (New York: Library of America, 1984), 973.

17. Further information about the National Digital Infrastructure for Information Preservation Program (NDIIPP) is available at: http://www.digitalpreservation.gov/. Accessed 2005-11-28.

18. NDIIPP's mission is discussed in greater detail at: http://www.digitalpreservation.gov/index.php?nav=1&subnav=1. Accessed 2005-11-28.

19. The initial NDIIPP announcement is available at: http://www.digitalpreservation.gov/about/pr_093004.html. Accessed 2005-11-28.

20. Richard Pearce-Moses and Joanne Kaczmarek, "An Arizona Model for Preservation and Access of Web Documents," in *Documents to the People, Newsletter of the Government Documents Roundtable*, 33, no. 1 (Spring 2005), 17-24.

21. A definition of 'original order' is supplied by University of Illinois at Urbana-Champaign Archives online at: http://web.library.uiuc.edu/ahx/define.htm. Accessed 2005-11-28.

22. Deborah Fallows, *Search Engine Users: Internet Searchers are Confident, Satisfied, and Trusting–But They are Also Unaware and Naïve* (Washington, DC: Pew Internet & American Life Project, 2005 January 23), available at: http://www.pewinternet.org/pdfs/PIP_Searchengine_users.pdf. Accessed 2005-11-28.

23. Robert L. Brubaker, *Archive-Library Relations*; ed., Robert L. Clark, Jr. (New York, NY: R.R. Bowker Company, 1976), 181-191.

doi:10.1300/J201v04n01_11

The Archivists' Toolkit:
Another Step Toward Streamlined
Archival Processing

Bradley D. Westbrook
Lee Mandell
Kelcy Shepherd
Brian Stevens
Jason Varghese

Bradley D. Westbrook, MA, MLS, is Metadata Librarian and Digital Archivist, University of California, San Diego Libraries. He can be reached at 17462 Matinal Rd., #4731, San Diego, CA 92127 (E-mail: bdwestbrook@ucsd.edu).

Lee Mandell is Programmer and Member of the New York University Digital library Development Team, 1 Fitchburg Street, B153, Somerville, MA 02143 (E-mail: lee@nyu.edu).

Kelcy Shepherd, MLIS, is Five College Project Archivist, W.E.B. DuBois Library, University of Massachusetts at Amherst, Greenfield, MA 01301 (E-mail: kshepher@library.umass.edu).

Brian Stevens, MLS, is Project Archivist, University Archives, New York University, 70 Washington Square South, New York, NY 10012 (E-mail: brian.stevens@nyu.edu).

Jason Varghese is Programmer/Analyst, New York University Digital Library Development Team and is currently pursuing his MBA. He can be reached at Digital Library Team, New York University, 70 Washington Square South, New York, NY 10012 (E-mail: jason.varghese@nyu.edu).

The authors would like to thank the Andrew W. Mellon Foundation and their university library administrators for their continuing support of the Archivists' Toolkit project and the persistent assistance of Robin Chandler and William Landis in preparing this article for publication. They owe thanks also to Arwen Hutt (UCSD) for her astute editing of the article.

[Haworth co-indexing entry note]: "The Archivists' Toolkit: Another Step Toward Streamlined Archival Processing." Westbrook, Bradley D. et al. Co-published simultaneously in *Journal of Archival Organization* (The Haworth Information Press, an imprint of The Haworth Press, Inc.) Vol. 4, No.1/2, 2006, pp. 229-253; and: *Archives and the Digital Library* (ed: William E. Landis, and Robin L. Chandler) The Haworth Information Press, an imprint of The Haworth Press, Inc., 2006, pp. 229-253. Single or multiple copies of this article are available for a fee from The Haworth Document Delivery Service [1-800-HAWORTH, 9:00 a.m. - 5:00 p.m. (EST). E-mail address: docdelivery@haworthpress.com].

Available online at http://jao.haworthpress.com
© 2006 by The Haworth Press, Inc. All rights reserved.
doi:10.1300/J201v04n01_12

229

SUMMARY. The Archivists' Toolkit is a software application currently in development and designed to support the creation and management of archival information. This article summarizes the development of the application, including some of the problems the application is designed to resolve. Primary emphasis is placed on describing the application's functional requirements and architecture, as well as options for its sustainability. doi:10.1300/J201v04n01_12 *[Article copies available for a fee from The Haworth Document Delivery Service: 1-800-HAWORTH. E-mail address: <docdelivery@haworthpress.com> Website: <http://www. HaworthPress.com> © 2006 by The Haworth Press, Inc. All rights reserved.]*

KEYWORDS. Archivists' Toolkit, archival information, archival information system, archival life cycle, archival workflow, database applications, processing efficiencies, open source software, software development, software specification, archival standards, use case methodology

INTRODUCTION

The Archivists' Toolkit (AT) will be an open source system for managing archival data in a single integrated software application. The objective of the Archivists' Toolkit project is to help streamline and improve efficiency of archival processing and to promote the standardization of archival information. This article discusses the need for the Toolkit, project staffing and methodology, features and application of the application, and possibilities for future development.

The Archivists' Toolkit project is a multiyear effort, which has just now entered its second year.[1] Consequently, the ensuing project description is primarily limited to the first year of the project, including accounts of some events leading up to and informing the project.

THE PROBLEM CONTEXT

The need for an integrated system to manage archival information has been recognized for decades. RLG began a project to develop an Archives and Museums Information System (AMIS) in 1988, hoping to assist archivists and museum professionals in managing their collections and daily operations. As envisioned, AMIS would integrate descriptive information, conservation histories, member and researcher data, exhibit information, and event schedules into a single system.[2] Due to lack of funding, the project ended in 1993 before a functional system could be developed. The need for an integrated system to manage archival information has only intensified as descriptive standards and technologies have evolved. In a large measure, the Archivists' Toolkit is a response to the advent of digital technologies and specifically to the establishment of the Encoded Archival Description (EAD)[3] standard and the subsequent proliferation of digital strategies and tools for producing EAD-compliant finding aids.

Twenty years ago the process of archival description was much simpler than it has become at the beginning of the digital era. Typically, archivists created inventories or finding aids for archival collections using a word processor or, in some cases, a typewriter. Administrative information–such as deeds of gift, accession records and action logs–was kept as printed forms in collection control files. Some repositories, those with sufficient staff expertise and access to an online bibliographic utility, created collection-level Machine-Readable Cataloging (MARC)[4] records for their archival holdings.

Beginning around 1990 and continuing over the course of the decade, the complexity of the descriptive practices increased dramatically as archivists began to experiment with the Internet as a tool for publicizing their collections to the research community. Archivists first utilized Gopher[5] and Wide Area Information Service (WAIS)[6] protocols to deliver American Standard Code for Information Interchange (ASCII)[7] versions of collection finding aids but quickly migrated to HTML-encoded finding aids once that encoding scheme was introduced in 1993. HTML served to improve the online presentation of finding aids; however, its limitations for facilitating searching and navigating online finding aids quickly became apparent to archivists. Furthermore, HTML did not help to promote consistent application of encoded data elements within or across repositories. Dissatisfaction with these drawbacks led to the development of a Standard Generalized Markup Language Document Type Definition (SGML DTD)[8] specifically for encoding archival collection descriptions and facilitating their publication online. This DTD, known as Encoded Archival Description (EAD), allows archivists to represent the hierarchical structure inherent in archival collections in an encoded format and then use this encoding for searching and navigating through a finding aid or a group of finding aids. EAD also makes possible the kind of data encoding standardization that access systems require to produce consistent and predictable results. The success of EAD quickly led to the construction of union databases of EAD-encoded finding aids, of which the Online Archive of California

(OAC) was the first. Similar statewide efforts have been implemented in New Mexico, Texas, Virginia, and North Carolina, and the Pacific Northwest states, not to mention RLG's Archive Grid, and several international projects.[9]

Undoubtedly, this development is highly laudable for it is a great benefit to the general research community. It has sparked the development of best practice guidelines for EAD encoding and a wide range of tools, of differing degrees of automation, for producing encoded finding aids. Several basic characteristics of these tools are noteworthy. First they are often under-utilized. A database, for example, may be used only to encode finding aids but not to support other archival tasks, such as accessioning of collections, tracking locations and sources of the materials, or even searching the finding aids. Second, the tools typically are not integrated. As in the previous print environment, each archival function or task typically has its own tool. There is a database for accessions, another database for collecting information about donors, a text document for listing the locations of collections, and so on. As a consequence, some data expressions, most obviously a resource title or identifier, need to be rekeyed several times and stored in different places. Updating the data often requires updating it at each unique storage point. Finally, the tools are highly localized and not designed in a manner that promotes standardization and interoperability beyond a repository's immediate institutional boundaries and needs.

The deployment of numerous, single-purpose tools increases the cost of archival processing in several ways. The workflow is inefficient because the same data has to be reentered at various times during the description process. Training costs are increased, as staff has to be knowledgeable about using each distinct tool. The breadth of skills and training required for proficiency with all the tools utilized in the descriptive process can prohibit assigning some descriptive work to lower staff levels. The tools have to be managed collectively and kept up to date.

There are hidden costs as well. For example, one consequence of encoding tools that do not sufficiently promote or enforce standardization is inconsistent data, and thus, union databases that cannot be searched or navigated at fine levels of granularity. As a result, the promise, or at least one of the promises, of the encoding is not realized. Additionally, increased costs for descriptive work absorb valuable resources from an archive's operational budget (rarely large), resources that could be used for other archival functions such as collection development, fundraising, and user services.

The development of a generally deployable digital application, such as the Archivists' Toolkit, to support archival processing work could serve to lower processing costs dramatically, to promote standardization of archival information, and to foster development of more robust union databases of archival information. Such an application could be designed to "softly force" adoption of and adherence to extant content standards, thereby assuring interoperability of finding aids and other standardized outputs produced from the application. The application could be constructed so that encoding standards are applied automatically in the production of outputs such as EAD encoded finding aids and Metadata Encoding and Transmission Standard (METS)[10] digital objects, thereby significantly reducing the need for and cost of training to utilize common standards. In addition, the application could be built to automate routines for managing archival information, thereby streamlining a repository's processing work. But most importantly, an application designed according to the objectives suggested here and described more fully below will lead to the inclusion of more compatible data streams into union databases and to more efficient and productive use of the those union databases. In short, such an application would foster and support good research, the basic mission for most archival repositories.

THE PROJECT

Funded by The Andrew W. Mellon Foundation, The Archivists' Toolkit is a multiyear, multi-institutional project to design and build a database application to support the processing and description of archival resources. Institutions participating in the project are the Five Colleges, Inc. (FC; comprising Amherst College, Hampshire College, Mount Holyoke College, Smith College, and the University of Massachusetts at Amherst), New York University (NYU), and the University of California, San Diego (UCSD). At present, the project includes five team members: Bradley Westbrook, Project Manager (UCSD); Lee Mandell, Design Team Manager (NYU); Jason Varghese, Programmer (NYU); Kelcy Shepherd, Archives Analyst (FC), and Brian Stevens, Archives Analyst (NYU). Carol Mandel, Dean of Libraries at NYU, and Brian Schottlaender, UCSD University Librarian, are co-Principal Investigators for the project. David Ackerman (NYU) and Luc Declerck (UCSD) provide additional administrative support for the project. The project anticipates hiring two short-term consultants, one for interface design and the other for usability testing, during the second part of the project.

Project Team members are distributed across several sub-teams. The Specification Team is comprised of the Project Manager and the two Archives Analysts, and it serves to elicit functional requirements from the project partners (see below) and express them as an application specification. The Design Team, consisting of the Design Team Manager and the Programmer, are responsible for transforming the application specification into a working application. The Documentation Team is charged with composing the application's documentation, which will include an installation guide, a user manual, in-context help and error messages, and stylesheets for rendering some of the outputs produced by the AT. The Testing Team will oversee functional testing and, in collaboration with project partners, usability testing of the completed application. Finally, the Senior Project Oversight Team, composed of the co-Principal Investigators, the NYU and UCSD Administrators, and the Project and Design Team Managers, is responsible for developing a plan for sustaining and developing the application after its initial release.

Seventeen archival repositories have agreed to assist the Project Team with formulating the functional requirements for the AT and, when the prototype is available, with testing the usability of the application's interface. These project partners were selected primarily on the basis of two factors: (1) the repository's proximity to the project sites and (2) the repository's ability to contribute to the project a different institutional perspective (e.g., academic archive versus museum archive) or archival data to be used in testing the application. The seventeen partners are:

Five Colleges, Inc.

- Amherst College Archives and Special Collections (Daria D'Arienzo, Peter Nelson)
- Hampshire College Archives (Susan Dayall)
- Mount Holyoke College Archives and Special Collections (Jennifer Gunter King)
- Smith College Archives (Nanci Young)
- Sophia Smith Collection, Smith College (Sherrill Redmon, Margaret Jessup)
- Special Collections and University Archives, University of Massachusetts Amherst, (Robert Cox, Danielle Kovacs)

Participating New England Area Archives

- The Edmund S. Muskie Archives and Special Collections Library, Bates College (Katherine Stefko)

New York University

- Fales Library, NYU (Ann Butler)
- NYU University Archives (Nancy Cricco)
- Tamiment Library, NYU (Mike Nash)

Participating New York City Archives

- The American Museum of Natural History (Barbara Mathé, Kristen Mable)
- The Brooklyn Museum of Art (Laura Peimer)
- Carnegie Hall (Kathleen Sabogal)
- The Center for Jewish History (Bob Sink, Stan Pesja)
- Manhattan College (Amy Surak)

University of California, San Diego

- Mandeville Special Collections Library (Steven Coy)
- Scripps Institution of Oceanography Archives (Deborah Day)

An Advisory Board composed of six expert archivists, archival educators, and digital library administrators serves the Project Team by providing guidance on the scope of the AT's initial development phase, appropriateness of the proposed functional requirements, overall application design, and marketing. The AT Advisory Board members are:

- Robin Chandler, California Digital Library
- Michael Fox, Minnesota Historical Society
- Merrilee Proffitt, Research Libraries Group
- Richard V. Szary, Yale University
- Guenter Waibel, Research Libraries Group
- Beth Yakel, University of Michigan

It should be noted that to a very large degree the objectives, high-level design, and initial scope for the AT application were established at two meetings sponsored by the Digital Library Federation (DLF) that took place prior to the start of the AT project. The outcomes of these meetings substantially informed the project proposal submitted to The Mellon Foundation. The first meeting took place in La Jolla at the University of California, San Diego on February 4-5, 2002 and was attended by twenty-one archivists and information technologists. The second meeting took place in South Hadley, Massachusetts, at Mount Holyoke College on

November 4-6, 2002, and was attended by ten archivists who had been present at the La Jolla meeting.[11]

THE APPLICATION OVERVIEW

Efforts during a little more than the first year of the project were devoted to three primary endeavors. First, the Project Team was assembled and equipped. Although the Specification Team was put in place at the start of the project, efforts to hire the Design Team members were delayed until the spring of 2005, to coincide with the scheduled completion of the first draft of the application specification. The second area of work involved eliciting functional requirements for the application from the AT project partners. The process for doing this relied on use case methodology.[12] Use cases describe the steps required to complete a certain task, such as recording an accession or locating an archival resource. The Specification Team constructed a straw-man use case for each of the application's prospective functional areas, which was then submitted to the partners, who were invited to revise the straw-man use case, either adding functional requirements, deleting them, or modifying their relationships. The Specification Team then reviewed the modifications proposed by the partners and synthesized them into a master use case for each functional area. Taking the completed use cases and transforming them into a formal software specification was the third major accomplishment of the project's first year. The software specification, written in compliance with *IEEE Recommended Practice for Software Requirements Specification, IEEE Std.830-1998*,[13] was released for public review on August 12, 2005. Subsequent to the specification's release, members of the AT Project Team presented it at the 2005 Society of American Archivists (SAA) annual meeting,[14] the 2005 New England Archivists fall meeting, the 2005 Museum Computer Network conference, and to the AT Advisory Board, the California Digital Library, and the partner repositories. These presentations resulted in several modifications being accepted for the AT specification, which is now in the process of being revised. The remainder of this article comprises a summary description of the AT application as it stands at the beginning of the design process.[15]

The Archivists' Toolkit is to be an open source database application that will support description of archival materials, and, moreover, will increase archival processing efficiency, lower the costs of archival description in several ways, and promote standardization for description of archival resources (see Figure 1). The application will:

- Satisfy and integrate key functions in the archival descriptive cycle, including accessioning, registering source information for archival resources, creating and applying name and topical headings to resources, managing resource locations and producing finding aids, collection guides, METS digital objects, and various administrative reports.
- Allow archival repositories to ingest extant metadata about collections in the form of EAD finding aids, MARC records, and electronic accession information into a centralized, integrated database, and store and process it along with newly created information about digital assets, accessions, and sources.

FIGURE 1. Archivists' Toolkit Context Diagram, which represents the various actors or individuals who will interact directly or indirectly with the data stored in the application. Note that these actors sometimes interact with one another independent of the application, but in a manner that might influence how the application is used.

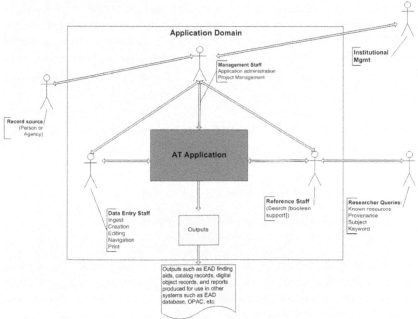

- Be deployable in a range of archival repositories from historical societies, college archives, museum archives, commercial archives, and other archives specializing in non-textual materials (sound or video archives, for example) on the one hand, and, on the other, in archives with a single staff member or in multirepository consortia such as the Five Colleges, Inc., or the Online Archive of California.

The ultimate objective of the AT is to reduce the costs of archival processing by facilitating more efficient workflows and quicker throughput of archival information,[16] by incorporating key archival functions into an integrated application environment. This will make it possible for data about archival materials to be more easily repurposed and output in different formats to support different needs.

In addition, by adhering to archival content standards, the AT will contribute to the standardization of archival information. Indeed, to promote its acceptance, usability, and development, the AT design is grounded in the standards essential to the creation and communication of archival information. The application is to be open source and modular. An open source design will facilitate collaboration, and modularity will allow repositories to use just the functional areas they require to support their local work, as well as define discrete sub-parts of the application where developers might target their contributions. The interfaces and outputs of the application will be customizable, leaving repositories to configure the application to conform to their workflows and staffing structures, rather than forcing them to adjust work practices to fit the design of an application.

Reducing archival processing costs and increasing data standardization will benefit researchers by allowing archival materials to be described more quickly, and by promoting standardized access tools for archives such as EAD finding aids and METS records.

GENERAL FEATURES OF THE APPLICATION

In brief, the AT is designed to support essential functions of the life cycle of archival materials, to promote community descriptive standards, to allow for increased efficiency in archival processing, and to be customizable to local work settings. The following page has a list of the application's high-level design objectives and attributes:

Integrated

- To streamline processing and support efficient retrieval of information, the application will be based on the entire life cycle of archival materials, beginning with initial contacts with the sources of materials and encompassing all work carried out on materials once they are received in a repository. This work includes accessioning, arrangement and description for archival resources, items, and digital objects; application of name and topical headings for creators and subjects; registration of sources; and location management.

Diverse Implementations

- The AT is being designed to be installed as a desktop application used by one archival worker or as a networked application used by multiple archival workers. The design goal is to support up to twenty-five simultaneous users. Two or more institutions using the same AT implementation will be able to share name and subject records.

Modular and Customizable

- Repositories will not be required to use all of the functional areas available in the first release of the Archivists' Toolkit. A repository will be able to use the application for creating and storing descriptions for processed archival resources and not use it for tracking accessions, managing locations, or recording source information, as needed by the repository. In addition, the application will allow repositories to modify the data entry templates, including the presentation of the template, the elements included on the template, and the arrangement or sequence of the elements. Reports and outputs will be capable of being modified, allowing repositories to add their own branding, as well as alter the amount and arrangement of information in a given report.

Intuitive User Interface

- Drawing on usability expertise, the Project Team will design an easy to use interface for the application. Use of the application should require minimal training at most staff levels, and it must be constructed to be usable by the lowest levels of staff.

Standardized and Output Neutral

- Data elements are designed to promote compliance with *Describing Archives: A Content Standard (DACS)*.[17] Data will be stored in an output neutral fashion consistent with the AT database schema. However, processes are to be formulated that will allow for users to produce outputs compliant with EAD, Encoded Archival Context (EAC),[18] METS, and other community data format standards. A minimal amount of data input is required to complete any particular task, such as accessioning a collection, and to assure that outputs are compliant with data format standards.

Data Consistency

- Users will be able to impose additional constraints on data input, for instance, restricting the application of names or subjects to the repository's archival resources as a whole or to certain subcategories or processing projects within a repository's holdings.

ARCHITECTURE

The Archivists' Toolkit application will be developed as an open source project and released in the second half of 2006 under an Open Source Initiative Certified License. Building the application as an open source application will make it possible to offer the application freely to the archival community and to evade costs and many of the restrictions present with proprietary software.

The AT project will be accessible through SourceForge[19] during the summer of 2006. At the time of that release, the programming community will be invited to contribute to the project. The overall hope is that a community of programmers interested in open source applications, archival information systems, or MySQL,[20] will form around the application and help to further its development. The Design Team will draw on the results of several open source software projects in building the Archivists' Toolkit. Two in particular pertain to the relational database back end of the AT application. One is MySQL, a robust database management application. Over the past few years, MySQL has become the most popular open source database application, and, through the efforts and contributions of a large developer community, the MySQL software has matured to a level satisfying enterprise database needs.

The other open source software project is Hibernate.[21] Hibernate is a persistence layer situated between the database and Java objects. The layer makes a group of application program interfaces (APIs) available that provide object/relational mapping between the database and Java objects. It also provides a query service that is independent of individual dialects of SQL (see Figure 2). This approach offers several advantages, one being that it enables the AT database to be more easily generated, thereby accelerating the design process. Moreover, Hibernate makes it much easier to replace the MySQL database with another SQL database application such as DB2, PostgreSQL, Oracle, Sybase, Microsoft SQL Server, Informix, or Ingres.[22] For instance, if a repository that is planning to implement the AT is already a well-skilled and licensed Oracle shop, then that repository could replace the MySQL database shipped with the AT application with an Oracle database.

In regard to the design process itself, Hibernate allows the AT Design Team to sidestep some of the problems deriving from the inherent mismatch between the relational database model and the object oriented model of Java and having to do with issues of granularity, identity, and association. Technically, this mismatch is referred to as the Object-Relational Impedance Mismatch.[23] There are four basic options for solving this incompatibility. One is to abandon the object-oriented features of Java and make the design look like a relational database. The second is to use an object-oriented database in place of a relational database. Third, and at the cost of substantially more effort, is to hand code the mapping between the relational database and the Java design. The last option is to write a unique, dynamic persistence layer between the relational database and the Java. None of these strategies are optimal, and exercising either of the last two would greatly lengthen the time required for the design process. Fortunately,

FIGURE 2. Archivists' Toolkit Layered Architecture

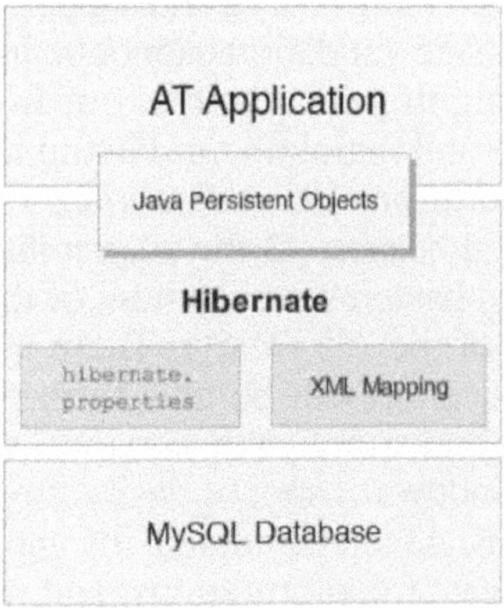

Hibernate, although a generic application, is a robust enough persistence layer that can be easily adapted to the AT project and resolve the tension between the application's back and front ends.

A relational database approach was chosen over other database technologies such as object-oriented and native XML databases[24] for two main reasons. First, relational database technology is quite mature, with a large number of excellent open source and commercial options. Many of these, such as Oracle and MySQL to name two, are enterprise-capable software and thus able to meet the maximum expectations for the Archivists' Toolkit application. Surveys of the partner repositories, as well as of the Online Archive of California EAD finding aid database, revealed that the number of described archival resources per repository ranges from 21 to 1,200. Exactly how many database records a given archival resource description would require is anybody's guess at this point. The AT Software Specification Team projects that if the AT application were implemented in a consortial setting, it might have to manage several million records and serve as many as fifty simultaneous users. But as the team well understands, those figures represent an extreme demand that will seldom, if ever, be placed on the application. Second, and almost as important, most information technology departments, especially those associated with archival repositories, are better equipped with relational database expertise than they are for working with object-oriented or XML databases. Because of this large number of relational database options and pool of skills, there are many existing open source projects and tools, such as the Hibernate application, that may provide shortcuts for building the AT.

The front end of the AT will be built with Java and will be a desktop client. Using a desktop client instead of a browser-based interface will yield a more functional user interface that can take advantage of Java's extensive Swing libraries.[25] Features such as drag and drop; tightly integrated, multiple windows; and client-side validation cannot be implemented in a Web-based system without significant quantities of JavaScript.[26] JavaScript can be difficult to write and maintain, and using it can result in browser incompatibilities. In addition, like the choice for relational database strategy, Java was chosen because of the availability of good open source tools, the opportunity to hasten development of the application, and the predominant expertise of the AT Design Team members.

Overall, the AT application will be able to run on Apple Mac OS X, Microsoft Windows 98 and subsequent versions, and Linux. Earlier versions of Mac OS and Windows cannot be easily supported due to poor Java support for those versions. As already noted, the application will be capable of implementation in several configurations, and it will ship with default interfaces for system/project administration, data entry, and searching. It is expected that repositories will be able to install and run the application with great ease. One requirement for installing the application will be for repositories to complete a repository record, which will store basic identifying information that serves to distinguish one repository's records from another, as well as to support data elements in EAD and METS headers.[27] Repositories will be able to restrict or constrain use of the application by requiring users to submit userIDs and passwords.

FUNCTIONAL AREAS

As mentioned earlier, the core functions that will be supported in the first release of the Archivists' Toolkit are accessioning and deaccessioning, description for archival resources and digital objects (including application of name and subject headings), and location tracking. These core functions represent the primary functional areas of the application, and they are illustrated and described in Figure 3.[28] The AT application includes an additional functional area, which is for managing the application and defining projects. The descriptions below reflect a few of the more salient features present in each functional area. A fuller description of each functional area–complete with tasks lists, data requirements, flow diagrams, and element definitions–is available in the software specification.

1. Application and Project Management

The application and project management functional area supports administration of the application and definition of projects. Application administration requires completion of a repository record in support of several outputs such as EAD, EAC, and METS, and it allows for establishing procedures and levels of use for accessing the application. It will also require recording the formula a repository uses for its accession numbers and resource identifiers. The administration function will also track the creation and last modification of each record in the AT.

Project management provides the means for customizing the application to reflect project parameters. These project parameters can be set at the level of the repository, a group of archival resources (for instance, to distinguish the university archives from the papers of persons), or at the level of the individual archival resource. Projects can be parameterized

FIGURE 3. Archivists' Toolkit Application Diagram illustrating the relationships among the Toolkit's functional modules and interfaces

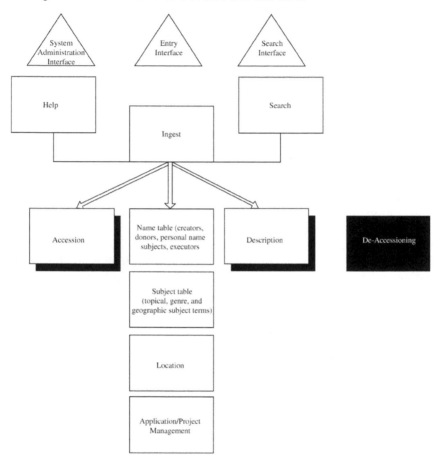

at two places in the AT application: at the data entry templates and at the outputs. For the data entry templates, repositories will be able to alter the elements that appear on the template, change the sequence and labels of elements, restrict the names and subjects that can be applied to a resource or set of resources, and change the overall presentation of the template. For outputs, a repository will be able to add institutional branding to reports and modify the kind and arrangement of data in some of the administrative reports. Repositories will not be permitted to alter the default database structure, however.

2. Ingest

To adhere to the goal of integrating systems and archival information, the AT will support ingest of legacy data in the form of EAD finding aids (version 2002), MARC XML[29] records, and either XML or delimited accession data. MARC XML records will be ingested when there is not a corresponding EAD and, when there is a corresponding EAD, as a source for harvesting name and subject access terms not present in the EAD. The name and subject access terms will be stored in the AT as name and subject records and linked to the corresponding archival resource description. Further, only MARC XML records for the archival resource, be it an item or a collection, will be ingested. It will not be possible to ingest a MARC record marked as a linked or child record.

3. Accessioning

The application will provide for the creation and editing of accession records. At its minimum, the accession record represents the accession transaction. But additional data elements are provided for basic collection management information such as a preliminary description of the resource and its condition, whether intellectual rights have been transferred or if restrictions constrain use of the resource, and whether acquisition agreements have been acquired and acknowledgment letters sent.

4. Deaccessioning

The application will also support tracking the removal of materials from accessions and from resources for those instances when accessions from different sources are compiled into a unified resource. Repositories will be able to record what materials were removed, how much was removed, why it was removed, what was done with the removed materials, and if the source of the materials was notified.

5. Description

The description functional area constitutes the largest part of the application. This functional area complies with *General International Standard Archival Description (ISAD(G))*[30] and *DACS* and will support the single and multilevel description(s) of archival resources (EAD hierarchical model) and of digital objects (generic parent-sibling-child hierarchical model) drawn from those resources. Repository staff will be able to import and, if necessary, edit information from accession records. The application will also provide twenty-seven descriptive notes, each of which can be applied once to every component level. In addition, it will be possible to describe multiple manifestations of an information object at the same component level. Thus, an original document, a microfilm version, and a digital image version can all be described at the same component level. For digital versions, it will be possible to record or extract, using a metadata extraction tool such as JHOVE,[31] technical metadata required to support preservation of technical objects.

A particular difficulty of the description functional area confronting the Design Team is to construct displays that represent the physical arrangement of a resource on the one hand and the resource's intellectual arrangement on the other. Data entry staff will then be able to toggle between the two displays, using either display to locate a record within the arrangement or using drag and drop functions associated with each display to modify the arrangement.

There are several functions that the AT will definitely not support in its first release. One is to maintain extensive technical metadata for audio and video formats, since technical metadata schemas for those formats have not yet been standardized. Another is to permit creation of component records, either for archival resources or for digital objects, without first creating a top-level resource record. All records in the description functional area must descend from or resolve to a top-level resource record that represents an archival resource, be it an item or a collection. Last, the application will not include functionality for managing, searching, and presenting the descriptive outputs it produces, such as EAD, MARC, or METS. As illustrated in Figure 1, these fall outside the application's domain and are to be supported by additional software applications.

6. Names

Name records in the AT are based on the *International Standard Archival Authority Record for Corporate Bodies, Persons, and Families (ISAAR (CPF))*[32] and are devised to facilitate the output of EAC-compliant name authority records. Repositories will be able to create name records for persons, families, or organizations and link them to accession and description records to indicate the agent who created, was the source of, or is the subject of the materials. Name records can also be linked to other non-established forms of the name ("see" references), to related names ("see also" references), and to contact information about the agent represented in the name record. The contact information will also contain a repeating general note for recording information about successive interactions with the agent named in the record.

7. Subjects

Descriptors for content or format characteristics are recorded in subject records in the AT, which can then be applied to accession or description records and output, for instance, as part of EAD and MARC records. The subject term element is designed primarily to accommodate simple terms or phrases such as "Boats" or "Boats and boating" and qualified terms such as "Boats and boating–Law and legislation." The record also facilitates recording the type of subject term (e.g., topical, geographic, genre), the authority source (e.g., AAT[33]), and a scope statement for the term that can be consulted during data entry.

8. Location

An important function for any integrated archival information system is to record and represent both permanent and temporary locations of archival materials. This is vital for tracking, since materials often migrate from permanent shelf locations to reading room locations, to exhibition locations, to conservation laboratories, and so forth. In its first release, the AT will only support recording the permanent location of archival materials, that is, the location at which archival materials are normally located when they are not in use for some purpose, or undergoing some treatment. It will be possible to create location records at the level of an archival resource or at the level of a component part such as a box, a microfilm reel, or a URL for a digital file.

9. Outputs

Generating a broad and useful range of information about archival holdings is a primary motive for the AT application. The current design for the application defines forty-one reports that the application will produce, as listed below:

- Ingest success report
- Ingest validation error report

- Accession receipt
- Accession report
- Accession processing report
- List of acquired accessions for a given time period
- List of accessions processed for a given time period
- List of unprocessed accessions
- List of uncataloged accessions
- Lists of accessions per acquisitions agreement
- List of accessions per intellectual rights status
- Container list
- Box labels
- Folder labels
- Printed finding aid
- EAD finding aid (for archival resource description)
- MARC XML record
- Metadata Object Description Schema (MODS)[34] record
- Dublin Core[35] record
- Open Archives Initiative (OAI)[36] record
- Metadata for Images in XML (MIX)[37] record
- Preservation Metadata Implementation Strategies (PREMIS)[38] record
- METS record (for digital object description)
- Location record for a resource component (i.e., box)
- Locations for a resource
- Shelf list for all resources
- EAC record
- List of names applied to a resource
- List of resources linked to a name
- List of non-preferred names for a name
- List of related names for a name
- Resource source record
- List of resource sources
- List of subject terms applied to a resource
- List of resources linked to a subject term
- Repository production report (extent of accessions acquired and processed and number of accessions cataloged for a specified time period)
- Repository guide (short list/description of archival holdings)
- Subject guide (including names applied as subjects)
- Object type inventory
- Genre/form inventory
- List of restricted resources and restrictions

10. Documentation

While not a functional area, it is worth mentioning that ample documentation will be provided for the Archivists' Toolkit. Documentation will include installation guidelines, a complete user manual bundled with the application and also available online independent of the application, a data dictionary, glossary of AT terms, and in-context help and error messages.

FUTURE DEVELOPMENT

Sustainability and development of the Archivists' Toolkit application will depend substantially on establishing the most effective business model for the application and eliciting from the user population key areas in which to extend the application's functionality. Repositories that consider using the application will want strong assurance that the application will be maintained and kept up to date with technology and relevant to archival work.

The AT Senior Project Oversight Team (SPOT) will convene in the early months of 2006 to select an open source license for governing use of the AT and, more importantly, to formulate a business model for sustaining and continuing development of the application. Discussions at the meeting will be concerned with discerning the needs and costs for different levels of support. For instance, support could be constrained simply to making the application available, with requisite documentation, for download and installation. But it is likely that support to only that degree is too limited and ignores, on the one hand, the needs of some repositories for ongoing support in the form of a help desk and on-site consultants who can help prepare a repository's legacy data for ingest into the AT application. On the other hand, the needs of the application to evolve forward with hardware and software technology and to increase its functional coverage of the archival life cycle must also be considered. Developing cost models for increased levels of support will be one objective of the SPOT meeting.

A corollary objective will be to develop effective revenue models. If the AT application is to persist and its development to be continued over time, it will be necessary to move the project from its reliance on temporary, short-term grant funding to something more enduring. Having a committed source of funding will provide for a stable staff and long-term planning for the application. Determining what is the most effective funding model for all concerned parties is the crux of the problem. There are several obvious possibilities to evaluate: (1) transfer oversight to an established library and/or software vendor, (2) form an institutional alliance, (3) form an application federation akin to the SAKAI Foundation[39] or the DSPace Federation,[40] or (4) institute a new start-up business. The SPOT team will sort through the advantages and disadvantages of each reasonable option to determine which one promises to provide the best means for sustaining the application well beyond its initial development phase.

The functional areas that are being built for the first release do not, of course, represent all the core functions of the archival life cycle. The Project Team expects that functionality of the application will be substantially expanded in subsequent development cycles of the Archivists' Toolkit, thereby making it an even more suitable application for a broader range of archival repositories. Archival repositories have already expressed a great deal of interest in two directions in which the application could be extended. One is to add a more robust collection management functional area to the application. This would likely require providing better means for recording rights and licensing information, for specifying and tracking completion of preservation actions, and for recording or linking to administrative documents such as purchase agreements and acknowledgment letters. A second possible extension would be to add functionality to the application for supporting the registration of onsite repository researchers and the tracking of their use of a repository's archival materials. Such functionality would be very valuable in support of arguments for the importance of archives to repository administrators. It would also be important for guiding ongoing development of a repository's collections.[41]

NOTES

1. The AT project Web site is located at http://archiviststoolkit.org/. Accessed 2006-03-17.

2. "The Research Libraries Group to Develop Information Management System for Museums and Archives," *Technical Services Quarterly* 9, no. 2 (1991), 65-66.

3. See the Encoded Archival Description (EAD) Official EAD Version 2002 Web Site at http://www.loc.gov/ead/. Accessed 2005-12-08.

4. See http://www.loc.gov/marc/. Accessed 2005-12-08.

5. Gopher is a network protocol for searching and retrieving distributed documents on the Internet. It has been almost completely superseded by the World Wide Web.

6. WAIS is a distributed searching system using the ANSI Z39.50 protocol. Few WAIS servers exist on the Internet today.

7. ASCII is a character set for the Roman alphabet, wherein each byte represents a single character. Unlike word processor files, ASCII files are plain text without any special formatting.

8. For more information about SGML and DTDs, see the Cover Pages at http://xml.coverpages.org/sgml.html. Accessed 2005-12-08.

9. See the Online Archive of California (http://www.oac.cdlib.org/), Online Archive of New Mexico (http://elibrary.unm.edu/oanm/), Texas Archival Resources Online (http://www.lib.utexas.edu/taro/), the Virginia Heritage Project (http://ead.lib. virginia.edu/vivaead/cgi-bin/eadform.pl), North Caroline Echo (http://www.ncecho.org/), the Northwest Digital Archive (http://nwda.wsulibs.wsu.edu/index.html), RLG Archive Grid (http://archivegrid.org/web/jsp/index.jsp), and the United Kingdom's A2A: Access to Archives (http://www.a2a.org.uk/). Accessed 2006-03-17.

10. See http://www.loc.gov/standards/mets/. Accessed 2005-12-08.

11. White papers, reports, and rosters for both meetings are posted at http://tpot. ucsd.edu/arc-bench/. Accessed 2006-03-17.

12. For an explanation of use case methodology, see Alistair Cockburn, "Use Cases in Theory and Practice" (http://alistair.cockburn.us/usecases/usecases.html) and his *Writing Effective Use Cases* (Boston: Addison-Wesley, 2001). For the value of use case methodology in established software functional requirements, see Dean Leffingwell and Don Widrig, *Managing Software Requirements: A Use Case Approach.* 2nd. Ed. (Boston: Addison-Wesley, 2003). URL accessed 2006-03-17.

13. Available at http://users.snip.net/~gbooker/INFO627/IEEE-830-1998.pdf. Accessed 2005-12-08.

14. The slides for the SAA presentation are available on the AT project Web site at http://archiviststoolkit.org/AT_SAA_2005/AT_presentation_SAA2005.pdf. 2006-03-17.

15. The application specification, which provides a complete description of the application, is available on the AT project site: http://archiviststoolkit.org/ATspecification/ index.html. Accessed 2006-03-17.

16. The detrimental effects of processing inefficiencies are also addressed in Mark A. Greene and Dennis Meissner, "More Product, Less Process: Revamping Traditional Archival Processing," *American Archivist* 68:2 (Fall/Winter 2005), 208-263 (a preprint of the article is available online at http://ahc.uwyo.edu/documents/faculty/greene/ papers/Greene-Meissner.pdf; accessed 2006-03-17). The strategies proposed by Greene and Meissner and those targeted for the Archivists' Toolkit are complementary.

17. *Describing Archives: A Content Standard* (Chicago: Society of American Archivists, 2004) is an SAA-approved standard for the description of archival materials.

18. More information about the Encoded Archival Context initiative can be found at http://www.iath.virginia.edu/eac/. Accessed 2005-12-08.

19. See http://sourceforge.net/. Accessed 2005-12-08.

20. See http://dev.mysql.com/. Accessed 2005-12-08.

21. See http://www.hibernate.org/. Accessed 2005-12-08.

22. For more information, see DB2 (http://www-306.ibm.com/software/data/db2/), PostgreSQL (http://www.postgresql.org/), Oracle (http://www.oracle.com/index.html), Sybase (http://www.sybase.com/), Microsoft SQL Server (http://www.microsoft.com/ sql/), Informix (http://www-306.ibm.com/software/data/informix/), and Ingres (http:// www.ingres.com/). Accessed 2005-12-08.

23. "The Object-Relational Impedance Mismatch refers to a set of conceptual and technical difficulties which are often encountered when a relational database is being used by a program written in an object-oriented programming language or style; particularly when objects and/or class definitions are mapped in a straightforward way to database tables and/or relational schemata." From *Wikipedia*, available online at http://en.wikipedia.org/wiki/Object-Relational_impedance_mismatch. Accessed 2006-03-17.

24. Native XML databases are those that store and index XML without translating the data to another format. This is a relatively new technology and has not reached the maturity of relational and even object-oriented databases. Object-oriented databases are those that are modeled after data objects in the same way that object-oriented programming languages are. This includes the concepts of classes, inheritance, properties, methods, polymorphism etc. More information can be found in "The Object-Oriented Database System Manifesto" located at http://www.cs.cmu.edu/People/clamen/OODBMS/Manifesto/htManifesto/Manifesto.html. Accessed 2006-03-17.

25. Swing, a toolkit of graphic user interface widgets for the Java programming language that facilitate uniform interface look and feel behaviors across multiple platforms. For more information, see the Wikipedia entry at http://en.wikipedia.org/wiki/Swing_%28Java%29. Accessed 2006-03-17.

26. Additional information about JavaScript is available at http://www.javascript.com/. Accessed 2006-03-17.

27. Both the EAD and METS standards include a header, which allows metadata about the document to be embedded within the document itself. This generally includes information about the publishing repository.

28. Note that while the functional areas for the initial release of the Archivists' Toolkit are firmly set, some of the details for each functional area, as described in this report and in the complete software specification, are subject to modification. Programming difficulty and time may not permit the application to ship with all of the features currently planned for it, or, conversely, the application might ship with a few additional features that are not now described in the specification.

29. Information about the MARC XML schema is available at http://www.loc.gov/standards/marcxml/. Accessed 2005-12-08.

30. *ISAD(G)* is an archival descriptive standard maintained by the International Council on Archives. The standard is available at http://www.ica.org/biblio/cds/isad_g_2e.pdf. Accessed 2005-12-08.

31. See http://hul.harvard.edu/jhove/ for a description of this application. Accessed 2006-03-17.

32. The *ISAAR(CPF)* standard is available at http://www.ica.org/biblio/isaar_eng.pdf. Accessed 2005-12-08.

33. See http://www.getty.edu/research/conducting_research/vocabularies/aat/. Accessed 2005-12-08.

34. More information is available at http://www.loc.gov/standards/mods/. Accessed 2005-12-08.

35. See the Dublin Core Metadata Initiative Web site at http://dublincore.org/. Accessed 2005-12-08.

36. The Open Archives Initiative establishes a protocol for harvesting metadata. More information is available at http://www.openarchives.org/. Accessed 2005-12-08.

37. See http://www.loc.gov/standards/mix/. Accessed 2005-12-08.

38. More information is available at http://www.oclc.org/research/projects/pmwg/. Accessed 2005-12-08.

39. See "Sakai Partners Launch Sakai Foundation for Open Source Software" (17 October 2005) at http://www.sakaiproject.org/index.php?option=com_content&task=view&id=297&Itemid=507. Accessed 2006-03-17.

40. See description of the DSpace Federation at http://dspace.org/federation/index.html. Accessed 2006-03-17.

41. We acknowledge that these two extensions will require more resources than the AT Project Team now has its disposal. These resources will have to come in the form of additional project funding and/or collaboration with archivists and programmers in the community. In addition, both these extensions will require considerably more community agreement about the basic information requirements for good collection management and user/use tracking. As far as we know, there are no initiatives underway to standardize collection management for archives. However, there is a international project, also funded by the Andrew W. Mellon Foundation, to establish and test metrics for archival users (http://www.si.umich.edu/ArchivalMetrics/Index.html). URL accessed 2006-03-17.

doi:10.1300/J201v04n01_12

Index

Page numbers followed by f indicate figures; those followed by t indicate tables.

© 2006 by The Haworth Press, Inc. All rights reserved.   *255*

Milton Keynes UK
Ingram Content Group UK Ltd.
UKHW022105141024
449569UK00031B/1778

9 780789 034380